WELCOME TO VOLUME ONE **OF** FIVE THINGS I SAW & HEARD THIS WEEK...

Five
Things
I Saw
& Heard
This
Week
Vol. 1

MWB MARTINWORKBENCH&CO.

This volume written between
February 2012 and April 2014,
in London, England

© Martin Colyer, 2018

Designed by martinworkbench&co.

Dedicated to Mimi, Jordi and Gabe x

Typeset in Hoefler & Frere-Jones' Sentinel

ISBN 978-1-78926-180-6

Printed by CreateSpace

Published by martinworkbench&co./
Independent Publishing Network

ONE THING FROM THE FUTURE (2017) LIL BUCK
DANCE is my Cultural Achilles Heel™ but I overcome it to
marvel at this*, filmed while the Shchukin collection was at
the Fondation Louis Vuitton in Paris. "I was born in Chicago,"
Lil Buck says, "Raised in Memphis, Tennessee..." Well, that's
a blues lyric right there. He continues, as he steps onto the
elevator: "It's a dance style that started with Memphis underground rap music, and that music, the way it was produced,
gave us a certain bounce. When I was around 16 years old I got
into ballet. We made a deal with this artistic director that we
would teach hip-hop, and they would teach us ballet..." There's
a moment at 2:45 in front of Picasso's *Three Women* that is
just astounding, but it's not the locale, or the music, or the
amazing art – this would be as strange and beguiling wherever
it was performed.

{*GOOGLE | "LIL BUCK FONDATION LOUIS VUITTON"}

Five
Things
I Saw
& Heard
This
Week
Vol. 1
Martin
Colyer

MARTINWORKBENCH&CO.

Foreword
Richard Williams

JUNE 2018

AS YOU MIGHT EXPECT FROM THE SON OF THE MAN WHO FIRST APPLIED the word "skiffle" to the rudimentary hybrid musical form that provided the bridge across which so many of us took our first steps towards rock and roll, Martin Colyer has a taste that is broad, deep and historically rich. The short items that form his weekly blog might seem to resemble the sort of flotsam and jetsam that you would expect to salvage from a net cast into popular music's rapid flow, but together they provide evidence of an acute, inquisitive, empathetic and coherent sensibility. In these pages you'll find Jimmy Webb and John Coltrane, Van Morrison and Trouble Funk, Sam Amidon and Allen Toussaint, Aimee Mann and Meshell Ndegeocello, the Alabama Shakes and Dave Brubeck. And Dylan. Always Dylan.

SOMETIMES THE PIECES TAKE THE FORM OF AN EXTENDED REMINISCENCE, A BRIEF ASIDE, OR A quote from an interview he's just read. He'll pick up an interesting letter from the morning newspaper, or give us the full text of a letter written to him by his friend Sam Charters about his experience of working with Harry Smith, of *Anthology of American Folk Music* fame ("a genuine horse's ass"). A trip to Paris yields a glimpse of Serge Gainsbourg's grave and a beautifully observed review of a Leonard Cohen concert at the venerable Olympia music hall.

IN THE 1980S MARTIN WAS A MEMBER OF A BAND CALLED HOT HOUSE, WHOSE SINGLES – NOTABLY "Don't Come to Stay" and "The Way That We Walk", featuring the voice of Heather Small, a future M Person – were outstanding examples of UK soul, and took him to the Muscle Shoals studio in Alabama for recording sessions with the band. In another life his studies at Chelsea School of Art were followed by a career as a graphic designer, mostly with magazines (*Radio Times*, *The Observer* and the *Reader's Digest*, among others), which is why this book looks so good. That also helps to explain the occasional digression into the visual arts; some of the items here are

NAT HENTOFF: Is It Libel or Blasphemy To Defame a Saint?
FOUND IT! at the COLONY
PROMPTLY SHIPPED
Comin' in on a Wing and a Prayer
The amazing guitar of Amos Garrett
ARD WILLIAMS
Country Music WAX MUSEUM and SHOPPING MALL
INSIDE DYLAN'S BRAIN
Fender lovin' care
WORDS & MUSIC
MUSIC SUPPLEMENT
CRAWDADDY!
The Magazine for Music Lovers
NEW WEST
The Making of 'HAMMETT' By Tim Hunter
AMERICAN BUFFALO
The Young Vic Studio
BOB DYLAN | I WAS YOUNG WHEN I LEFT HOME
ALMOST RELEASED SONGS AND OUTTAKES FROM BOB'S CAREER 1961-1967
Brownie McGhee
Sonny Terry

the result of his ability to use his eyes as he goes through the world. He has a story about Arthur Rothstein's "Dust Storm in Cimarron County, Oklahoma, 1936", the cover photograph of Woody Guthrie's *Dust Bowl Ballads*, and a withering little dismissal of the painter Marlene Dumas's much-hyped portrait of Amy Winehouse.

Did I tell you that he was a childhood playmate of Sid Vicious? And that he can name the great records made in an anonymous stucco building – now a financial services office, or something like that – a few yards from Marble Arch? **That he once put together the best Dylan bootleg I've ever seen? Or that he caught Prince's plectrum at the end of his stunning London debut at the Lyceum in 1981?**

READING THESE PIECES IS LIKE GETTING PHONE CALLS FROM A FRIEND. YOU might not share every one of their obsessions, but they're never going to waste your time. And in Martin's case, you'll be encouraged to listen to or look at something new, or something you've been ignoring, with a sharpened appreciation. Even if I didn't know him, I'd think of him as a friend. And so will you.

Richard Williams.

Richard Williams

From the Beginning: Why Five Things Seen & Heard?

I WANTED TO TALK ABOUT BRUNO MARS' BASS PLAYER. THAT'S ALL. Watching that performance at the BRITS one night in 2012, I thought – *that should be written about*. A great moment, but one that falls through the cracks. Music journalism doesn't approach the subject that way. In a world of *New Releases!* and PR'd interviews, something small like that would have come – and be gone. Those small moments can be treasurable or illuminating, and I wanted to capture them.

I REALISED YEARS AGO THAT I REALLY LIKE MUSICIANS, THE RESULT OF being raised in a house that was often a musicians' crash pad. So rescuing from obscurity, even in a small way, contributions that were vital to the creation of something good seemed a worthwhile pursuit. So pursue it I did. I heard songs being used on adverts and tv show soundtracks, lyrics referenced in cop show dialogue, a variety of weird and brilliant soundscapes, and exhibitions built around musicians' stories. I saw posters from the past still as vivid as the day they were printed, and watched pop videos of genius. Five seemed the right number to make it work – sometimes perfectly so, sometimes a struggle, especially if a large amount of transcription was required. I'm a lousy typist.

Five Things is mostly a love letter to musicians. Those whose work I've loved. Those who are unsung journeymen. **At other times it's a letter to my dad, or to Sam Charters, written here to be preserved.**

SINCE I WAS A TEENAGER I'VE CUT GREAT WRITING OUT OF MAGAZINES, GATHERED MEMORABILIA and liberated fabulous photographs from picture agencies that were closing down. I still have boxes full of cuttings, but of course the clipping in your hand in 1973 didn't lead anywhere easily... whereas the internet, well the internet can lead anywhere, and there can be the greatest fun in the discovery, the stumbling upon, the going down the rabbit hole. Looking up one thing would lead to another – to Lowell George's US sitcom cameo, Bowie's police mugshots, the intense performances at a school fundraiser of a faded eighties rocker. I wanted to create a scrapbook of the inspiring thoughts and writings of others, too, which accounts for a fair number of excerpts from newspapers and magazines. The book has been edited by my wonderful and literate friend Rick Ball, a book editor in New York. We've added explanatory notes to set up entries that were blind, and Rick's been invaluable in discarding the less compelling entries (that's why not every date has five entries).

VOLUME ONE COVERS 2012–2014. I HAD PLANNED TO MAKE A BOOK OF *FIVE YEARS OF FIVE THINGS*, but Amazon's CreateSpace platform has a page limit of 212 at this size of book. Of course, five years would have meant a book of around 600 pages, so best be thankful. *Volume 2* may follow in due course. For *Volume 1*, I'd like to thank these constant writing inspirations: Laura Barton, Mick Brown, Joan Didion, Michael Gray, Peter Guralnick, Barney Hoskyns, Marinas Hyde and O'Loughlin, Michael Jackson (the *wine* one), Anthony Lane, Greil Marcus, Mark Myers, Amanda Petrusich, Alex Ross, John Jeremiah Sullivan, Ed Ward, Richard Williams and Peter York.

THERE WERE ALSO THOSE WHO BECAME CORRESPONDENTS IN VARIOUS LOCALES – JOHN CUNEO, for reporting and illustrating Woodstock, Mick Gold for his roving mind and film notes, and cartoonist Steve Way for his Van/Football/Montmartre missives. There are friends who have pointed me towards fascinating things: Tim Clifford, companion and instigator in many adventures that made these pages, Gray Lovatt for running the radio station [THE ECLECTIC EEL] that would have been the *Five Things* station if there were such a thing, Marcel Ashby for the odd "odd thing", Bob Gumpert for picking up strands of wonder from all corners of the internet, Lloyd Clater for his interest in all things stringed, Calum Storrie for sharing his taste in outré music with me, and John L. Walters at *Eye* magazine for being such a great editor. Not forgetting Steve Carr [EVERYRECORDTELLSASTORY], Paul Kerr [BLABBER 'N' SMOKE] and Thom Hickey [THE IMMORTAL JUKEBOX]. Everyone at ROCKSBACKPAGES. COM deserves thanks, as does Hugh Kyle – ex-*Record Mirror*! – my co-worker for ten entertaining years.

{KEN COLYER | "SPORTIN' LIFE" †}

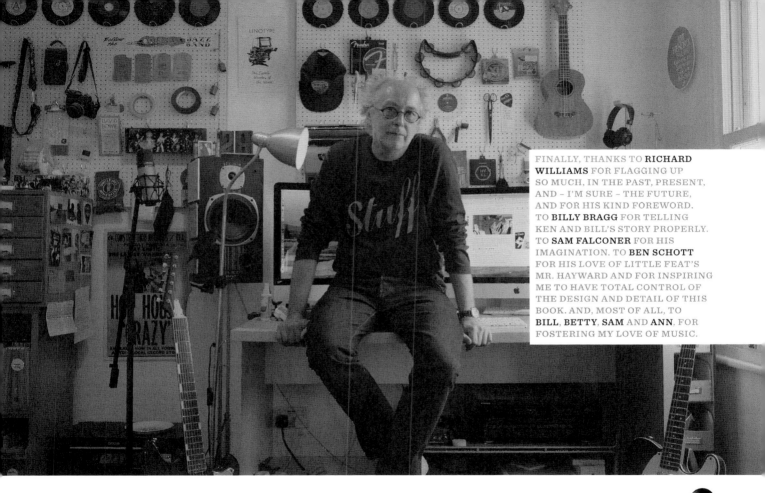

FINALLY, THANKS TO **RICHARD WILLIAMS** FOR FLAGGING UP SO MUCH, IN THE PAST, PRESENT, AND – I'M SURE – THE FUTURE, AND FOR HIS KIND FOREWORD. TO **BILLY BRAGG** FOR TELLING KEN AND BILL'S STORY PROPERLY. TO **SAM FALCONER** FOR HIS IMAGINATION. TO **BEN SCHOTT** FOR HIS LOVE OF LITTLE FEAT'S MR. HAYWARD AND FOR INSPIRING ME TO HAVE TOTAL CONTROL OF THE DESIGN AND DETAIL OF THIS BOOK. AND, MOST OF ALL, TO **BILL**, **BETTY**, **SAM** AND **ANN**, FOR FOSTERING MY LOVE OF MUSIC.

SOME REGULAR APPEARANCES...

¶ HOT HOUSE was a group I was in from around 1983 'til its demise in 1990. Wildly unsuccessful and unfashionable (we liked cutting live in an era where machine-tooled soul was the dish of the day) we managed to record in both Muscle Shoals and Malibu and spend £1.3m of RCA's money. Our records are currently out-of-print although there are videos on the HotHouseChannel at YOUTUBE.COM and a brief history at THEHOTHOUSESTORY. COM. Our singer, Heather Small, went onto huge success with M People.

¶ My co-conspirator in Hot House was MARK PRINGLE, musician extraordinaire and now Chief Archivist at the music journalism website, ROCKSBACKPAGES.COM, that we founded alongside BARNEY HOSKYNS. I first met Barney through his obituary of Bill Graham in *The Guardian,* where he mentioned that he was working on a book about The Band. Of such connections are lifelong friendships made.

¶ My relationship from childhood with ANN and SAM CHARTERS was hugely influential. Ann is an author and university professor, Jack Kerouac's biographer and the first person to record Scott Joplin's rags at their proper tempo. Sam, whose compilation *Really! The Country Blues* was a critical work in the rediscovery by the 60s generation of early blues, wrote on an astonishingly wide range of music. He produced albums for Skip James, Buddy Guy and Junior Wells, Dave Van Ronk and Country Joe & The Fish, among others.

¶ My uncle was the British jazz trumpeter, KEN COLYER. His brother – my father, BILL COLYER – was a massive fan of American blues and jazz, and found on his return from the Army that his kid brother had a) become obsessed with the music that he'd collected on 78s, and b) had started playing the trumpet. Ken's talent soon became apparent, and his obsession grew to the point where he re-joined the Merchant Navy with the express intention of getting to New Orleans, the source of the music he loved. He stayed for a few months, played with the somewhat stunned locals (*who was this 22-year-old white boy from across the ocean who knew their music so well?*) and ended up in the Parish Prison. His letters home to Bill led to a weird and tiny sort of celebrity when they were published in the *Melody Maker.* He came back to a band put together for him that included Alexis Korner, Chris Barber and Lonnie Donegan, and their interval turn with guitars and washboards was seminal in fuelling the Skiffle boom.

† AT THE FOOT OF THE PAGES...

you'll find RECOMMENDED SONGS, relevant to a piece on that page. Most can be found on Spotify or YouTube, but where the songs are super obscure and hard to find, there's a type mark, †, which tells you that the song is part of a ZIP FILE that I will happily send if you email me.

2012

DISCOVERING THE CHALLENGE OF FINDING *JUST* FIVE THINGS | OR, SOMETIMES, *EVEN* FIVE THINGS

The First Blog:
Wednesday, February 29

ONE BRUNO MARS' BASS PLAYER. THE BRITS

Unassumingly, but assuredly, the coolest man to take the stage on the night, and by a country mile. Bruno Mars – nice Little Willie John look and fine pompadour – played the Wonder-ish "Just the Way You Are", and his bassman rose to the challenge. Digging playing at the show, hands bopping over the fretboard like Jamerson reincarnated, Jamareo Artis didn't put a beat or a note wrong, even when double-stepping the dance moves. The final high flourish as the song ended was the sublime icing on the cake, sliding his right hand down the fretboard to dampen the last note, before hooking his thumb jauntily in his hip pocket.

TWO WHITNEY HOUSTON, R.I.P. THE BRITS

Watching the jarringly brusque tribute on this year's BRITS, my mind flashed back to an earlier time: 1987, in a Park Lane hotel ballroom. Whitney sang her hit du jour, "How Will I Know", dancing awkwardly to a backing track on a stage more suited to an army base than an awards show. We were ten yards away, pushing bad food around our plates, and could hear Whitney acoustically as well as through the PA. She gave it her all and, as the track started to fade, was so into the performance that she continued for a good fifteen seconds, not backing off her volume at all. Jaws hit the table as the most thrilling sound vaulted over us. For those fifteen seconds, she was a blissful and transported teenager, singing in the Lord's House. In that fakest of environments – an awards show – something real.

THREE WEIRD IPOD SYNCHRONICITY PT 1

On the bus going up Park Lane, approaching Speakers' Corner at Hyde Park yesterday morning, iPod on random. A Dylan track, from a bootleg I haven't even bothered listening to (it comes from a period I don't care for, around the time of *Under the Red Sky*). It's a shuffle, pretty badly mixed, with what sounds like Randy Jackson's rubbery basslines bubbling along.

"One time in London I'd gone out for a walk
At the place called Hyde Park, where people talk
Get up on a platform and they tell their point of view
To anyone who's there, that's who they're talkin' to
There was a man on a platform, talking to some folks
About TV being evil, he wasn't telling jokes"

Leaving aside the obviously low, McGonagallesque quality of these lines – possibly some of the worst Bob's ever penned – how strange is that? I remember asking Randy Jackson (he played on the sessions for Hot House's second album) about that time, and he said that they were pretty weird sessions. To keep things fresh, producer Don Was would line-up different bands of players each time Dylan came to the studio. No one had the first clue what they were meant to be doing. A production technique, I guess...

FOUR **THANK YOU, BONNIE RAITT**

That's the song "Thank You" from her early days, although it's entirely appropriate to thank Bonnie for one of American music's most satisfying careers. Justin Vernon (Bon Iver) drew attention last year to her sublime "I Can't Make You Love Me", but there's so much in Bonnie's past that's fine, just waiting for rediscovery.

"Thank You" † is on *The Lost Broadcast: Philadelphia 1972* (through an EU loophole, Amazon are selling CDs of US radio broadcasts, including Dylan, Waits and Cohen).

Bonnie: "For all you unseen people out there, I'm just going to move to the piano to show how versatile I am. Haven't played a piano for months now, didn't play it before that since I was a little kid, pubescing in Los Angeles. Playing Dick Dale runs [finger down keyboard] – 'Wipeout'! Anyway, this is a tune I wrote over the summer. Ready?"

It's not a perfect song – part Jackson Browne, part Eric Kaz, a little Philly soul (the taping took place at the legendary Sigma Sound studios), even some Toussaint in the piano melody – but this performance, with Freebo on bass and T.J. Tindall on slithery, chiming guitar, is a tiny gem. As she glides her beautiful tones over the phrase "I was all you'd ever need", hear one of the great American voices – unforced, unglitzy, true.

FIVE **THE ADELE GAP**

Phrase describing the difference between a performer's singing and speaking voices. For instance, "There is no Adele Gap in

the case of Leonard Cohen." See *TIME* magazine's mishearing of Adele's Grammy exclamation "Mum! Girl done good!" here.

Week Two: Wednesday, March 7

ONE **BUSKER, CHARING CROSS TUBE STATION**

An alto saxist playing Ewan MacColl's "The First Time Ever I Saw Your Face", every phrase so extended that it took the entire length of the subway corridor for the tune to fall into place, which it did, rather beautifully.

TWO **DARK AGES FAN COMMUNICATION**

Found in a folder of old things: this returned envelope from a simpler, less efficient time. I attempted to join the Levon Helm Organization, for the 8x10 glossy and a quarterly newsletter. For $6. Myspace, Facebook, Twitter? What? Who needs 'em? NB for illustration fans: the early Isabelle Dervaux rub-

ber stamps are trumped by a great United States Post Office RETURNED TO SENDER.

THREE **CLOSE UP TO A CLARINET**

I'm working on a book with a great musician, Sammy Rimington. Sammy's played clarinet over the years with some of the greats of the jazz world, as well as with the likes of Muddy Waters and Ry Cooder, and I asked if he'd bring his clarinet the next time we met to work on the book, a scrapbook of his life. He obliged and, sitting two feet away from him as I pushed the record button, I was struck by how good it felt to be in such proximity to (a) a great musician and (b) that most gorgeously fluid and smoky-sounding instrument.

FOUR **PRO-RATA MUSIC DOCUMENTARIES**

Talking with my friend Steve Way about the Gerry Rafferty documentary on BBC Four, he proposed that future music documentaries should be made in appropriate formats: e.g. Punk Rock documentaries should be very short, preferably under three minutes; Prog Rock documentaries should be extremely long and in multiple parts (the "Gatefold Sleeve" approach).

FIVE **KASABIAN VS LOU REED**

The Graham Norton Show, BBC One. Kasabian are so bad, so indie dishwater bland, they make me want to crawl into a hole and die. All the moves, all the thin jeans and pointy shoes and shades in the world couldn't rescue the flaccid strumming and the la-la-la's. Goldie Hawn attempted to describe this sorry mess, causing the singer (looking for all the world like someone's dodgy bearded uncle) to reference "Be My Baby" and Roy Orbison.

Oh, Please.

Fuck. And Off.

Over on BBC Two a few minutes later, there was a discussion about Lou Reed reaching seventy. After a clip from *Later*, of Lou with Metallica, writer Christina Patterson made this observation: "I kind of think, why should he carry on doing the same stuff? He did some stuff absolutely brilliantly. That's more than most of us do in a lifetime and it's a great temptation for artists to do the same thing again and again. And I think *good on him*... to try and do something fresh. Personally, I think it's disastrous, but I don't see there's anything wrong in the quest."

Absolutely spot on. But then Lou's done something great in the first place, unlike Kasabian. Result? Victory for Lou!

Wednesday, March 14

ONE DAVID WHITAKER

The death, at 81, of the man responsible for the strings that were sampled by The Verve for "Bittersweet Symphony" brought forth this excellent little nugget, recounted by Bob Stanley in his *Guardian* obit: "He spent much of his time in Paris working with the cream of the country's 'yé-yé' scene, including Johnny Hallyday, Sylvie Vartan... and Serge Gainsbourg. Gainsbourg's song 'Comic Strip' was recorded in London, with Brigitte Bardot providing back-up vocals. Whitaker later explained how they decided where they worked: 'If Serge wanted some new clothes, we recorded in London, and if I wanted some we recorded in Paris.'" Ha! There are, by the way, excellent waxworks of both Johnny and Serge in the Musée Grévin in Paris.

THREE DO YOU REMEMBER THE TYLA GANG?

At lunch with friends on Sunday it turns out that Weston's brother Mike was the drummer in The Tyla Gang. We had a fine time reminiscing about the Nashville Rooms and Bees Make Honey and the London music scene of the early seventies, and Mike had great stories to tell of his times with Brian Eno and Sean Tyla. I saw Ducks Deluxe, Tyla's band before the Gang, many times at the Fulham Greyhound. Most of my memories of Fulham Palace Road are pretty fuzzy, centering around Nazareth and Heads Hands & Feet. Oh, and being shouted at by Ian Dury: "Oi, Four Eyes... get your beer off my fucking amp".

FOUR IT'S BILL WITHERS' WORLD: WE JUST LIVE IN IT... THE WONDERFUL *STILL BILL*

Everyone is hereby urged to see this fine, fine piece of work, less a music documentary than a meditation on how to live a life. Best human moment: Bill's visit to an educational project helping kids who stutter (Withers stuttered until he was 28). Best musical moment: a toss-up between Raul Midón and Bill on the telephone and, at a tribute concert, Bill watching guitarist Cornell Dupree glide 'n' slide through "Grandma's Hands", talent undimmed by illness (he has an oxygen tube on).

Bill steps onto the stage and sings a verse, but then, as Barney Hoskyns wrote: "as if concerned not to upstage the ailing but grinning Dupree – one of soul music's greatest guitar players – he almost immediately sat down beside him, continuing to sing but deferring to Dupree." And with his hand resting on Cornell's knee.

Wednesday, March 21

ONE *HOMELAND*'S SOUND DESIGN

British dramas tend to have clean, neat soundtracks. I don't mean the musical elements, but more the overall soundscape.

Brilliant atmospherics and great music scoring, but generally pristine voice recording and Foley (sound effect) work. US programmes on the whole have a funkier sound. It may be partly a technical thing, but I'm no expert.

However, *Homeland* has taken funky to new levels. It's oppressively, brilliantly, noisy – all cicadas and compression. [COMPRESSION |kəm pre sh ən| *noun*. Compression in audio recording lessens the dynamic range of the audio by reducing the level of the louder parts, resulting in an "in your face" sound. The proper use of compression will bring out the quieter parts of the audio and make the entire piece sound louder.]

In each scene, the outside seems as loud as the inside – just witness the crickets at night in the episode where Carrie sleeps at her sister's house and the same background sounds run into a cut to Brody's house. Air conditioners whirr, fridges hum, interview rooms seem to throb. There's no escape...

THREE eMUSIC FIND OF THE MONTH

Late Late Party, a compilation of songs recorded by The Pac-Keys and The Martinis at Stax in Memphis in the mid-sixties. Both bands featured sax player Packy Axton, son of the label's founders. Like a frat-boy version of Booker T. & The MGs. Fantastic. Hear "Greasy Pumpkin" and wonder how they came up

with that title. If you like that, hear the rest. (The wonderful photo on the left shows Packy Axton, Don Nix, Duck Dunn and Steve Cropper.)

FOUR WHITE ON WHITE

I hadn't reread *The White Album* by Joan Didion for years. But it's extraordinary. Against a backdrop of California, Manson and her own mental issues, it's filled with brilliant passages like this one. After Manzarek and Morrison discuss, in a circular way, where they might rehearse the next day... "I counted the control knobs on the electronic console. There were seventy-six. I was unsure in whose favor the dialogue had been resolved, or if it had been resolved at all. Robby Krieger picked at his guitar, and said that he needed a fuzz box. The producer suggested that he borrow one from the Buffalo Springfield, who were recording in the next studio. Krieger shrugged.

"Morrison sat down again on the leather couch and leaned back. He lit a match. He studied the flame awhile and then very slowly, very deliberately, lowered it to the fly of his black vinyl pants. Manzarek watched him. The girl who was rubbing Manzarek's shoulders did not look at anyone. There was a sense that no one was going to leave the room, ever. It would be some weeks before The Doors finished recording this album. I did not see it through." Read anything about music that good recently?

Wednesday, March 28

ONE **FROM MADISON AVENUE TO GILLIAN HILLS**

That hysterical "Zou Bisou Bisou" birthday party scene! *Mad Men*'s musical mojo has not deserted it. The band (all Fender instruments present and correct) groove quietly on Dobie Gray's – or Ramsey Lewis's if you prefer – 1965 smash "The 'In' Crowd" (of course). Megan, Don's wife, then gives it her best yé-yé on 16-year-old Gillian Hills' 1960 poptastic smash – "Zou Bisou Bisou".

I always think of The Band's Robbie Robertson when I watch Jon Hamm as Don Draper. He's watchful, taking in the surroundings, rarely speaking. He's also the creative one they all circle around, who brings out all the others' talents. And he keeps his counsel, because as both Abe Lincoln and Ronnie Hawkins said, in different ways, "Better to remain silent and be thought a fool than to speak out and remove all doubt."

TWO **DALE ROGERS & TRIGGER**

Clint Black introduction on *Songwriters' Circle* at the BBC: "This is a song really inspired by Roy Rogers, who I had the pleasure of gettin' to know a little bit – recorded a song with him and got to spend a couple o' years with him, off and on. And he said lots of great stuff – and his wife, too, Dale. A great lady. And the one thing that stuck out above everything else... she was kinda secretly hoping that Roy would pass first, because she really, truly, was afraid... that he might have her stuffed."

YÉS-YÉS, MEGAN!

FOUR **VOX POP**

The Voice, Saturday Nights. Favourite Judge: will.i.am. Who knew he was so much fun? There's almost a Dr Seuss-like quality to his looks, eyes scanning the other judges like a fawn in the forest. Quirky, impish, arrogance undercut by a winning vulnerability. Best Song Choice: "Come Together" rammed into "Lose Yourself". One of the great songs of the sixties b/w one of the great songs of the noughties. Impressive that Judge Danny knew all the words and rapped along perfectly. Most Agonised Judge: the excellent Jessie J, taking the whole thing *waaaaaaay* too seriously.

{ EMINEM | "LOSE YOURSELF" – *one of the best songs ever written about the power of music*}

FIVE $ADE

Sade outearned every touring British act in the world last year. Even Adele. Extraordinary. Under the radar, not courting press, just selling out a rare tour. I confess that the only time I've actually fallen asleep at a live gig was when I saw Sade at, I think, the Hammersmith Odeon in the eighties. My wife had modelled dresses designed by her friend Sarah and Sade when they were at St Martin's (the short-lived label was Lubel and Adu and the dresses were shot silk and beautiful), so I guess that's why we went. But, as mid-tempo ballad followed mid-tempo ballad, my eyes grew heavy. Nice, lovely songs, but not my speed.

Wednesday, April 4

ONE **ACOUSTIXX...**

Could you sound like The xx with just a cheap acoustic guitar and a cassette tape machine meant for accompanying karaoke? Willis Earl Beal can. Young, black, Southern, heartbroken, can draw, could soundtrack *Juno*. "Evening Kiss" is beautiful, insistent, mournful, touching. He says, "This record was recorded on bad equipment. I like it that way." Amen to that.

TWO **CHURN, CHURN, CHURN**

To everything there is a season... and it seems that right now it's a fashion season belonging to Flo and Lana. It used to take a good few years for pop or rock stars to get sucked into other orbits such as film or literature, but now the career path is Voguealicious. Is this diversification, to make the Fame Moment™ last longer? We've had Florence and Karl [Lagerfeld], sittin' in a tree, yet *Stylist*'s cover story this week says that "despite two Number 1 albums and 18 awards, Florence Welch is a reluctant star". Really? Reluctant? It sure doesn't look it, in the 327 full-page pictures they've run of her.

To be fair, it's a good interview that paints her as someone who accepts all of this so that she can do the work she cares about... And Lana, first whispered about in September last year, now (already!) the recipient of the fashion equivalent of the Légion d'honneur, a Mulberry bag named after her, because of her – are you ready? – "retrospective look". As for the bag, it's straight out of W. Eugene Smith's *Life* magazine story "Country Doctor".

THREE **THE SOUND OF DOBELL'S**

"Every Jazz fan is born within the sound of Dobell's!" ran the catchy tagline on the record shop's bags, playing on the Cockney/Bow Bells interface. I get an email from Leon Parker announcing the launch of his resource dedicated to Britain's hugely influential record shops. Charlie Gillett introduced us because of the Dobell's shops on Charing Cross Road (built by my dad Bill, and where I worked as a teenager). There are some nice reminiscences on the site and I particularly liked Rob Hall's: "It was an ambition of mine to own all the albums featured on the bags they used."

{*Think you don't like Lana? Check out this song...* | "WEST COAST"}

My dad had selected the albums and had them photographed by an advertising guy he knew in Soho, who shot on lith film for better reproduction. Accidental design, it still looks good today.

FOUR **PICK OF THE WEEK**

"Sometimes, if I crave silence I turn to my Land 250. The experience of taking Polaroids connects me with the moment. They are souvenirs of a joyful solitude." – Patti Smith. I thought that maybe I'd lost this Patti plectrum, a sweet souvenir from an installation at Fondation Cartier in Paris that "reflected 40 years of her more personal visual art-making and creative expression," but it turned up this week. Here's a fake Polaroid of it. And it will never be used in anger, of course.

Wednesday, April 11

ONE **LIONEL RICHIE, WHAT I'VE LEARNED, *US ESQUIRE*, APRIL ISSUE**

"If what's happening now in America had happened in the sixties, we would have protests like you've never seen before. But in 2011, people can name every player on the football team, but they can't tell you how badly they're being taken advantage of and by whom. They know what Gaga's doing, but they don't know what the government's doing. Everyone's on Facebook and Myspace and Yourspace and Theirspace and Twitter and Tweeter. Great, fantastic! But anybody paying attention?" From Tuskegee, Alabama, to 1600 Penn Ave – Lionel for Vice President, 2012!

TWO eMUSIC FIND OF THE MONTH

Hayes Carll's album *Kmag Yoyo* (military acronym, "Kiss My Ass Guys, You're On Your Own"), which features the beautiful, Willie Nelson-esque "Chances Are". "Chances are I took the wrong turn, every time I had a turn to take." Every so often a classic country song is just what you need. And the title track's "Subterranean Homesick" feel is pretty cool, too.

THREE HAVENLY

News that Rumer is to cover "It Could Be the First Day" by Richie Havens sent me back to *Stonehenge*, one of the albums Richie made in the late sixties, which also featured his great covers of "I Started a Joke" and "It's All Over Now, Baby Blue". Richie also features on *An Album to Benefit Preservation Hall*, which rounds up some usual and unusual suspects (Paolo Nutini, Andrew Bird, Tom Waits, Pete Seeger, Merle Haggard, Dr John, Steve Earle) in support of this venerable New Orleans institution, and his track may just be the best thing on it. "Trouble in Mind" is a totally gorgeous version of an old chestnut – with soft horns, walking bass, sad Dobro and sandpaper clarinet underpinning Havens' stoic vocal.

FOUR IN A WHITE ROOM...

We were talking at work about the surviving Abbey Road letters (as seen on the back of the *Abbey Road* album) that featured on the memorabilia and auction show *Four Rooms*, and discussing what item of rock memorabilia we'd most like to

own. Suggestions? The Jayne Mansfield cutout from *Sgt Pepper*? Brian Wilson's sandpit? The guitar on the cover of *Joan Baez/5*? My favourite choice was Simon H's: Nick Drake's cape/blanket, *Way to Blue* cover.

FIVE GIRL TALK, GIRL TALK

Speaking of muted horns, "Trouble in Mind" prompted me to find a tape recording I'd made in the late seventies. I had, rather unfashionably for 1977, gone to Ronnie Scott's with my tutor-cum-landlord, Dennis Bailey, to see Panama Francis And His Savoy Sultans. Dennis insisted we see a bit of jazz history, and

THE WESTMINSTER REFERENCE LIBRARY, JUST OFF LEICESTER SQUARE. I used to do my homework there. Tonight it's the venue for the Sam Amidon Experience, purveyors of historical American Music.

A power trio unlike any you've ever heard. Sam makes the melodies of these old, old folk songs a kind of plainsong – flattened out and dessicated, almost. By repeating and intensifying phrases, voice totally in sync with his unique guitar style, he makes the tunes move forward and shift gears. Behind him, like mad scientists tiptoeing through the cables, his genius accompanists moved from Slingerland drumkit to computer, from bass to prepared guitar. Take a bow, Shahzad Ismaily and Chris Vatalaro.

With these two beyond-talented collaborators the show swayed from free jazz to beat poetry to Appalachian ballads (one of which, "Prodigal Son", Amidon dedicated to Rick Santorum*: "When I left my father's house, I was well supplied, I made a mistake and I did run, I'm dissatisfied ... I believe I'll go back home, I believe I'll go back home, I believe I'll go back home, Acknowledge I done wrong.") Sam's wife-to-be, Beth Orton, harmonised beautifully on some of the tunes.

I took my mum. She found it equal parts beguiling and baffling. She loved the final medley of "Climbing High Mountains" with R. Kelly's "Relief", where the audience sang the refrain like a hymn. She'd like to have heard more Beth Orton. Mothers, eh?

*US politician who was running for the Republican nomination in that year's presidential election.

we weren't disappointed. To hear a (little) Big Band in a small club is an experience not to be forgotten, but what stayed with me was a glorious take on the torchy "Girl Talk", a song composed by Neal Hefti, with lyrics by Bobby Troup, written for the 1965 film *Harlow*, a biopic starring Carroll "Baby Doll" Baker.

The song has been described by Michael Feinstein as the "last great male chauvinistic song written in the 60's," but hey, an instrumental version equals no one offended! Panama lays out a sifty undertow on his kit, the horns spread out and one of the great melodies takes shape. By the time the second chorus comes round, they've put the burners on and the whole thing is glowing and swinging and Dennis is shouting yes! yes! and we're laughing with sheer joy, enveloped by the sound of beautifully burnished brass. NB: Julie London does my favourite vocal version, and Feinstein's right – it is a staggering chauvinistic lyric.

Wednesday, April 18

ONE *NEWSNIGHT* VS ODD FUTURE WOLF GANG KILL THEM ALL

Oh dear. Old media fails again to report properly on new phenomena... From Stephen Smith's bizarre "Is this the future of Rock 'n' Roll?" opening line it was *The Day Today* all the way. After the bonkersly named group's manager, Brick Stowell, explained that he made 300 T-shirts for the pop-up shop (OFWGKTA are paying their way by selling stuff rather than

music at this point), Smith's supposedly snark aside was: "Are there any washing instructions on here?" How lame is that?

A pointlessly combative interview with OFetc., followed, before Smith's coup de grâce: "Some say the band are a case of new wine in old bottles, or is that a case of old dope in new bongs?" If that's the level of discourse, if that's how you're going to attempt to impart information in the six-minute time slot that *Newsnight* will allow – then why bother? As the kids would say: Jam Yo Hype, *Newsnight*!

THREE **MYSTIC MALVINA**

"There were some good things at the Monterey Folk Festival – you must have missed them, or they didn't appeal to you... A girl named Janis Joplin, square built, impassive, singing blues in a high, skin-prickling voice like a flamenco woman... When thousands of kids are doing something with diligence and devotion, there are going to be some geniuses among them – it figures mathematically. And something is coming of this. Bob Dylan is a sign."

An excerpt from a wonderful letter that Malvina Reynolds (composer of "Little Boxes") wrote to Ralph J. Gleason, published by Jeff Gold on his Recordmecca blog*. As Jeff says, "Boy, did she ever get that right." Big Brother & The Holding Company are three years in the future, and this was Dylan's first time on the West Coast. "He, too, was almost completely unknown, and for Reynolds to invoke the genius-word was pretty prescient – and daring, indeed." Jeff follows this with a letter from a woman called Donna, about Dylan's 1965 San Francisco press conference which is just as good. These primary sources ring with the resonance of a time and place, not with hindsight or a critical straitjacket to tie them up in.

Wednesday, April 25

This week's entry was written just after the death of Levon Helm, drummer of The Band, and dedicated to him.

ONE THE FIRST TIME I EVER HEARD THE BAND...
... was when Sam Charters came through London in 1969, leaving America behind. He gave me his five favourite albums, one of which was *Music from Big Pink*...

TWO LEVON ALWAYS REMINDED ME...
... of my dad. Wiry. Ornery. Absolutely lived for music and drink-fuelled good times. Had a great turn of phrase. Who was the man who made the party happen – wherever he happened to be. So whenever I watch any footage of Levon, I'm always put in mind of Bill.

THREE THE SONG THAT MEANT THE MOST
"The melody – too beautiful and out of reach for any words I have – spins the chorus into the pastoral with a feel for nature that is really hedonistic –

'Corn in the field

Listen to the rice as the wind blows cross the water
King Harvest has surely come...'

– and a desperate, ominous rhythm slams the verses back to the slum streets that harbour the refugees of the pastoral disaster." – Greil Marcus, *Mystery Train*

"'King Harvest' was one of his greatest, most intuitive performances, and the sound of his kit more than did it justice. Levon: 'That was where I got my drums sounding the way I always wanted them. There's enough wood in the sound, and you could hear the stick and the bell of the cymbal.' Jon Carroll wrote that Levon was 'the only drummer who can make you cry,' and listening to him on 'King Harvest' – the anguished fills and rolls, the perfect ride cymbal figure accompanying the line Scarecrow and a yellow moon, pretty soon a carnival on the edge of town – it's hard to disagree." – Barney Hoskyns, *Across the Great Divide*

FOUR TWO BITS A SHOT
In the nineties, in the early days of *Rock's Back Pages* [ROCKS-BACKPAGES.COM], Barney and a group of us were pitching ideas to Malcolm Gerrie (creator of *The Tube*) for magazine TV shows about music. My most unlikely idea was to almost fetishistically examine great musicians' instruments... and of course the opening feature would have been Levon's wood-rimmed kit, with the harvest scene painted on the bass drum, filmed from the inside out...

FIVE LEVON HELM, THANK YOU KINDLY...

"They took me out to the location [for *Coal Miner's Daughter*, the biopic of Loretta Lynn], and it was like going back in time: The film crew had rebuilt Butcher Hollow, Loretta's hometown...

We started work late in February and filmed for about six weeks, until old Ted Webb [Loretta's father, whom Levon was playing] passes away... I was sad when my character died and my part of the movie was over.

"I didn't really want to get in the coffin for the big wake scene, but I also didn't want to be thought of as superstitious or 'difficult'. So I told Michael Apted he'd have to get in first to show me how to look. So he kind of warmed the thing up for me, good sport that he is. As the 'mourners' gathered around to sing 'Amazing Grace', I had to sit bolt upright. It was like coming back to life.

Cut!

"'It's my funeral,' I told them, 'and if you're gonna sing "Amazing Grace", it's gotta be the old-fashioned, traditional way.' And I taught 'em in my dead man's makeup how to do it shape-note style like they would've back in the holler in those days. Some of the ladies they'd hired as extras turned out to be church choir singers, so once we'd got it off the ground it didn't sound too bad.

"We rehearsed it a few times, then I got back in the coffin, and we shot the scene."
– Levon Helm (with Stephen Davis) in his autobiography, *This Wheel's on Fire*

Wednesday, May 2

ONE MILES DAVIS, THE "MY FUNNY VALENTINE" SCENE, *HOMELAND*

Carrie presses play on her music system and Miles' trumpet entwines round the next five minutes, as the would-be dinner à deux fails to materialize. She puts on lipstick, walks past the painting of a jazz trumpeter on the stairs. Brody's at the door. Their clothes rustle, the ever-present cicadas throb as the background sounds are foregrounded. She pours wine. "Miles Davis!" she barks. "Do you like jazz?" "I don't know anything about it." He tells her why he's there, he leaves, the double bass climbs, she ditches the wine.

As the title melody resurfaces, the camera cuts to Brody getting into his car and staring out the windscreen, then back to Carrie, wretched in her kitchen, then to Saul. He's the only one who knows about Brody and Carrie's relationship, has a tangled relationship of his own with Carrie as her mentor, and now he's staring into a CIA fridge filled with all the things that office fridges always contain: medicines and mustard and peanut butter...

The tune stretches as Saul walks back to his office and sighs, realising he's forgotten a knife. He looks in his desk drawer and pulls out a ruler to spread the peanut butter, and at 5 minutes, 10 seconds, with the song only 50 seconds away from finishing, it cuts into an electronic bass hum / high-pitched drone and a child's drawing in a mansion window, as the next day dawns – and brings with it the fateful surveillance operation in the square.

TWO FREAK OUT!

In a particularly wide-ranging segment of Jools Holland's *Later* comes the incandescent Annie Clark – a refreshingly fresh singer and a considerable guitarist. I was so-so about the song, but the guitar playing! Well, great joy! Not since seeing the latest Chili Peppers guitarist (Josh Klinghoffer) has someone stopped me in my tracks like that. "As of late 2011, her pedal board includes the following: DBA Interstellar Overdriver Supreme, ZVex Mastotron Fuzz, Eventide Pitchfactor, Eventide Space. She usually plays with a 60s Harmony H-15V Bobkat guitar." – *Wikipedia*

FOUR OLLY: LIFE ON MURS

The fabulous poptastic late-night treats continue. Here's a programme possibly commissioned for the Title Pun alone.

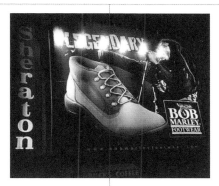

We follow cheeky chappy Olly (a cut-price Robbie Williams) as he tours. The most memorable moment is the huddle just before they hit the stage. Rather than Madonna's prayer circle, a raucous New Orleans-style number led by the horn players as the band leap around singing "I feel like fuckin' it up, I feel like fuckin' it up." Brilliant.

FIVE JOPLIN. GRAVE. SPINNING.

Not since I saw a poster in Times Square for Bob Marley Footwear has something clothes-based seemed so fundamentally wrong. A reissue of Joplin's *Pearl* had this flyer inside: "Made for Pearl is part gypsy rambler, and part cosmic cowgirl... a bit of joyful rebellion. MFP has produced clothing and accessories as enduringly modern, beautiful and timeless as Joplin's colourful legacy." Not to be indelicate – but who writes this shit?

Wednesday, May 9

TWO JANIS JOPLIN, "GET IT WHILE YOU CAN" (TAKE 3), JULY 27, 1970

"Everybody I know is crazy, except President Nixon... and *that's* his problem." This is take 3 of the great Jerry Ragovoy / Mort Shuman song, still not quite polished, still raw and free. When they reconvene on September 11 to finally record it, they're more focused – "brighter", in producer Paul Rothchild's words. But take 3 still has the edge: a more pleading vocal and a coda of "No No NoNoNo NO..." that is absolutely moving, and missing from the final take.

THREE A MESSAGE FROM CHUCK!
A couple of weeks ago I'd heard that legendary bassist Chuck Rainey was ill, and that there was an appeal to help with his medical bills. On behalf of all the readers of *Five Things* I contributed, and received this...

FOUR ALABAMA SHAKES, ELECTRIC BRIXTON
In the sleeve notes to an album by one of Alabama's greatest musical talents, Eddie Hinton, that fine Memphis journalist Robert Gordon wrote, "If a frayed rope could sing, it would sound like only two people, and since Otis is dead, that leaves Eddie." And since Eddie is dead, that leaves Brittany Howard. Janis is the cheap 'n' easy invokee – but Howard's models seem

be those two men, especially when you factor in her tone.

After I'd first seen the Shakes, when the excellent Laura Barton wrote about a lone YouTube video in The Guardian last year, I'd deliberately avoided listening to them, but I bought tickets anyway. As my daughter Jordi said: that way you're not just anticipating the couple of songs you know and therefore not listening properly. So we let it wash over us and tried to ignore the ******* hipsters talking at the bar and the drunks hollering next to us (hard to do in the moodily quiet numbers).

Punching her guitar, stomping her boots and seemingly conducting the songs by shakes of her head, Brittany Howard lives up to the hype, and the band are just slick enough to make it work, but not so slick that it sounds mechanical – you just wish you could be watching them at the Lamplighter, outside of Muscle Shoals. Oh, one other thing: the name. It's not easy to do a great band name these days – see Noel Gallagher's High Flying Birds – but this is most excellent, both geographical locator and mission statement.

FIVE VAN THE MAN SATNAV
Driving with my friend Steve Way to a cartoon festival, when he was taken with the Irish voice on our car's satnav and started doing guidance in the style of Van Morrison. Genius! Approaching roundabouts has never been so entertaining. Googling to see if anyone had already thought of this, I could find only one reference, from a thread on Julian Cope's *The Modern Antiquarian...* "My Van Morrison Sat Nav has caused

me to flood my brakes in the slipstream and I'm now stuck between two viaducts..."

Wednesday, May 16

ONE DONALD "DUCK" DUNN, RAH, APRIL 15, 1970

In the middle of his set supporting Creedence Clearwater Revival at the Albert Hall, Tony Joe White introduced his band: two of the Dixie Flyers (Mike Utley, organ, and Sammy Creason, drums) and on bass, ladies and gentlemen – the legendary Donald "Duck" Dunn, Memphis maestro! You know, Booker T. & the MGs, Otis, Eddie, Wilson et al.

Not content with Duck's luminous, numinous credits, Tony Joe informed the audience that we had a champion in the house (my memory fails me with the precise details, but it was something like All-State Tennessee Hall of Fame Champion). Yes, Duck is a champion of... the yo-yo!

And there, on the stage of the Royal Albert Hall, Duck walked the dog. He hopped the fence. He went around the world. He looped the loop and – after a stunned few seconds – three thousand people whooped for joy and gave him a standing ovation.

TWO JULIE DELPY, *THE FILM PROGRAMME*

In a really entertaining interview by Francine Stock on Radio 4, Julie Delpy talks about her new film, in which the action takes place over 48 hours. "I like the unity of time, maybe because I'm not very good at storytelling in time-lapse, and I hate the time-lapse sequence of montage with, like, music. The typical one was a nice trendy song of the time, then you have a montage of time passing or whatever (laughs) – I just can't do that! I like unity of time, like when shit hits the fan it really usually happens in a very short period of time... In *Before Sunset* the idea of doing it in real time, a hour and a half, came from me..."

THREE A VETERAN VIBE

Aimlessly flipping from channel to channel, a great juxtaposition: Charles Aznavour (now 87, at the time of this recording of "She", 57) and Engelbert Humperdinck (formerly Gerry Dorsey, 76). Aznavour sings like a piano player, jamming words together in entirely unnatural fits and starts, cramming then letting one word run long. It's mesmerising, especially as the camera holds the same closeup of his face throughout the song.

Humperdinck sings Britain's Eurovision Song Contest entry, "Love Will Set You Free", and leaving aside whether the song is derivative or not – what would you expect? – he gave it some going over. The voice was strong, his pitch was dead-on, and he negotiated the tricky key change (a Eurovision must) with aplomb. All the best for Baku, Eng!

FIVE ALBERTO Y LOST TRIOS PARANOIAS?

Simon was saying that I should be aware of The Cardiacs, a band I'd entirely missed in the nineties. On their *Wikipedia* entry I noticed a name from the past – listed as an inspiration – and it's a name you don't forget. Alberto Y Lost Trios Paranoias

were a band I happily watched countless times (mostly, I think, at the Marquee) as they purveyed a wildly cynical take on the music business.

It's hard to describe their shows. Look at the contact sheet of a roll I shot at the Marquee and you'll get a sense of what they were like. See drummer Bruce Mitchell – widest shoulders this side of Dick Tracy plus huge wooden nude-girl tie! The worrying balaclava-and-gun look! That alarming codpiece!

C.P. Lee, here wearing a Peter Cook–like belted raincoat and playing a Stars & Stripes guitar, went on to academia, and to write a great book about Dylan's infamous '66 Manchester Free Trade Hall gig, *Like the Night*. The Albertos were a one-off – they were really good musicians and were also hysterically funny. There's not many bands you could say that about.

Wednesday, May 23

ONE MODERN FAMILY ROCKS! OR SOFT ROCKS?
Ty Burrell as Phil just gets better and better. Daughter Haley

{BOB DYLAN & THE HAWKS | "TELL ME MOMMA"}

EXTRA! "I'M A WIZARD, NOT A MUSICIAN". WILLIS EARL BEAL AT THE TABERNACLE

Tim and I ventured out, on the back of one small article in The Guardian *about a new cat in town. This is how it went down.*

1 The Look John Carlos, Mexico City 1968. One black-gloved hand. (On the right hand, though Carlos's was on the left, but he looks more like Carlos than Smith). Cross that with Aaron Neville in his muscle/t-shirt days. Sunglasses. Tight jeans. Cowboy boots. Occasional wearing of a sheet as a cape. Sheet starts evening covering up AKAI reel-to-reel.

2 The Poses With cape, and standing on chair, superhero. Stalking stage with mic: Grace Jones meets Emo Philips. Albequerque-back-porch-stretched-out-almost-horizontal-feet-crossed for one song.

3 The Voice Paul Robeson. Tom Waits. The Mavericks' Raul Malo. Something of James Carr. Just trying to give pointers. He doesn't really sing/sound like any of 'em.

4 The Tools Simple. Shaker Simple in comparison to most. Aforementioned reel-to-reel tape recorder (gotta love a performer whose set list is contained on a reel of tape). Open-tuned electric guitar, played on lap with strings fretted by thumb, Richie Havens-style, and amp. Rum and Coca Cola. Belt, taken off and used to whip chair at one point.

5 The Songs Some are no more than a backing track of cheap synth beat overlaid by buzzing insect sound, here mutated into a compelling signal to noise. One of the guitar songs is

almost a classic Southern Soul Ballad. I don't know what their titles are, I'd only heard one track before going, but all are declaimed with a frightening intensity, and as we're all sitting/standing very close, it's a little like watching performance art.

I love an act that grabs the evening by the scruff of the neck and, by force of will, carries an audience – even as they're trying to get a handle on what the hell's been put in front of them. And ends it with: "We need you to buy the album, *Acousmatic Sorcery*... [long pause] ...the action figures [long pause] ...the pencils... [long pause] ...and if you do, I will then personally come to your house and give you benediction."

{WILLIS EARL BEAL | "TAKE ME AWAY" & "EVENING'S KISS"}

has been ripped off, and her dad gets ready to confront the perpetrator. Phil: "Yeah I got a plan. Either he gives us the money or he gets a private performance from (holds up left fist) England Dan and (right fist) John Ford Coley." Later, he amends this to "Crosby (left fist), Stills (right fist), Nash (knee) and Young (kicks out his foot)." Baby Boomer scripting par excellence.

TWO I MISSED THE RADIO DOC ABOUT THE MISSING BOBBIE GENTRY

I only found out after the broadcast, and then – just as my finger was hovering over the play triangle on iPlayer – it disappeared. I can only hope it featured the wonderful Jill Sobule song "Where Is Bobbie Gentry?" Set to a clever melody closely modelled on "Ode to Billie Jo", it tells of a fan's devotion…

> *"Out in the desert where the skin slowly cures deep brown / She's got a little shack, a pickup truck parked out on the edge of town… Where is Bobbie Gentry?*
> *Up in Alaska, Hollywood or maybe in Japan / I bet that she's still beautiful, goes barefoot everywhere she can / Does she still play guitar or write a song or two? / Maybe that was over; she's got better things to do…"*

Then a true fan's middle eight…

> *"If I could just find you, I would love you, then I'd leave you alone"*

THREE NILE 'N' MILES

Fascinating piece hidden in *The Guardian*'s Money section, by the always interesting Nile Rodgers, in a regular column called My Greatest Mistake. He tells of the many occasions on which Miles Davis would ask Rodgers to write him a song.

Nile: "This is a great man who changed my life – and he wanted me to help change his… I believe he kept asking me for about two years, and all that time I couldn't believe he was serious… He had a funny coding system for when we spoke on the phone at night, like I was calling the president of the US: I had to ring three times and ask for so and so and then he would know it was me…

"I kept doing jazz fusion demos and whenever Miles heard them he'd say to me: 'I can do that myself. I want a motherfucking "Good Times".' Miles Davis was 100% clear but I didn't hear him… He was completely sincere and had opened himself up by asking for my help. If I wasn't so stupid I might have done it."

FIVE BOB DYLAN BOOT LEG

From horn player Bobby Keys's autobiography *Every Night's a Saturday Night* we learn that the feet poking out from the Rolls-Royce on the cover of Delaney & Bonnie & Friends: On Tour with Eric Clapton are Bob's. And the Rolls? Albert Grossman's.

Wednesday, May 30

ONE PETE DOHERTY INTERVIEW

Geoffrey Macnab, *The Guardian*. Ah, poor Pete, treated badly by everybody as he makes his film debut in Confession of a Child of the Century. Take Charlotte Gainsbourg. She "wasn't 'all that happy' about the production, which he says he knows because he snuck into her room and looked at her journal [!]... It was freezing cold on location. Between takes, assistants would 'leap on her with loads of blankets and hot-water bottles and I was stood there in 19th-century cotton with lots of holes in it'." And in prison: "It's horrible. There are lots of aggressive, money-oriented, very masculine people, but at the same time, there is really nasty homoerotic violence. It's not the place to be if you are a freethinking man." And now – film critics! Reviews have been overwhelmingly negative, with Doherty's own performance deemed "catastrophic" and "calamitous".

I have no great opinion of Doherty's songwriting and I wasn't impressed by The Libertines, but I saw him play a song at Hal Willner's Disney night, *Forest of No Return* – part of Jarvis Cocker's *Meltdown* – at the Festival Hall in 2007. With a lineup of luminaries ranging from Nick Cave to Grace Jones (The Jungle Book's "Trust in Me" – terrifying!), Pete took the stage to sing "Chim Chim Cheree".

We were sitting just behind the model Kate Moss, Pete's then-inamorata, who was busy taking photos. One of the few performers to have memorised the words, strumming a bat-

TWO BEST EUROVISION MOMENT

After Albania's rather terrifying sub-Bjork performance, Graham Norton waited a beat, then said:

"I'm pretty sure that, if they get her medication right, that need never happen again..."

tered acoustic, he totally inhabited the song, and – singing beautifully – essayed a perfect and tender version, rescuing it from the clutches of Dick Van Dyke. And that's no mean feat.

THREE A NIGHT AT THE OPERA

Puccini's *Madam Butterfly*. English National Opera. Anthony Minghella's production. Visually stunning. Rousing, expressive music. Awful story, outdated, verging on distasteful. Terrible clunky hard-to-sing language (Pinkerton: "I bought this house for nine hundred and ninety-nine years, but with the option, at every month, to cancel the contract! I must say, in this country, the houses and the contracts are elastic!"). And sung with seeming disregard for the melodies of the music underneath. Interview this week with Emma Rice, director of theatre group Kneehigh: Is there an artform you don't relate to? "Opera. It's a dreadful sound. It just doesn't sound like the human voice."

Wednesday, June 6

It's quite hard to explain how weird this outdoor concert in front of Buckingham Palace was. Here's my attempt.

ONE QUEEN'S JUBILEE CONCERT SONG CHOICES

CLIFF RICHARD. "Devil Woman". Wronged-man song. "She's just a devil woman, with evil on her mind." *Give that man a knighthood! Oh, they did...*

ROBBIE WILLIAMS. "Mack The Knife". Song about a murderer. "Now on the sidewalk... whoo, sunny mornin', Lies a body just oozin' life..." *Don't harsh my mellow, Rob!*

ED SHEERAN. "The A Team". Song about a junkie prostitute. "Goes mad for a couple grams... in a pipe she flies to the motherland, and sells love to another man". *Thanks for coming, Ed!*

TOM JONES. "Mama Told Me Not to Come". Song about a drug-fuelled party. "That cigarette you're smoking 'bout to scare me half to death." "Delilah". Song about death and adultery. "She stood there laughing – I felt the knife in my hand and she laughed no more." *Loving the imagery, Sir Tom!*

Stevie Wonder. "Superstition". "Thirteen-month-old baby, broke the lookin' glass, Seven years of bad luck..." *Hmmmm...*

TWO NO RESPITE, EVEN IN THE CLASSICS

RENEE FLEMING. "Un bel di, vedremo" (from Madama Butterfly). Deluded woman waits for philandering, unpleasant husband to return. *Sorry, no comment.*

THREE THE HIGH POINT

GRACE JONES. "Slave to the Rhythm". The Hula-Hoop. The core strength. The Mad Headdress... *Enough said!*
{GOOGLE | GRACE JONES JUBILEE}

FOUR THE GENIUS OF *SPY* MAGAZINE, NOW COMPLETE & ONLINE

Spy magazine's influence was huge on both editors and art directors, but no one ever really made something like that work in Britain. Here, Al Hirshfeld draws the British editors who made their careers in NYC in the nineties. Diggin' Anna Wintour as Paul McCartney!

From left: Vogue's Anna Wintour, The New Yorker's Tina Brown, The New Republic's Andrew Sullivan and Harper's Bazaar's Liz Tilberis

{GRACE JONES | "WILLIAMS' BLOOD". *Not Prince William's, ovbs!*}

Wednesday, June 13

ONE RICK DANKO, "UNFAITHFUL SERVANT", LOS ANGELES, 1979: "EASY WITH HIM, HE'S A HUMAN..."
As Eric Andersen wrote in a wonderful farewell letter to Rick: "Your singing remains one of the everlasting glories of American music." And, though it's ragged and rough, this is as glorious as it gets. A sweaty club, a febrile atmosphere (it's not beautifully recorded, but the room fairly crackles – I've rarely heard something sound so *present*).

Blondie Chaplin, ex-Beach Boy, is on piano, Rick just singing, not playing bass, someone loosely slapping a tambourine. The crowd is rowdy, inappropriate for such a heartfelt song. There's an Elvis-like foldback on the vocal mike, almost sounding like it's hitting the back wall and touring the room.

From "Caledonia Mission" to "It Makes No Difference", Rick defined a way of ballad singing that's unique – a high, white, hilltop soul man, singing American music, and here he leans in hard, perhaps as a response to the low-down, boozed-up crowd. He fumbles some lyrics, oversings others, but as a performance it's fantastic.

Just after he sings "Farewell to my other side, Well, I'd best just take it in stride", he makes the above plea to the boisterous crowd, but doesn't miss a beat. The crowd whistles and whoops and Rick turns it on until the words run out and Paul Butterfield steps up front to take the song home with a searing harp solo.

FOUR WEIRD IPOD SYNCHRONICITY PT 2
June 12, Victoria Station, London. A song I don't recognise comes on, a bluesy shufflin' riff with Beatles-y overtones, as I turn to the Guardian's G2 section. Steve Miller starts singing: "Way down in Alabama there's a girl just a waitin' for me / She don't have to worry, she don't have to hurry / Lord, I keep her so happy, she's my..." And at this point I read the Guardian cover line: THIS DRUG RUINS LIVES: HOW SUGAR BECAME A LETHAL ADDICTION. And Steve sings: "Sugar baby, Sugar, sugar baby..."

FIVE REALLY? REALLY?
I have to admit, I'm gobsmacked by this table...

WORLD'S RICHEST DJS		NET WORTH
10	Moby	$28 million
9	Daft Punk	$30 million (each)
8	Pete Tong	$30 million
7	Judge Jules	$40 million
6	Sasha	$40 million
5	Armin Van Buuren	$40 million
4	John Digweed	$45 million
3	Paul van Dyk	$50 million
2	Paul Oakenfold	$55 million
1	Tiësto	$65 million

{TOM JONES | "ELVIS PRESLEY BLUES" – *a fine cover of Gillian Welch's song about Tom's old friend*}

Wednesday, June 20

ONE SCHOOL'S OUT (FOR EVER?)

"Baby taking her GCSEs. Passing of time is wonderful. Means never again will I hear a school choir sing 'I Believe I Can Fly'. **Thank Christ.**" – Alison Moyet on Twitter.

It's unsettling *and* amusing that R. Kelly is responsible for the modern school anthem of positivity and inspiration. Google R. Kelly to find out why. For a change, schools could switch to his "Relief". Great tune, beautifully covered by Sam Amidon as a folk ballad. It has that anthem thing going on, a shout-out to the Man Upstairs, and is teeming with hope, if not quite actualité.

> *The storm is over, and I'm so glad the sun is shining*
> *Confusion everywhere, without a clue how to make things better*
> *A toast to the man upstairs, he puts the pieces back together*
> *Now let's step to a new tune, 'cause everything is ok*
> *You're alright, and I'm alright, well, let's celebrate.*
> *What a relief to know that – we are one*
> *What a relief to know that – the war is over*
> *What a relief to know that – there is an angel in the sky*
> *What a relief to know that – love is still alive*

Just imagine a hundred ten-year-olds singing that.

TWO NOSTALGIA TIME ONE

Mixing desk, Vanguard Studios, NYC, 1968. Our old friend Sam Charters has been staying with us and I looked out pictures of Sam, among them this little gem – a three-track recording desk (very cutting edge, apparently), a vacant studio in Midtown, a twelve-year-old wannabe engineer. On the reels: Buddy Guy and Junior Wells.

THREE THE POETRY OF AARON COPLAND

Came across this beautifully written piece I'd ripped out of *The New Yorker* years ago, by Alex Ross: "There is an affecting recording of the elderly Copland rehearsing 'Appalachian Spring' with the Columbia Chamber Ensemble. When he reaches the ending, an evocation of the American frontier in ageless majesty, his reedy, confident Brooklyn voice turns sweet and sentimental: 'Softer, *sul tasto, misterioso,* great mood here... That's my favourite place in the whole piece... Organlike. It should have a very special quality, as if you weren't moving your bows... That sounds too timid. It should sound rounder and more satisfying. Not distant. Quietly present. No diminuendos, like an organ sound. Take it freshly again, like an Amen.' Copland conjures a perfect American Sunday in which the music of all peoples streams from the open doors of a white-steepled church that does not yet exist."

FOUR EMILY, WHEREVER THEY MAY FIND HER

From *The Trichordist*: "Recently Emily White, an intern at NPR All Songs Considered... wrote a post on the NPR blog in which she acknowledged that while she had 11,000 songs in her music library, she's only paid for 15 CDs in her life. Our intention is not to embarrass or shame her. We believe young people like Emily White who are fully engaged in the music scene are the artist's biggest allies."

David Lowery (of Camper Van Beethoven and Cracker) wrote this open letter. An excerpt: "Why do we gladly give our money to some of the largest richest corporations in the world but not the companies and individuals who create and sell music? This is a bit of hyperbole to emphasize the point. But it's as if...

NETWORKS
Giant mega corporations. Cool! Have some money!
HARDWARE
Giant mega corporations. Cool! Have some money!
ARTISTS
99.9% lower middle class. Screw you, you greedy bastards!

Congratulations, your generation is the first generation in history to rebel by *unsticking* it to the man and instead sticking it to the weirdo freak musicians!"

FIVE NOSTALGIA TIME TWO: SID VICIOUS STOLE MY CORGI TOYS

Nah, he didn't, really. But the *Punk Britannia* series on BBC

{SEX PISTOLS | "GOD SAVE THE QUEEN"}

Four put me in mind of Sid, or as I knew him, John Simon Ritchie, an extremely nice playmate. My mother's friend Rene was Anne Beverley's sister and was often called on to help a fairly troubled woman navigate her messy life. We lived in the same block as Rene and her son David, and Simon – a shy kid – spent time there when the need arose. I remember long after-

OH, SID...

noons spent on our hands and knees with Corgi cars in David's tiny bedroom...

At some point he stopped coming round to play and we all moved on to other things.

I saw Simon twice more. Once on Shaftesbury Avenue, looking in the window of a music shop, wearing a long army-style greatcoat with hair cut like Bowie, fidgeting, mumbling, smiling. And then as Sid, on a tube train – in the summer of 77, I'm guessing, definitely by then a member of the Pistols, all leather and chains – when I felt too intimidated to say anything, but we exchanged a glance and sort-of-knew that in some previous life we had known each other.

Wednesday, June 27

ONE HALL & QUOTES (OUCH!)

Rebecca Hall interview, *Stylist*.

STYLIST: *There's a rumour you're a total music geek...*

REBECCA HALL: "Yes, that's true. This is how much of a music geek I am; if I have a day with nothing to do, one of my favourite things is to just sit at my computer and make playlists of pretty much anything. If I could be a musician, I'd do it. I love singing."

STYLIST: *Is there one song you think everyone should listen to?*

REBECCA HALL: "That's a really tough question. Do you mean the song or the version? I always go back to Ella Fitzgerald singing 'My Man' at the Montreux Jazz Festival 1977. It's not necessarily the song, and it's not even necessarily her, it's that particular recording. For some reason, it always gets to me. And I've got a bunch of those, but that's the first that comes off the top of my head."

Well, I'm a sucker for actually bothering to listen to things that people recommend (in all those *My Playlist*, or *Favourite Saturday Night/Sunday Morning Record* magazine features), and that's such an interesting response: the song or the version? Sometimes there are particular versions of songs that just work for you.

For instance, Rick Danko singing "Unfaithful Servant" (part of last week's post). That's not the version I'd play anyone if I were trying to convince them of the brilliance of the song (that would be the original Band version, if you're interested). It's not even the second version I'd play them (that's the *Rock of Ages* one if you're still interested). But it is the one that moves me now and makes me hear the song anew.

Anyhow, I go to iTunes to get Ella's Montreux version and find this:

Do explicit songs get a 20p surcharge? No, because "I Let a Song Go Out of My Heart" apparently doesn't have swearing and is 99p. WHAT IS THIS SWEARING? So I buy it. "My Man" is lovely, throaty and intense (the last time through, Ella hits the title phrase like a tenor sax), starting with a deep breath as Tommy Flanagan picks out the intro. It has all her signatures, and a beautiful virtuoso ending, and I can see why Rebecca Hall loves it. I've listened to Ella's "Come Rain or Come Shine" and damned if I can find any @#%&*! swearing.

If anything, Ella sings like she has a broad smile for the whole song. For me, this song is owned by Ray Charles' glacial take, so I don't find Ella's "My Man" a version for the ages. It's just a version with a 20p surcharge.

THREE TIN PAN ALLEY, STEFAN GROSSMAN, SOUND TECHNIQUES

Sound Techniques was a studio housed in an old dairy building between Chelsea Embankment and the Kings Road. I'm thinking about it because I walked past a guitar shop on Denmark Street and idly glanced at a beautiful inlaid Martin acoustic, priced at £4,179. I looked closer and realised it was a Stefan Grossman signature model. Stefan was, and is, an extremely brilliant guitarist.

I had been talking about him with Sam Charters, who was tasked in the mid-seventies with making a mainstream Grossman record by Transatlantic Records' Nat Joseph. To this end he hired Alan White, Danny Thompson and Richard Thomp-

son to play. When Sam was in town producing, I would hang around the studio after work or college, just enjoying watching the creative process and soaking up the atmosphere (Nick Drake's albums were recorded at Sound Techniques), looking down from the control booth to the live room below.

I have two memories of those particular sessions: one is watching Sam and Stefan patiently making the curly-headed Richard Thompson overdub a single electric guitar part for hour after hour, trying to get him to play it more aggressively. Difference between a session man and an artist in his own right – a session man will say, "You want this? Or this? Or how about this?" Richard just tried to play it better each time. And the other memory was of picking up a comic that was lying in Alan White's drum case and being given very short shrift by the Plastic Ono Band drummer for not asking first.

Wednesday, July 4

ONE TAKE A GIANT STEP AROUND THE BLOCK

In the office Hugh started singing "Goin' Back" (I can't remember why; nor can he) and I said, "Oh, The Monkees did the original version of that," and he said he was sure it was Dusty Springfield. We were both convinced it was written by Goffin and King (we were right), but a short search later it turned out that Dusty's was the first released (although Goldie of Goldie & The Gingerbreads had recorded it first, before falling out with Goffin and King over some changes she'd made to the lyrics).

Anyway... the song I was actually thinking of was "Take a Giant Step", also by Goffin and King, that was on The Monkees' first album. Then I said, "Oh, that was recorded around the corner, at the Philips recording studios at Marble Arch." As it was, as well as "You Don't Have to Say You Love Me" and "If You Go Away". It also hosted The Walker Brothers for "Make It Easy on Yourself" and "The Sun Ain't Gonna Shine Anymore".

Philips Studios opened in 1956 in the basement of Stanhope House, close to Marble Arch. By 1983 the studio had become part of the Polygram group, was put on the market and was bought by Paul Weller, who renamed it Solid Bond. He found that the studio was out of time...

Paul Weller: "Dusty Springfield, The Walker Brothers and all that. And then all of a sudden this desk wasn't 'any good' any more and this tape machine wasn't 'any good' any more and everything had to be digital. And as soon as we all went digital, man, everyone sounded the fucking same. From country & western to funk to rock 'n' roll or whatever, everybody sounded glassy and linear. A technical thing, but it's true." And so, through lack of bookings, he sold it and all the equipment.

Well, I went down the road to see what was still there. I passed Le Pain Quotidien – where we had lunch the other day and, bizarrely, Paul Weller walked past with some dry cleaning – and negotiated safe passage past the machine-gun-wielding cops outside Tony Blair's house in Connaught Square*.

Besides an imposing set of steps leading to Stanhope House, I found an excellent resprayed sixties Mini – can't you just see

Dusty holding down her bouffant to squeeze into it?

A Middle Eastern electronics shop selling translated copies of Tony Blair's biography, next to some irons and hair trimmers; and next door, a shop whose purpose I couldn't pin down. There were replicas of the creature from Alien, some crash helmets and motorcycle cowlings with airbrushed women on. There were TVs and mobile phones. There was a five-string G&L bass. So I asked how much the bass was. "Ah, that's not for

{SHELBY LYNNE | "I DON'T WANT TO HEAR IT ANYMORE" – *from her Dusty covers album*}

sale. It's in the window to attract attention." It's things like this – it was the least attention-grabbing part of the display (except to me, that is) – that make me love Edgware Road.

TWO DUSTY VS SCOTTY

I love when you dig out something that you loved as a teenager and it still sounds as great, in every way, as you remembered it. I'm picking tracks for a DJ set for illustration collective Art School Disco – I know, what were they thinking? I've never DJ'd in my life, but they said I didn't have to stand there actually doing anything clever, I could just give them a CD. They're pitching up at Boxpark in Shoreditch to illustrate to the Sounds of Disco for the day, so I was looking for stuff we loved at Chelsea School of Art, played as we worked in the Manresa Road studios from '75 to '79.

We loved Scotty for "Draw Your Brakes" from the *Harder They Come* soundtrack, and for the most fabulous and wonderful "Skank in Bed". YouTube it. Over a version of "Breakfast in Bed" (as heard on *Dusty in Memphis*, written by Eddie Hinton and Donnie "Flipside" Fritts) Scotty sings, shouts and pleads with Lorna – who did the version of the song that Scotty is freaking out over – and then breaks off to admonish his musicians in a, frankly, indescribable way. Majestically bonkers.

THREE ANOTHER MAG DONE GONE

"Sad news, sad news, come to me where I sit." *The Word* magazine closed this week. Now who's going to interview all those amazing and interesting characters that no one else has the brains to talk to? And provide a home for the peerless Rob Fitzpatrick, whose writing about the end of music just gets better and better:

ON NEIL YOUNG'S *Americana*: "But if you remove the comfort blanket of (in this case entirely unwanted) hero worship for a moment – and I love Neil Young dearly – what you're left with is a record that no one in their right mind could possibly want to play more than once or twice. There is a great deal to be said for recording quickly and intuitively, but not much for bashing through everything once and then calling it a day."

ON THE MYTH OF SCOTT WALKER: "A discourse on the song 'Patriot (A Single)' runs aground when the writer can't decide what Walker really meant in a particular line. 'It's virtually impossible to say,' they admit, 'and Walker has always been sparing with his explanations...' All of which makes me think, Well, if you don't know and he won't, or can't, say, what is the point of all this? What are we doing here? Sometimes it's important to step back and open a window and remember that this is pop music; it's not meant to hurt this much."

ON THE SHELF LIFE OF BANDS: "If I were a musician, the question I hope I would ask myself more than any other is: who cares?... The facts are simple: a hundred years of recorded music is available at the touch of a button to anyone who cares to listen. Are you really sure it's necessary to put out another LP? It is more than ten years since The Cranberries released a record, but despite no one on Earth missing them, they have decided to make another. Sadly, 30 seconds into the first tremulous, ponderous, say-nothing, waltz-time, half-arsed shrug of a track you will be screaming at the sky."

HERE'S CAST: "John Power's relentless lack of imagination makes Beady Eye sound like Sun Ra. Criticising Guided by Voices is a bit like criticising weather – momentarily distracting, but entirely pointless when it just keeps coming anyway."

ON KAREN DALTON'S 1966: "In 1966 Dalton was 29 years old and had left New York to live in a remote cabin in Colorado with her husband, Richard Tucker, and children. Most nights they would gather around a log fire and sing, and on one of those nights a friend called Carl Baron, who'd sweated up to this address-free outpost with his precious reel-to-reel tape recorder, captured the songs as they were sung. Forty-five years later, the ghosts of that evening have finally been let loose.

"Dalton certainly doesn't seem to be performing these songs; this is eavesdropping on a grand scale and it has all the dark thrill and guilty tang that comes with that behaviour. We are the unseen watchers, the eyes at the window, the ears at the wall, and there is, I think, a psychic cost involved in that deal. Friends and lovers trading songs around a sparking grate is one

thing: having those same moments digitally disseminated decades after your death is quite another. The covers and the traditional songs that inhabit this exquisitely presented recording are deeply moving and I wouldn't want to be without them, but rarely, if ever, have I been as haunted by a collection as I am by 1966… On 1966 [Dalton] sounds relaxed. Safe. At peace. Whether you're willing to risk disturbing that hard-won peace by listening in is, of course, entirely up to you."

I'm bereft.

FIVE INAPPROPRIATE MUSICAL ILLUSTRATION

Ripped from the sketchbook, illustrator John Cuneo's visceral visual reaction to the Carly Rae Jepsen song that has been driving America mad (judging by the comments after John's post). NB: John has informed me that "I draw to praise that song, not to bury it".

Wednesday, July 11

ONE POLIÇA/"DARK STAR"

REASONS TO HATE: Huge amounts of reverb. Achingly trendy/hipster friendly. Arty double-tracked female vocal. Iconic Grateful Dead title. (Dangerous to pilfer Iconic Grateful

{KAREN DALTON | "IN A STATION", *Richard Manuel's gorgeous "George Harrison" song* ✝}

Dead titles.) REASONS TO LOVE: Wonderful live drumming with a huge open-room sound. Sometimes there's nothing better than a pummelling four-on-the-floor (hey, even Take That's "Shine" has a fabulous drum track, all RAK Studios circa Mickie Most). Cracking tune.

And the arty double-tracked vocal really works, weaving in and out of unison. It reminds me of Al Green singing around and off himself in "How Can You Mend a Broken Heart?" Add all this to some great twanging bass and slightly out-of-focus horns and it's a winner. Granted, this could end up wearing thin over more than a few tracks, but "Dark Star" and "Lay Your Cards Out" (for another great melody and truly insane drumming) are absolutely terrific.

TWO **SEVEN IS THE MAGIC NUMBER**

A review of a new version of Sophocles' *Antigone* by Anne Carson (Antigonick) in *The New Yorker* printed this fine single-verse version of the siege of Thebes: "Seven gates / and in each gate a man / and in each man a death / at the seventh gate." Seven is a lyrical number – especially in country blues. There's Muddy Waters, singing Willie Dixon's "Hoochie Coochie Man": "On the seventh hour / On the seventh day / On the seventh month / The seven doctors say / He was born for good luck / And that you'll see / I got seven hundred dollars / Don't you mess with me." Or Dylan's "Ballad of Hollis Brown": "There's seven breezes a-blowin' / All around the cabin door / Seven shots sing out / Like the ocean's pounding roar / There's

seven people dead / On a South Dakota farm / Somewhere in the distance / There's seven new people born."

THREE **NORA EPHRON (& SUSAN EDMISTON) INTERVIEW BOB DYLAN, ALBERT GROSSMAN'S OFFICE, LATE SUMMER, 1965**

Q: *But negro rhythm and blues has been around underground for at least twelve years. What brought it out now?*
A: "The English did that. They brought it out. They hipped everybody. You read an interview asking who the Beatles' favourite singer was and they say Chuck Berry. You never used to hear Chuck Berry records on the radio – hard blues. The English did that. England is great and beautiful, though in other ways kinda messy. Though not outside London."
Q: *In what way messy?*
A: "There's a snobbishness. What you see people doing to other people. It's not only class. It's not that simple. It's a kind of Queen kind of thing. Some people are royalty and some are not."

Plus ça change...

FOUR **THE BEST THING I READ ABOUT THE GRACELANDS CONTROVERSY**

Following Stuart Jeffries' *Guardian* review of the 25th-anniversary documentary, where he concluded that Paul Simon should have left the music alone: "It gave the chance to hear unsullied the South African music that thrilled Simon 25 years ago. How lovely to hear, for instance, accordionist Forere Motloheloa laying down a groove without Paul Simon singing over it. If only it had remained the music Simon loved, rather than the music he, having loved, used."*

Widlow, posting on the *Guardian* blog, answered with this: "Paul Simon clearly was a politically naive, contrary, slightly obsessive, perfectionist artist, who may have thought himself above such things as needing permission from the ANC. But what he produced was akin to Jesse Owens at the 1936 Olympics: a body of work that incarnated the exact opposite of the Apartheid philosophy, that sang out 'Mixing cultures is good', that proclaimed 'These musicians are virtuosos and their culture is vibrant', that put Black and White people into the same studio and had them eating and drinking together and using the same toilets and calling each other Brother..."

This footage of the original 1985 sessions was extraordinary. There were children and babies sitting on the studio floor as the guitarists danced around the backing singers, vaulting their legs over their guitars (!) with the monumental bass and accordion lines of what became "Boy in the Bubble" booming out.

Wednesday, July 18

ONE **WOODROW WILSON "WOODY" GUTHRIE, BORN 14 JULY, 1912**
My favourite photograph of a musician is this [above], a shot of Woody Guthrie, kindly given to me by the peerless Bob Gump-

{BOB DYLAN | "LAST THOUGHTS ON WOODY GUTHRIE" – *from the NYC Town Hall, 1963*}

ert. It's my favourite because it has all the essential ingredients for a great music photo: An icon. A cigarette. A great location. A wide-angle that puts you right there. An acolyte, absolutely in the moment of playing with a trailblazer. A curious crowd, all looking about fifteen. Their expressions are priceless.

I asked Bob how he came to have the picture:

"It was taken by a photographer named Art Dubinsky – I am guessing the late fifties – early sixties in Washington Square Park in Greenwich Village, NYC. The other guitar player is Ramblin' Jack Elliott. Art was a friend, a generous man who was a far better photographer than he got credit for.

He lived in NYC at the time – at least I think so. I met him when he lived in LA and I was working in a rental darkroom, time behind the counter for time at the enlarger.

"He came in one day to use the darkroom, as his home had burned down. We got to talking and became friends. He put me in contact with the National Lawyers Guild, which led first to my photographing farmworker housing at Gallo wine – housing that Gallo said they didn't have – and then to Harlan County, Kentucky, for three months of photographing a coal miners' strike.

"And that in turn led to everything else. Sorry – I guess that is really more about Art and I and not the photo. He gave me the image, probably for no other reason than I liked it and had said so."

A perfectly appropriate tale to celebrate Woody's centenary birthday – a story of friendship, inspiration and workers' rights.

TWO POOR OLD DONOVAN, DESTINED TO BE DISSED BY DYLAN COMPARISON FOREVER*

The always-amusing Barney Ronay on André Villas-Boas, Spurs manager, *The Guardian*: "There was something oddly heartening about the return of André Villas-Boas, now formally in place as the new head coach of Tottenham Hotspur, and appearing, austerely suited in the middle of all this wretchedness, like an unexpected knock at the door from the local curate, who against all expectation you find yourself delightedly ushering inside.

"It has become fashionable to see Villas-Boas as a rather tarnished figure, to recall the frictions of his time at Chelsea [and] to portray him instead as a kind of weak-chinned, own brand José Mourinho, Donovan to Mourinho's Dylan, a provincial Wimpy bar to Mourinho's gleaming McDonald's, a managerial Sindy doll of prodigious inauthenticity.

"This is more than a little unfair. If nothing else there is much to admire in the way Villas-Boas is still out there... displaying the unshakable backseat extroversion that all the best managers have, as he winces and struts centre stage in skinny-trousered splendour, looking each time a little more like a tiny little dancing soldier on top of a wedding cake, or, increasingly, like a particularly convincing waxwork of himself."

Donovan doesn't see it this way himself – there's not much humility going on in his autobiography, The Hurdy Gurdy Man. *The evidence of* Dont Look Back [correct spelling] *doesn't lie, however: "It's All Over Now, Baby Blue" vs "To Sing for You"?*

THREE **ROLL AWAY THE STONE**

The Stones played their first gig at the Marquee Club 50 years ago this week. Bill Wyman, in his book, *Stone Alone*: "On 3 March 1963 we played an afternoon session at the Ken Colyer Club, Studio 51, in Soho.

"It was ironic that we were given a great welcome by the ladies, Vi and Pat, who ran this stronghold of New Orleans-style jazz, whereas the jazz snobs at the Marquee and elsewhere saw us as upstarts who should not be encouraged."

The Stones went on to play Ken's club most Sundays for a year. On September 10, 1963, through a chance meeting with Stones' manager Andrew Loog Oldham in Charing Cross Road, The Beatles visited them in rehearsal at the 51. They presented them with a new, unfinished song, "I Wanna Be Your Man". On hearing that the Stones liked the song and wanted to record it as their next single, John and Paul went into Ken's office and finished it off.

FOUR **THE SOUND OF** *THE GREAT GATSBY*

Ben Williams is onstage through the whole of Elevator Repair Service's production *Gatz* (so that's about six and a half hours in all), sitting at a desk off to one side, controlling the sound effects and cues, as well as playing various characters. He does a stunning job – intensifying the drama, or broadening it with humour – running the gamut from car crashes and gunshots to air-conditioner hums and vaudeville turns.

One of the most (unexpectedly) moving moments comes when Mike Iveson, playing Gatsby's houseguest Klipspringer, turns the office sofa into a piano and mimes the gestures of a pianist, playing along to Williams' tape. He abruptly stops and sings, a cappella, the only words in *Gatz* which don't come from Fitzgerald's book, the song "The Love Nest":

Building houses still goes on
Now as well as then
Ancient Jack and Jill are gone,
Yet return again.
Ever comes the question old,
"Shall we build for pride? Or,
Shall brick and mortar hold
warmth and love inside?"

Just a love nest, cozy and warm,
Like a dove rest, down on the farm,
A veranda with some sort of clinging vine,
Then a kitchen where some rambler roses twine.

In an exquisite rendition, Iveson turns the theme from the

George Burns and Gracie Allen Show, a pretty but standard twenties musical number, into a complex, achingly poignant commentary on the emptiness at the heart of Gatsby's mansion.

FIVE M.I.A.'S "BAD GIRLS" VIDEO

As recommended this week in *Metro* by Shirley Manson from Garbage. Words are extraneous. Just go to 2:03. Go on. Think of the insurance quote… if they bothered to get insurance.

Wednesday, July 25

ONE THE BIG MAN ON THE BASS

Sad news that Bob Babbitt ("Midnight Train to Georgia", "Rubberband Man", "Signed, Sealed, Delivered I'm Yours", "Inner City Blues", "Band of Gold", "Tears of a Clown", "Copacabana", "Never Can Say Goodbye" – wow!) has passed away. Watch *Standing in the Shadows of Motown* and thrill to his pulse, precision and groove. He's totally on it, whether negotiating James Jamerson's iconic lines or his own. Watch him – in a moment caught on videocam – reflected in Meshell Ndegeocello's sunglasses, as he tearfully talks about the assassination of Martin Luther King, saying of the other musicians who made up The Funk Brothers, "I felt as sad as they did. I was one of them."

TWO "SHE CAME WITH HER SPINDLY LITTLE LEGS AND HER MENTAL HAIR…

…and sang her heart out." *Amy Winehouse: The Day She Came to Dingle*. Philip King, producer: "There's something about singers. They're odd, you know. They carry songs with them. How many songs is any singer singing at one time?… If you talk to a great jazz singer they'll say 'I know five hundred songs but I'm singing thirty of them at the minute'… Certainly, the way that she sang that night, Amy sang the blues away…

She used her gift to still her trembling soul. She used her gift as a way to explain herself to herself. To entertain people, sure, but to sing the blues and to give herself some relief."

On bass, Dale Davis. On guitar, Robin Banerjee. Singing stunningly, Amy Winehouse. There are too many great moments to list, but watch for the Ray Charles interview, an exquisite "Me & Mr Jones," the way Amy's eyes light up when she talks about The Shangri-Las, and the way she sings the word door in "You Know That I'm No Good". If you love music, watch this film.

FOUR EURO 2012: A THRILLER. IMOGEN HEAP'S VERSION: NOT SO MUCH

Now, I love a re-visioned MJ classic as much as the next person (Evidence for the Prosecution: Robbie Fulks' "Billie Jean") but it has to make sense. This usual end-of-tournament slo-mo roundup-with-music was typically well edited and included all the moments of high tension and goals to die for that are prerequisite. It was soundtracked by Imogen Heap (who I like and admire) doing an acoustic cover of "Thriller" – nice piano playing and lyrically some strike/hand/paralyzed-type links for relevant footage. But "Billie Jean" with an impassioned, paranoid delivery atop a slinky bolero beat = goal. "Thriller" with all the thrills drained out, replaced with slightly hammy over-emoting = horrific penalty shoot-out miss.

FIVE TONIGHT THE BLACKBIRD DIES

Despite really liking Low and seeing them live last year, I was ashamed to discover I'd never heard "Monkey", which blasts out over the opening of a cracking (but modest) B-picture, *Killshot*, based on Elmore Leonard's book of the same name, one of the great modern-day crime novels. The song is fantastic – "Tonight you will be mine, tonight the monkey dies..."

Nice to see a Hollywood film about hitmen that's not excessive and stupid, but tight and realistic instead. Mickey Rourke is in finest *Wrestler* mode as Armand "Blackbird" Degas, Diane Lane is excellent, and Joseph Gordon-Levitt as Richie Nix is really fine. The behind-camera lineup is impressive: directed by John Madden, photographed by Caleb Deschanel, thanks to Anthony Minghella and Sydney Pollack in the credits. Of course, it never got a cinema release in Britain.

Wednesday, August 1

ONE BUSKER, WATERLOO STATION, JULY 29

Playing Jimi Hendrix riffs. Not songs – just riffs. I figure he thinks the most anyone hears is about 25 seconds, and so sticks to what he does best – flashy hand waving and facial grimacing. I gave him £1 for the way he fluttered his hand away from the strings after playing a particularly nice "Purple Haze" pastiche.

TWO STAND UP FOR SENEGAL!

Alone among the national anthems that I've heard at the 2102 Olympics, the Senegalese don't have militaristic percussion and brassy horns. It actually has a pretty, pastoral tune, which seemed to float round the stadium rather than bounce off the metal girders, as Uruguay's did. Senegal went on to float past the Uruguayan defence and win 2–0, playing with ten men for most of the match.

THREE SOUNDS IN SILENCE

Re-parking the car late the other night. The street is eerily quiet, as is the car, and the radio unexpectedly leaps into life at top volume. Jesus! But it's only our old friends Simon and Garfunkel singing "The Sound of Silence" in the Tom Wilson "Folk Rock Overdub Mix". I'm not sure that I've ever really listened to this but it's great. Subtly done, albeit in a chart-friendly kind of way, with Bobby Gregg particularly good on drums as he follows Simon's fingerpicked acoustic. But it's such a strange notion, isn't it – to, without the knowledge, cooperation or consent of the act, reshape the track so radically? And, in the process, re-form the act and help to make it huge.

FOUR HOW WE MADE... *THE PIANO*

From *The Guardian*. Jane Campion, director: "The only brief I gave Michael was to compose quite a few pieces that we could choose from. I let him have free rein, but we'd discuss what he'd done and I'd tell him if something could be sadder or happier. When he first visited, I hired a piano thinking he'd want to work through a few ideas, but he sat down, played a couple of notes, and said: 'Let's go shopping!' I assumed this was a musical genius at work, so decided I'd better go along with it. I trailed him all afternoon, while he bought a shirt and watched some cricket. Finally, I asked if he'd had any thoughts and he said he'd decided to research Scottish folk songs. I knew immediately that this was perfect."

FIVE BOWIE: BACKSIDES/MUGSHOTS

Stumbled across two David Bowie artifacts this week. First: a bootleg of a 1980 TV show recorded at the Marquee Club, Wardour Street, London, in late October 1973 for the American TV show *Midnight Special*. I remember that somehow we got tickets and queued down the Soho street for hours to get in.

I wasn't a great Bowie aficionado but I do remember the show, with all its stop/start filming and endless retakes, as being really thrilling. Bowie was backed by The Spiders from Mars, but with Aynsley Dunbar on drums.

Luckily, Mick Rock, who was photographing it, wrote about

it for *Music Scene*: "The space in the Marquee is too limited to permit the requisite number of cameras to film simultaneously, so each song had to be reshot from different angles. This entailed as many as six performances of the same song... The atmosphere generated by Bowie's own unique craziness swiftly transformed the clubhouse into something closely resembling a circus ring – Dali-style.

"Throughout Bowie was very patient, very up. He filled in the intervals between takes rapping with the audience, teasing, laughing. After each song he would disappear immediately, reappearing dramatically on cue for the next one in a new costume. Bowie was joined by Marianne Faithfull, in a nun's cowl and black cape, for the last song, the old Sonny and Cher hit, "I Got You Babe". He frolicked about in the true spirit of the song while Marianne watched him, deadpan throughout. During one long break between takes she turned and left the stage, and paraded a pretty bare bottom, as the split in her cape flew open." I remember that quite vividly.

Second: this, the most composed, fashion-forward police mugshot of all time. "David Bowie, Iggy Pop and two female friends were busted for felony possession of half a pound of marijuana back in March of 1976 at the Americana Hotel in Rochester, NY, following a nearby concert. Bowie was held in the Monroe County jail for a few hours before being freed on bail – but this swanky mug shot wasn't taken until he returned a few days later to face arraignment. The four ended up skating on all charges." – Joe Robinson, Diffuser [diffuser.fm].

Wednesday, August 8

ONE **KILLING ME SOFTLY...**

Now the second season of *The Killing* has ended I'll hear no more the striking and enigmatic theme, my current favourite piece of TV music. Some Great Detectiveness (© Bob Burden's genius *Flaming Carrot*) leads me to find that it was written by a couple of London-based musicians (see Alabama 3/*The Sopranos* for similar US-TV/London-based-musician interface). Richard File and Wendy Rae Fowler perform as We Fell to Earth – name and logo courtesy of the Nic Roeg/David Bowie film *The Man Who Fell to Earth*. I resolve to find out more...

TWO **READERS/WRITERS**

Aditya Chakrabortty in *The Guardian*. This week Aditya read David Remnick's profile of Bruce Springsteen and wondered: "Is it a sign of age when you read a music piece not because you like the singer, but the journalist?" I don't think it is. My guide to the quality of writing in a magazine has always been the same – how many pieces have I read here that are about subjects that are of no, or little, interest to me? The higher the number, the better the writing.

THREE **"SARO" BY SAM AMIDON**

In this performance [VIMEO.COM/40238069] with Bill Frisell live at the Poisson Rouge on Vimeo, Sam essays the song's chords on an old dust-bowl-dull Martin, a professorial Frisell to his left as they take this beautiful ballad for a stroll down by a clear flowing stream. Frisell is such an inspirational player and, playing off Sam's elegant and affecting plainsong, wraps his fearless, serpentine lines around the vocal. It's a wonderfully open-hearted performance, Bill's smile at the end treasurable.

FOUR **THE MUSICAL LIFE, *THE NEW YORKER***

"Watts said the difference between playing jazz in clubs and playing rock and roll with the Stones was the volume. 'Also, in jazz you're closer,' he said. 'In a football stadium, you can't say you're closely knit together. It's difficult to know what Mick's up to when you can't even see him. He's gone around the corner and he's half a mile away.'" – Alec Wilkinson

FIVE **OLYMPIC MUSIC**

The BBC have pulled out their Battles and the xx mp3s with a vengeance for the Olympics, to track short films about rowers and cyclists, but the overwhelming memory of music at the Games will be Vangelis' bloody "Chariots of Fire". At first I thought the IOC had just done away with the national anthems altogether in the medal ceremonies and gone with the uplifting and triumphant™ Britfilm classic, but it turns out that it soundtracks the start of the presentation, before ending with the winner's anthem. Vangelis' royalty cheque should make interesting reading.

Wednesday, August 15

ONE eMUSIC FIND OF THE WEEK

"My name is Dale Hawkins, and I wanna dedicate this song to the three cities... that I, uh, had the pleasure of recording this tune in! Give a listen and you'll hear 'em." – Dale Hawkins, cousin to Ronnie and creator of the fabulous "Susie Q". (If you haven't heard it in years, download it now! James Burton's guitar – out-of-this-world!)

This is from "L.A., Memphis & Tyler, Texas," title song of Hawkins' obscure late-sixties release, with Burton, Ry Cooder, Taj Mahal, Dan Penn and Spooner Oldham all playing. It's on the great compilation *Country Funk 1969–1975*. "Ain't no bum trip, man," he drawls over a particularly out-of-place flute solo. "It just goes to show ya, man, you can take the soul pickers out of the soul country, but you can't take the soul out of the pickers..." As *Pitchfork* says, "Weird, in a totally wonderful way," and it's hard to disagree.

TWO FROM DAKAR TO KAMPALA!

We started two weeks ago at the football with Senegal's lovely anthem and, in some excellent circularity, ended with "Oh Uganda" – "a musical treat" according to *The Guardian*'s Peter Bradshaw – at the final medal ceremony, in honour of Stephen Kiprotich's stunning gold-medal run in the marathon. And a musical treat it is – I'd pay good money to hear either Randy Newman or Garth Hudson do an arrangement of it.

THREE BEST COAST, 100 CLUB

I hadn't been to the 100 since it was saved by Converse's sponsorship. Very happy to see that nothing much had changed – remarkably branding-free and still sweaty, loud and rocking.

My cousin's son, Brett, was playing bass and guitar with Best Coast, and I took his picture by the plaque that's there for my uncle, his great-grandfather, Ken.

Wednesday, August 22

ONE GARNER-A-GO-GO!

"This is Jim Rockford; at the tone leave your name and message – I'll get back to you..." Talking to Aimee Mann about her new album, she mentioned being drawn to analogue synthesizers and gnarly guitars after revisiting the early-eighties pop-synth era. Among obvious markers like The Cars and Blondie, it was great to hear her namecheck the terrific theme to *The Rockford Files* by Mike Post and Pete Carpenter… and to hear her quote it at the end of the title track of *Charmers*.

TWO BITS OF BOB

As excerpts of *Tempest* (not *The Tempest* – that's Mr Shakespeare's, according to Bob himself) filter out, we hear "Early Roman Kings" (fabulous title) soundtracking some dreary-looking US TV series, *Strike Back*. The song itself is a default Dylan accordion-led twelve-bar that gives the band little room. Now that Charlie Sexton's back, this is disappointing: at Hammersmith last year he showboated so much it could have been called THE CHARLIE SEXTON SHOW *featuring Bob Dylan*, as he fired riff after riff into every available space, absolutely thrillingly…

THREE LYLE LOVETT, WHAT I'VE LEARNED

From *US Esquire*: "The inspiration and excitement that you get from being amazed when you give a vague direction to a guitar player like Dean Parks – 'Make it sound a little more purple' – and then hear him play exactly the right thing."

FIVE PHOTOGRAPHERS ON MUSIC: BRILLIANT!

The advent of blogging has revealed that photographers (a) are really thoughtful and smart about their work, the world, the price of coffee, etc, and (b) can really write. Here's two I came across this week. First, Chris Floyd, writing on his blog *Clean Living Under Difficult Circumstances*, about a complex quick-turnaround shot of Olympic cycling gold medallist Laura Trott:

"I close my eyes and I think of the canon. The canon are the photographers I draw on in times of doubt. They give me comfort, solace and inspiration. They include Richard Avedon, Helmut Newton, Bruce Weber, Lee Friedlander, Sally Mann, Corrine Day, Glen Luchford, Erwin Blumenfeld, Harry Callahan and, in this case, Irving Penn…

"I go through the rolodex in my head thinking of them all until I find the one that instinctively feels like the inspirational match for the task at hand. That's not to say I set about slavishly ripping them off. I use them as my starting point… They are my photographic moral compass. They show me the light, guide the way and keep me company. Once I push off and get underway I'm then going forward under my own steam. By the time I get to the other side I will have, hopefully, added enough of my own ingredients to the dish for it to taste new and different.

To understand what I mean then check this out:
"Bad Penny Blues" by Humphrey Lyttelton (1956).
then this:
"Lady Madonna" by The Beatles (1968).
Each of them are great but one was a jumping-off point for the other. I love it. You can hear the lineage right there."

I also stumbled, via the *Black Eyewear* blog, across *Perous Secret Diary*, by Perou, photographer to the stars, and read this fantastic account of his experience of seeing Elizabeth (Cocteau Twins) Fraser at Meltdown. If only more music writing was this good, or this well laid out:

"i am sitting on my own due to a late ticket purchase.

but i'm three rows from the stage.

we all make the mistake of sitting through 30 minutes of support act: four people doing acapella, harmonised, medieval chanting.

all songs sound exactly the same.

unexpectedly, it makes me want to punch someone: almost certainly not what this music was designed for.

elizabeth arrives on stage: a demure, grey haired lady with the voice of an angel.

during the second song: a reworking of a cocteau twins track, i feel tears on my face and i'm glad i'm sitting on my own.

i have crazy tingles over my spine.

but then...

behind elizabeth i notice the bald keyboard player who looks like richard o'brien in the crystal maze, wearing a sparkly, tinsel, double-width, pointed shoulder-padded outfit, postulating between two stacks of keyboards like a prog-rock nightmare.

he is more than a little distracting.

and begins the downfall of my evening's entertainment.

the audience are annoying.

in between songs, old men shout out 'we love you liz'. 'marry me' and 'where have you been?'

there is a lesbian couple in front of me who try to dance though seated through all the cocteau twins songs.

one of these women also keeps trying to take photos of elizabeth on an iphone and keeps getting told by the ushers 'NO PHOTOS'

i am no longer able to enjoy the performance when a girl arrives four songs before the end of the show to take her empty seat next to mine.

she is wearing an overpowering fragrance that smells like a combination of mountain pine fresh toilet duck and lemon fresh toilet duck.

i don't know if she bathed in it pre-show or if she's been drinking it, but i am unable to think about anything else now.

i am concerned my nasal passages will be permanently damaged by sitting next to this person.

there are two standing ovations.

i sit through the first one

i stand through the second so that i am able to leave swiftly.

for the second encore elizabeth does a version of one of my favourite songs: 'song to the siren' which she did with 'this mortal coil' (a tim buckley cover)

and it is not so good.

i leave the royal festival hall a little disappointed.

sarah texts from the train station.

she'd left with steve before the first encore '... the memories were better.'"

Wednesday, August 29

ONE LET ME TAKE YOU BY THE HAND, AND...
Simon left a CD on my desk, sent in by a publicist, of a Ralph McTell sampler, featuring – of course – "Streets of London", with a Post-it note on, saying "You'll probably like this." I had to disabuse him of that, and then we had a great fifteen minutes watching the fantastic "Streets of London" sketch from *Big Train*, where Kevin Eldon plays a singer-songwriter whose audience won't allow him to play anything other than the eponymous tune. It not only painfully highlights the one-song career but brilliantly skewers the tyranny of a change-resistant audience.

TWO *MARK GOES TO MEMPHIS*, R2
In this compelling documentary [full disclosure – it was made by my brother-in-law] Mark Kermode and his band, The Dodge Brothers, head to Memphis to record at the legendary Sun Studios. There's a lovely interview with Matt Ross-Spang, Sun's in-house engineer.

"This room is like your garage – white tile, you're five feet away from the other person, there's no booths and you gotta play quiet so's you can hear the singer, and I don't let you use headphones and you just put a good tape echo on it and call it done. Sam Philips, to me... was on a mission. Took me a long time to figure out, but I started limiting myself to what he had in the fities, a few extra mikes or somethin', and once I figured out how we can get that feeling, that fifties vibe...

"[The Dodge Brothers] came in and the first song they did was "Number 9" by Tarheel Slim, which is an old Sun song. Nobody knows that record... and they start playing it and I's like 'Oh, that's Tarheel Slim, "Number 9"... No one has ever known who sang that!' Of course, I'm a rockabilly freak, so I know, but it's nice to be able to have that conversation with somebody. Cause you don't get to talk about Tarheel Slim to your girlfriend or anything... or anybody, you know?"

THREE WEIRD IPOD SYNCHRONICITY PT 3: AUGUST 23, VICTORIA STATION, LONDON
Just got to Irvine Welsh's pick of Five Films in the *Metro* newspaper where he chooses *Double Indemnity* and then *Eraserhead*, when David Lynch's "Pinky's Dream" explodes into my headphones.

The song is a noir-sounding updating of Jan & Dean's "Dead Man's Curve" with Karen O sobbing/pleading... "Pinky, what do you see? Flying down the road... Pinky, tell me, are you laughing, or are you crying? Please, Pinky, watch the road. Please, Pinky, watch the road..." as guitars judder and lurch like an out-of-control Dodge careering down Mulholland Drive.

"People go on about David Lynch's visuals but one of the things he does better than anybody is his work with sound," says Welsh, spot on.

No. of tracks on iPod: 1,057.

No. of tracks by D. Lynch: One.

FOUR NOW, A MESSAGE FROM OUR SPONSORS

Every advert on TV is poptastic at the moment. Every one. If it isn't Lily Allen's appropriation of Professor Longhair's "Big Chief" in her song "Knock 'Em Out" (Kinder chocolate eggs, of course), it's The Trailer Trash Tracys' "You Wish You Were Red" soundtracking Renault's new spot. It sounds "like an unholy mix of Best Coast's 'Boyfriend', 'Sweet Jane' and 'Baba O'Riley'," as correspondents on the excellent website TV Ad Music [tvadmusic.co.uk] point out. They also point out that The Trailer Trash Tracys are "hotly-tipped and rubbish-named".

Wednesday, September 5

ONE BLACK TIE, WHITE NOISE

Evening Standard, last week. Bowie disputes claims made in *The Observer* by the V&A that he is co-curating the Bowie Costumes show. "Contrary to recently published reports [I] did not participate in any decisions relating to the exhibition... A close friend of mine tells me that I am neither 'devastated,' 'heartbroken' nor made 'uncontrollably furious' by this news item."

TWO REALLY?

Interview with Kevin Macdonald, director of *Touching the Void* and *Marley*:

Q: Why do you think Marley's music has proved so enduring?

A: He wrote incredibly good tunes. Bob wrote more standards than almost anybody else, apart from Lennon and McCartney."

{EARL HINES & LOUIS ARMSTRONG | "WEATHER BIRD"}

Did he? Standards? "I Shot the Sheriff", "Redemption Song", "One Love", "Three Little Birds", "No Woman, No Cry", sure, but are his songs covered regularly in the way that standards are? Marley's number 211 on the SecondHandSongs database, a pretty comprehensive list of the most-covered songwriters, some way below Ozzy Osbourne and Marvin Gaye.

THREE I CAN HEAR THAT WHISTLE BLOWIN'...

My friend Steve Way on "Duquesne Whistle": "Dylan vid weird. Like Bob is doing a phone ad song, and the director is doing a Sundance lo-fi Korean remake." True say, Steve, but the world may be a better place for having this song in it – the chorus and thick, dirty riff are just joyous. Duquesne is a city along the Monongahela River in Allegheny County, Pennsylvania. Earl Hines, legendary jazz pianist, was born there. He signed my autograph book once. He was with *Jazz Journal* editor Sinclair Traill and they swapped their surnames for fun.

FOUR "EVEN CATHY BERBERIAN KNOWS / THERE'S ONE ROULADE SHE CAN'T SING."

The wonderfully titled *Berberian Sound Studio* featuring Toby Jones opens this week. It's named for Cathy Berberian, American soprano of the avant-garde. With Umberto Eco she translated works by Jules Feiffer and Woody Allen into Italian. You couldn't make that sort of detail up. Eco nicknamed her MAGNIFICATHY. Steely Dan paid her tribute in the lyric above, from "Your Gold Teeth" on the *Countdown to Ecstasy* album.

FIVE MUSICAL MARYLEBONE

Only a few streets separate Joe Strummer's monstrous urban flyover and John Lennon's rather luxe pad. Of course, John's background was considerably more flyover than Joe's...

Extra! September 12

ONE WHEN HARRY MET SAMMY

I don't normally like these posts to be long, but as a piece of writing this is too good to edit down. I was reminded that things are rarely as they seem, or as simple as outsiders perceive. Those at the centre of events always have a much more complex perspective, and their primary recollections sing.

It started when Barney let me know a couple of months ago about an upcoming conference, *America Changed Through Music: Harry Smith's Anthology of American Folk Music at 60*, taking place this Saturday, September 15. It's hosted by the University of East Anglia's School of American Studies and will explore the impact and ongoing legacy of an extraordinary cultural artifact – whew!

I emailed one of the co-directors, Thomas Ruys Smith, as I'd been talking to Sam and Ann Charters about their time with Moe Asch at Folkways Records (*pictured right, Moe and Sam*) and offered to put him in touch. He said he'd be delighted to hear Sam's view. And then Sam emailed me with his view, which is brilliant (if off-message, conference-wise):

Sam Charters: "I've had a long, complicated relationship with Harry's set. I first heard it in New Orleans in 1952 just after it first came out – a folk singer named Billy Faier in the French Quarter had it – then when Annie and I first began living together in 1957 the first thing we bought together was the Harry Smith set. $35 – a lot of money for us.

{CLARENCE ASHLEY | "THE COO COO BIRD" *from the Anthology* †}

A LETTER FROM SAM TO FOLKWAYS CO-FOUNDER, MARIAN DISTLER

Houston, Texas
Jan.16, 1959

Marian,

I've found and recorded the legendary Lightning Hopkins. It's been a hell of a struggle, but I got an l.p out of him.

When I told Moe there was a chance that I'd find Lightning but that he'd probably take money Moe said go ahead; so I have. He's used to the kind of recording fees the major outfits have paid him in the past - he's recorded on Gold Star, Alladin, Herald, and Score - and we had a long weary afternoon. I was able to get him for $300. It took nearly every cent I had, but it was nothing compared to what he used to get from Gold Star and Alladin.

There were other singers Moe and I talked about, but Lightning is the only important one. He's got this sudden reputation among the folk singers, which the Score l.p. has helped, even though it's the old Alladin material. He's the best, without much question; so I'm not going to record anyone else. If anyone's interested in managing him; let me know. There's money here.

I'll be able to talk to Blind Lemon's family and get back to New Orleans, but at that point I'll be completely without money. I'll need the $300. I don't know how this catches you. There was/time for me to call.

How quickly do you want the tapes? I think you should get this out as quickly as possible. No matter what has to be delayed. He's pretty hot at this moment, and after we listened to the play-back we both f........'d never sung better. I can get the notes to you .... ys.

.... m staying with Mack McCormick in Houston.

.... ress is about the best I can do, but it

Regards,

Sam Charters

very

"I liked some of it – some of it I already knew – and it all seemed to be just part of what had been going on with the reissues of old jazz and blues recordings since the 1930s. Fred Ramsey was doing a 12-volume LP reissue for Moe Asch of the history of jazz at the same time and his volume 1 had a lot of the same kinds of material.

"When I began working with Moe he said that he had been helping support Harry and they both were junking old 78s on 6th Avenue, just around the corner from the Folkways office. All the records in the collection were up in the office and half of the records that went into the set were his. He said that he and Harry had talked a lot about what they wanted from the set and of course it followed the outlines that the Lomaxes had set up in their folk song anthologies. The LPs were fine and fun – but no big deal.

"But – for all those sixties teenagers the world began with Bob Dylan, and if he listened to the set it had to be the roots of everything that ever happened in America. Harry was living in the Chelsea Hotel all this time and in all my experiences with him he was a genuine horse's ass. I had to shut him up some-times when I was trying to record people in the Village, and he kept drifting into Moe's office begging for money.

"All his films were there as well, but I had seen a lot of experimental film and I didn't think these were very exciting. His great things seemed to be the collection of painted Russian Easter Eggs in his hotel room, and his unending repertoire of string games. I edited an album of Allen Ginsberg's readings and singing from tapes that Harry made in the hotel room, and at least he got a decent sound.

"He made some scrawled notes for a volume 4 and I was given the luckless task of trying to figure out what he wanted to include from his list – which drew down upon my head the wrath of everyone whose lives had begun with the original three volumes.

"Harry finally couldn't pay his hotel bill, so Allen moved him in and supported him, which meant that Harry now became an iconic figure, since Allen always made it known that he only hung out with important figures. Before he died Allen set up in his will a legacy to pay for promotion of the Harry Smith legend. The woman who had the job was a fire-eater who often expressed her dislike for me, but I always felt that she was just doing what she was paid to do.

"There was eventually a Harry Smith celebration at the St. Mark's Church on the Lower East Side where Harry was presented as the only person anyone knew who was probably at least as important as Jesus.

"So that's me and Harry – I wish some of these people could somehow see that what happened in the 1950s was just a continuation of the gathering and collecting of vernacular music in the South that had been going on for nearly a century. Everything I learned was from what people like Fred Ramsey and Bill Russell had done in New Orleans and the South in the 1930s – their recordings of musicians like Leadbelly and Bunk

Johnson and Jelly Roll Morton – the books and articles and eventually LPs and films.

"Why does Harry get the credit for something that was much larger than his set? I dunno. I did a radio interview yesterday with someone in America who had just read *The Country Blues* and he wasn't really aware that these things could have happened so long ago. At least the people obsessed with the blues don't go on about Harry – they want to talk about the Stones and the other Brits. I try always to talk about other things, but there is always a silence. At least he didn't ask me about Dylan. You can certainly pass this on to Tom – a small muted protest."

Thankfully, Tom felt that it was "a priceless perspective to get on things – a rich account from a significant individual." As it is. My dad used to include a couple of the tracks from the *Anthology* when he did record recitals around the country in the late fifties. I found these notes he made about Richard "Rabbit" Brown's "James Alley Blues".

FOUR **ON MY IPOD, DANNY O'DONOGHUE,** *METRO*

"Fire and Rain" by James Taylor. "This is such an emotional song and without doubt one of his best. It's about the time he spent with junkies, in particular a girl called Suzanne." Ah, Danny, with his simple, inaccurate view of the world...

The song actually chronicled Taylor's experiences in institutions, such as McLean Hospital in Massachusetts, as a senior in high school and his battle with addiction ('fire' in the title refers to his shock therapy).

"Suzanne the plans they made put an end to you" refers to Suzanne Schnerr, a childhood friend of his who committed suicide while he was away in London recording his first album for Apple Records. Friends at home, concerned that it might distract Taylor from his big break, kept the news from him, and he only found out six months later.

FIVE **"WHERE'S MY HARMONICA, ALBERT?" WHY, IN BEAK STREET, BOB,**

... at your pop-up store, located just past the corner of Carnaby and Beak. Truth be told, it's fairly underwhelming. I bump into Mark Ellen, whose two-time-listen opinion of *Tempest* is "Five good songs". Dead-on. Or as my friend Lloyd said, "It's like a Theme-Time Radio Show – but it's just him..."

Wednesday, September 19

ONE **OH, LIGHTEN UP MAN!**

Wynton Marsalis, responding to *Mojo*'s questionnaire, in their November issue (NB: It's just the opening of each answer):

What, if push comes to shove, is your all-time favourite album?
"I don't have a favourite album."
What was the first record you ever bought?
"Bought? I don't think I've ever bought a record."
Which musician, other than yourself, have you ever wanted to be?
"I've never wanted to be another musician."
What do you sing in the shower?
"I never sing in the shower."
What is your favourite Saturday night record?
"I don't think I've ever played a record on a Saturday night – I've played a gig almost every Saturday night since I was 13."

To be fair, the rest of the answer to "Which musician have you ever wanted to be?" is interesting: "You have no idea what they've had to deal with. The person I rate for something musical might have had an endless headache, or a back pain. Every person has something you can't imagine to deal with."

TWO **CLASSIFIED AD MANN**

So I've just filed an interview with Aimee Mann to *Rock's Back Pages* and it has this reference to a movie she's going to make: "I'm actually doing a little indie movie. Joe Henry is involved in – it's based on a *This American Life* episode [TAL is a weekly public-radio show broadcast on more than 500 stations, telling stories from everyday life] about this journalist who thinks: suppose she got a bunch of musicians from Craigslist, just kind of randomly posting 'Looking for musicians,' and forms a band and puts them in a studio for a day – what would that look like? So I'm playing that woman. And Joe Henry's going to be in it, and John Doe is going to be in it and Loudon Wainwright… and Joe is doing the music for it. So it sounds interesting, right? Too bad I don't know how to act…"

THREE HARRY SMITH CONF: A POSTSCRIPT

Esteemed writer and documentary maker Mick Gold emails about the conference: "Harry Smith conference had good stuff. Very detailed history of 'Moonshiners Dance Part One' from *Anthology*, which was a funny history of Minneapolis/St Paul. Rani Singh [director of the Harry Smith Archives] said that when they were reissuing the Anthology in 1997, they asked Alan Lomax for a comment. Lomax's reply was dismissive, similar to Charters' – Smith was a nasty piece of work, his *Anthology* wasn't that important, he ripped people off.

"Clearly there are political tensions in how this old music was presented historically, and the message it conveyed. Remember that when Irwin Silber got involved in running Folkways in the 1960s, he changed the Anthology cover, substituting a Ben Shahn FSA [Farm Security Administration] shot of a poor farmer for Fludd's celestial monochord. Perhaps

{AIMEE MANN | "BARFLY"}

THREE DUQUESNE BY BOB GUMPERT

Following last week's mention of "Duquesne Whistle",
Bob sends these intense photos of the town and
its abandoned Steel Mill, shot in 1986.

ONE FRIDAY: PUBLIC PIANO, EUROSTAR TERMINAL

A kind of omen, as we walk through the train terminal – a man starts playing a lovely, stately version of "Hallelujah", Len's now-most-famous song. As he finishes we say thanks for starting our trip off in such perfect style. He says it's obviously a sign and advises us to buy a lottery ticket.

TWO SUNDAY: MONTPARNASSE CEMETERY

A small detour to the tombs of Man Ray, de Beauvoir and Sartre, and here, covered in metro tokens, roses, kisses and poor pencil drawings, the grave of Serge Gainsbourg.

THREE SUNDAY: THE OLYMPIA MUSIC HALL

The couple sitting next to us met at a Cohen concert at Leeds University on his first tour in May 1970. And here they were, celebrating at the Paris Olympia 42 years later. And the grey fedora? Adopted, I was assured, long before Len.

FOUR THE CONCERT: IN NUMBERS

Thirty-three songs.

Three hours, 40 minutes.

Three encores comprising seven songs.

Ten musicians, made up of three women and seven men – two singers from Kent, England; one from Los Angeles, USA; one from Montreal, Canada; one drummer from Mexico City, Mexico; one keyboardist from Florida, USA; one guitarist from Texas, USA; one bassist from New York State, USA; one violinist from Moldova; one multi-instrumental string player from Zaragoza, Spain.

THE CONCERT: FIVE GREAT MOMENTS

1 A brilliant performance of "Everybody Knows", every verse a work of genius, every verse a still-accurate assessment of human weakness and failure. Co-writer Sharon Robinson later sings a glorious solo version of "Alexandra Leaving".

2 A bravura moment at the last verse of "The Future" where Leonard sings the "There'll be fires on the road / and the white man dancing," and bassist Roscoe Beck does a stately pirouette, which is followed by LC singing "And all the lousy little poets / coming round / tryin' to sound like Charlie Manson / and the white girls dancing," whereupon the Webb Sisters turn away from their mikes, take one step back and, synchronised, do perfect cartwheels...

off before the band (including half of Was Not Was and Robben Ford) came in. Tonight, Javier Mas was the star turn, a master-class in flamenco, playing the bandurria like a man possessed, the elastic strings rolling and tumbling to a frenzied crescendo.

EXTRA! THE CONCERT: SOME OBSERVATIONS
You have to make your peace with the fact that a certain amount of drama is missed by muting the drums quite this much. The sound is perfect and balanced, intentionally allowing every word to ring clearly through. To make up for the lack of beat, Larsen's churchy Hammond B3, Alex Bublitchi's muscular violin and Javier Mas's extraordinary Laud provide thrilling dynamics.

Mitch Watkins on guitar provides structure, architecture and blues – his moaning slur at the end of a Wes Montgomery-like solo on "Amen" the coup de grâce.

The older-type singers (the ones who aren't Mick Jagger, anyway) are very fond of the prizefighter pose. Len takes this even further than the bob-and-weave and sings at least half the set on his knees on the patterned rugs that cover the stage, James Brown-style. It also emphasised the supplicant nature of many of the songs: to God, to poetry, to lust, love, the musicians and to the audience, who he always addresses as "Friends". His ability to get back up from his knees with grace is very impressive.

The only singer with a deeper voice than Len is Barry White. That is a stone-cold fact.

3 Leonard soloing on a Jew's harp, that most American of instruments, on the hoedown breaks of "Closing Time", one of two songs ("Heart with No Companion" being the other) where he sounds uncannily like Tom T. Hall, only deeper. Also, "Take This Waltz" in a Weimar-ish arrangement, has a hint of The Sensational Alex Harvey Band. Honest.
4 "Night Comes On". I hadn't dared to hope that I'd hear Leonard sing my favourite song. And sing it he does, causing some spontaneous tears in the audience, its mournful melody letting the words cascade in their stoic and weary way, on the cushion of warmth the band create.
5 I remember catching a version of "Who By Fire" † in the late eighties in a hotel room in LA by chance. It was on *Night Music*, a show hosted by David Sanborn, with Hal Willner and Jools Holland involved – a precursor to *Later*. Sonny Rollins joined Leonard and played an unaccompanied intro that tore the roof

Alchemical versus Popular Front perspective."

Mick had earlier told me that in his opinion, Greil Marcus "created Harry Smith the Magus. Why? Because Harry offered Greil a completely different narrative on the uncovering & collecting of traditional songs & blues from the 'voice of the people,' oppressed blacks, Lomax, popular front orthodoxy. Harry offered alchemy, esoteric magic, mystification, and he came from the West, all big pluses in the eyes of Greil. Hence *Invisible Republic*."

Wednesday, September 26

ONE THEN, OUR NEXT FIXTURE IS JETHRO TULL OF WIESBADEN...

Montpellier football boss René Girard was angered that his side had to play Arsenal in the Champions League on Tuesday evening and then face Saint-Etienne just a couple of days later on Friday. "I am not paranoid. I simply say that it's a question of fairness. We played Arsenal, one of the best sides in Europe; we did not play Pink Floyd of Kiev," Girard said scathingly. (I'm guessing that this is an amusing reference to Young Boys of Bern, who recently played Liverpool in the Europa League.)

TWO MUSE, LATER, SEPTEMBER 25

Playing "Madness". Reined in and tight to the chest, they sounded for all the world like the house band in a bar in a Philip K. Dick novel, with disco overtones. A Triumph!

THREE I SAW THE SPLENDOUR OF THE MOONLIGHT, ON HONOLULU BAY

We had a uke moment in 1968, with the great Richard Perry–produced *God Bless Tiny Tim* album, then again in '72 on Arlo Guthrie's wonderful *Hobo's Lullaby*. There were few sightings until Evan Hurd [great photographer!] gave us Israel Kamakawiwo'ole and his extraordinary "OK, this one's for Gabby"* version of "Over the Rainbow / What a Wonderful World" in the early nineties. But now we have The Ukulele Orchestra of Great Britain for all our ukelele requirements, busting their way through Ennio Morricone, Handel and Lady Gaga in a smorgasbord of styles and genres.

At the Albert Hall on Friday they revisited the site of their Proms triumph of last year. Showing someone who'd never

FOUR STEPHEN COLLINS VS MUMFORD & SONS. THE MAN'S A GENIUS!

heard of them a clip on YouTube, I was thrilled to catch sight of Lloyd and me strumming Beethoven's "Ode to Joy" along with 1,006 other ukes.

That's Gabby Pahinui, whose slack-key guitar playing so inspired Ry Cooder that he flew to Hawaii to make a record with him. He features on Cooder's album Chicken Skin Music.

FIVE VAN THE MAN SATNAV: A STEP CLOSER

My friend Steve phones up one evening, the sound of jazz behind him as he leaves a message on the Ansaphone: "Hi Martin, it's Steve. I'm playing Van live and I just sort of realised the way to do the satnav is to just play it and let me do it live... not that I can sing like him but you can do it if you're listening to him, 'cos stuff occurs.

But if you're sitting there cold with a blank piece of paper you can't do it. You realise when you're listening to the tracks, like 'Tupelo Honey' – 'Well, you can take the A45' or whatever... and you can do it to the tune so it's real. That's the way we'll do it, alright? Cheers!" So I download the set of instructions from the TomTom site and all I have to do is record Steve and figure out how to save the commands as Ogg Vorbis files [what!?!]. More anon...

Wednesday, October 3

ONE TOM MORELLO, RAGING

From *Rolling Stone* magazine: "[Paul] Ryan claims that he likes Rage [Against the Machine, Morello's band]'s sound but not the lyrics. Well, I don't care for Paul Ryan's sound *or* his lyrics... Basically, the only thing he's not raging against is the privileged elite he's grovelling in front of for campaign contributions. You see, the super-rich must rationalize having more than they could ever spend while millions of children in the US go to bed hungry every night." Excellent Raging against the Republican Machine in a magazine that veers worryingly between *Tiger Beat*–style fawning over sundry popstrels and top-notch political reportage and comment. For instance, read Matt Taibbi on Mitt Romney and weep.

TWO *HOMELAND* TRAILERS, CHANNEL 4

The first one is filled to the brim with all the creeping paranoia of the series, as a children's choir sings "The Star-Spangled Banner", before clattering drumming (military? Middle Eastern?) drowns it out in a series of shots of the characters all at different places, screaming...

The second, using Johnny Cash and Rick Rubin's "God's Gonna Cut You Down" is even better, and is mostly about Claire Danes' eyes... "Go tell that long-tongued liar / Go and tell that midnight rider / Tell the rambler, the gambler, the backbiter / Tell 'em that God's gonna cut 'em down / Tell 'em that God's gonna cut 'em down." Of course, the only question is: Whose God?

THREE MORE DUQUESNE...

In Paris to see Leonard Cohen I found this vintage Martinique Rum keyring in the Vanves antiques market. Is there a pun on de Cane (sugar) here?

FOUR HOUND DOG POSTER, AU PASSAGE

I've been listening to Hound Dog Taylor lately, and who should I find on the walls of an artfully lo-fi restaurant in Paris but the man himself, complete with a great quote: "He couldn't play shit, but he sure made it sound good!" I should point out that these were his own words, prefaced with "When I die, they'll say..."

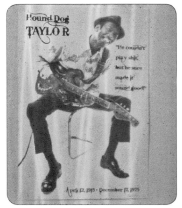

FIVE 1976: THE FIRST TIME I SAW LEONARD

After Paris, I thought back to the first time. It was on the south coast of England.

MY PHOTO OF LEONARD ON TOUR IN 1976

A friend of my mother's was managing the hotel where Leonard and his musicians were staying and had tickets to his show. I didn't really know much about his music then, but this was World Music before it had a name, with the flamenco melodies, the gypsy violin and the Moorish oud. Backstage for a meet-and-greet, we were struck dumb. The next morning, having breakfast at the next table, we were even more tongue-tied.

Wednesday, October 10

ONE GENIUS IDEA OF THE WEEK

Nick Paumgarten writes about record producer Scott Litt, *The New Yorker*, October 1. "When Scott Litt built a recording studio in back of his house, in Venice, California, seven years ago, he did it with Bob Dylan in mind. He pictured Dylan sitting there at the Hammond organ, accompanied by nothing but drums and a standup bass. Or maybe in an arrangement featuring a banjo and a trumpet. 'I always imagined him having a Louis Armstrong "Hello, Dolly" sound,' Litt said the other day. 'Musically, that's as American as it gets.' Sadly, when Litt was hired to engineer Bob's latest, *Tempest*, and "got up the nerve to mention his 'Hello, Dolly' idea, it didn't go over very well. [Bob] just went, 'Heh heh heh – "Hello, Dolly".'"

TWO THIS, FROM THE VERY WONDERFUL
LETTERS OF NOTE

In 1919 (at which point he was just nine years old) Samuel Barber wrote the following letter to his mother and left it on his desk for her to find. She did, and a year later Barber began to compose his first opera, *The Rose Tree*. He was still only 26 years of age when, in 1936, he finished his most famous work, *Adagio for Strings*.

"NOTICE *to Mother and nobody else*
Dear Mother: I have written this to tell you my worrying secret.
Now don't cry when you read it because it is neither yours nor
my fault. I suppose I will have to tell it now without any nonsense.
To begin with I was not meant to be an athlet [sic]. I was meant
to be a composer, and will be I'm sure.
I'll ask you one more thing. – Don't ask me to try to forget this
unpleasant thing and go play football. – Please – Sometimes
I've been worrying about this so much that it makes me mad
(not very),
Love,
Sam Barber II"

THREE ROLL ON, JOHN
Stanley Reynolds' piece for *The Guardian* from June 3, 1963, was reprinted this week: "Inside the club, down CND symbol smeared walls to a dark and bronchial cave, the dancers have originated the Cavern Stomp, because they did not have room enough to twist. In the dressing room off stage a steady flow of rock artistes come to talk with Mr Bob Wooler, the Cavern's full-time disc jockey whose visiting card tells you, with Dickensian charm, that he is 'a rhythm and blues consultant.'

"That is The Cavern, duffel coats and feigned boredom. On tour it is like a Hollywood success story. At the Odeon, Manchester, in the Beatles' dressing room, the four boys were asking a reporter from a disc magazine to please see if she could do something to stop girls from sending them jelly babies. She had once said they liked them. 'We've got two ton of them now,' John Lennon said. 'Tell them to send us E-type Jaguars or button-down shirts.' Someone came in and said two girls had won them in a contest. 'Just who are these girls who won us?' John Lennon asked. 'I mean, how long have they won us for?'"

Wednesday, October 17

ONE ROCK ME, DAVY!
1972, Fulham. Tony Cane-Honeysett calls me over to his record player. "Listen to this!" he says. The 45 starts with a snarly riff, before going into a moody, groovy blues, with snappy drums and hooky fuzz guitars. The singer sounds both pop and familiar. After a few minutes I tumble. It's David Cassidy, essaying a new, more grown-up direction, trying to move on from teen fandom to a kind of rock/blues. In May of '72 he'll pose nearly naked for Annie Leibovitz in *Rolling Stone*.

This week in 2012, four of Cassidy's albums from this period are re-released. Not sure I'll check them out, but for old times' sake (Hey, Tone!) I re-listen to "Rock Me Baby", and it's great. The Wrecking Crew rhythm section – Hal Blaine on drums and Joe Osborn on bass – get down while Mike Melvoin (father of Wendy) prowls around the edges on piano. In the centre of the soundstage Larry Carlton and Dean Parks strut and fret, combining to brew up a nasty Southern Rock snarl. It's just great, and I'm back in Anselm Road with Tony…

TWO SEAMUS RYAN SINGS "LIVERPOOL LOU" TO BILLY CONNOLLY

We had 12 minutes to photograph Billy Connolly in a room in a painfully Boutique Hotel™ this week. Photographer (to the stars) Seamus breaks the ice and makes a connection by revealing that he's Dominic Behan's godson, and Billy, famously, once decked Dominic in a bar, a fight broken up by Ronnie Drew of The Dubliners.

Billy remembers the incident in some detail, including the fact that he apologised the next morning to Dominic (sober throughout the whole fracas). At one point in the 12 minutes Seamus sings a few bars of "Liverpool Lou", one of his godfather's most famous songs (he also wrote "The Patriot Game") very prettily. On a recent *Desert Island Discs*, Yoko Ono selected "Liverpool Lou" as one of her choices, remembering that her husband had sung it to their son as a lullaby. Oh, and if you're worried, Seamus delivered, as always.

THREE NOW THIS SOUNDS INTRIGUING...

The Coen brothers' next film is *Inside Llewyn Davis*, about a struggling folk musician in the Village at the height of the 1960s folk scene. Apparently, the film's title character is based on Dave Van Ronk. Bob Sheldon called him the Mayor of MacDougal Street (also the name of Van Ronk's autobiography, written with Elijah Wald) and everyone who went through Greenwich Village at that time seems to owe him a debt, most famously Dylan. John Goodman was interviewed in US *Esquire* this month by Scott Raab, and talked about it:

Raab: *What are you shooting in New York?*

Goodman: "*Inside Llewyn Davis*. I'm playing a junkie jazz musician for Joel and Ethan Coen. I haven't worked with them since *O Brother, Where Art Thou?* – 15 years. Boy, it's great to be back with them again. We have a real good comfort zone. I just adore being with those guys. It's like hanging around with high school guys or something."

Raab: *I've heard the film is based on folk singer Dave Van Ronk's life. So it's set in Greenwich Village in the '60s?*

Goodman: "Right on the cusp of Dylan's big explosion."

Raab: *I'm probably one of the few people who's seen* Masked and Anonymous, *the movie you were in with Dylan, half a dozen times. It's such a strange movie, and it has so many moving parts. It's a fascinating film. How was Dylan on set?*

Goodman: "Being around Bob was a trip. I just hung back and watched him. When the cats had downtime, they'd go somewhere and play together. And I'd listen to that. The film got a god-awful reception at Sundance. There were a lot of walkouts, but who cares? It was kind of an absurdist, futurist piece. It was fun. And I got to work with Jeff Bridges again. I got to stand next to the fabulous Penélope Cruz for a little while. That was worth the price of admission. Senorita Cruz."

FOUR MORTIFICATION CORNER

1) *From the Diane Krall website:* "Diana Krall has collaborated with Academy Award winning costume designer Colleen

Atwood and acclaimed photographer Mark Seliger to create a series of beautiful and striking images for Krall's new album, *Glad Rag Doll*. They are inspired by Alfred Cheney Johnston's pictures of the girls of the Ziegfeld Follies taken during the 1920s." Well, if you say so...

2) Pity poor Art Garfunkel as he sits on the sofa being interviewed by the *One Show* dolts while they implore the Mrs Robinsons in their audience to text photos of themselves, preferably with toy boys. Art tried to modify the disdain in his expression, but didn't quite succeed.

Wednesday, October 24

ONE **YOU CAN'T ALWAYS GET WHAT YOU WANT**

"I had the idea immediately, the idea of somebody sticking their tongue out. The difficulty for me was how to portray that visually, as a disembodied mouth. So I tried straight on, I tried a profile – different views of it, different versions. And obviously I was trying to get something that looked a bit pop and looked

a bit cartoony, but also something that looked luscious. And I just kept re-drawing it until I came up with the version as it is now, the original. That's what I presented to Jagger, and he said he really liked it." – That's from a recent interview I did with John Pasche about the Lips & Tongue logo. He also said, "I find it difficult to look at the versions of it – as a designer it just irks me a bit. But I have to say, I think it has been used quite cleverly over the years in different forms on the various tours. And I think that's probably Jagger again." Gird your loins, John, here it comes for another round...

TWO **SOMETIMES ONLY MOR WILL DO**

Michael Hann on Kirsty MacColl, *The Observer*: "Since her dad [folk singer Ewan McColl] was absent, MacColl could sing along to her brother Hamish's singles, apparently teaching herself the vocal harmony parts to the Beach Boys' 'Good Vibrations' when she was seven." Her mother remembers Kirsty waiting for the musical interludes in Andy Williams' TV show: "Kirsty would take her violin out of the case and accompany him. I would have a quiet laugh to myself, but she took it very seriously. Then she'd put the violin away until Andy Williams came out for another song, and out would come the violin."

Like a palate cleanser between courses, listening to MOR provides a respite from less smooth music. I've always been drawn to Bacharach and David (the *Butch Cassidy* soundtrack is a favourite), Dean Martin and Andy Williams. A few months before Williams' death, BBC Four ran compilations of songs from his shows, and the duets showed his mastery of harmony lines, timing and plain fitting-in with his illustrious guests.

None was finer than Judy Garland, with an astonishing performance singing – of course – "Over the Rainbow". Halting

THREE "HERD OF MORONS." BRILLIANT.

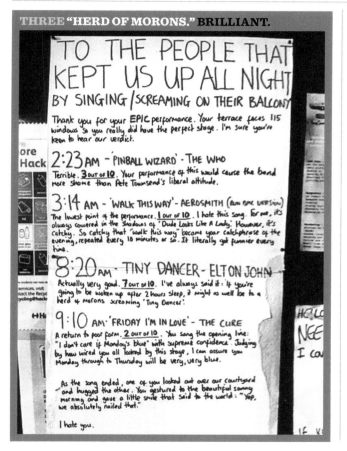

and hoarse, she eases her way into the song tentatively, staring the camera (and audience) down, like it's an enemy out to get her. As she gets into her stride she suddenly powers into the chorus like a trouper, before pulling back on *...birds fly over the rainbow*, sung *so* beautifully. Andy joins in on the final two lines ("If happy little bluebirds fly / beyond the rainbow, why, oh, why can't IIIIIIIIIIIIIIII...") to tenderly wind the song down.

THREE ON MY IPOD, LISA HANNIGAN, *METRO*

"Bells of Harlem" by The Dave Rawlings Machine. "My friends are sick of me banging on about this tune but I think it's perfect."

I'm with Lisa. A melody so beautiful, the first time I heard it I immediately looped the intro to use as a ringtone on my phone. Plangent and plaintive, it's up there with "People Get Ready" as a great song about the Civil Rights movement, with a clever and sharp-eyed lyric... "Far down the streets, I see the signs / The crowd is breathing faster / Some must have walked a hundred blocks / I see the flocks and pastors."

Wednesday, October 31st

ONE DANNY BAKER, *SHORTLIST* Q & A

Who's the most overrated band of your lifetime? "Queen. A dreadful group. They were neither Led Zeppelin nor Bowie and they played that middle ground in between. Punk rock didn't come around because of prog rock or anything like that, it came around because of Queen. ABBA, Queen and ELO – that was what people were trying to move away from. You can find everything Queen did better elsewhere."

TWO BOB DYLAN & THE POETRY OF THE BLUES

Michael Gray, pretty much my favourite writer on Bob Dylan, gives a talk in Canterbury, close enough to drive to. Mick Gold comes with me, supplying an excellent compilation CD and fascinating conversation for our tiny road trip. Michael's presentation is terrific – funny and revelatory. Over a meal afterwards we talk about the fact that Freddy Koella is both Michael's and my favourite Dylan guitarslinger. Mick reveals that the night before, Freddy had guested for two songs at Bob's Santa Barbara gig – the first time since he was a member of the Never Ending Tour Band in 2004.

Michael: "Freddy was Dylan's best-ever lead electric guitarist (and just might be the best electric guitarist altogether since the heyday of Hubert Sumlin). Robbie Robertson was near sublime – the next best, a very close second – but Freddy was better. And in The Band all the other musicians were crucial too, whereas in Dylan's band Freddy had to carry the whole front line. Of course, you could say Mike Bloomfield was right up there, but he was, though a virtuoso, essentially more limited (Dylan had to tell him, for 'Like a Rolling Stone', to play 'none of that B.B. King shit'); and G.E. Smith was terrific, but safe. You never wondered excitedly what he might do next.

"Whereas Freddy played by living on the edge, like Bob, fusing Django Reinhardt and Carl Perkins and playing as if it

were 1957 now. He was the electric lead guitarist Dylan himself would have been, had Dylan ever bothered to master the instrument." That line is fantastic, and spot on – "playing as if it were 1957 now".

THREE PAPA NEZ'S BLUES

To the Queen Elizabeth Hall with my mum to see her old fave, Mike Nesmith (the First & Second National Band stuff, not The Monkees, just so's you know). I seem to be making it a point lately to see only Senior Citizens Of Rock™ but it's just coincidental. It's instructive to compare and contrast the approaches, however.

LEONARD "LADIES' MAN" COHEN, 78, four years into his latest group of tours, is in fantastic voice, essaying three-and-a-half-hour shows with some of the finest musicians on God's earth and playing versions of his songs that make the original tracks seem pale shadows. It is, in all senses, not just another show. It's a proper summation of a life's work.

IAN "MOTT TO TROT" HUNTER, 73, belts out his impressive and rockin' back catalogue with ferocious intent, fronting a hell-for-leather combo, The Rant Band. On lead guitar, Mark Bosch is a passionate and note/feel-perfect seventies/eighties Noo Yawk (think Leslie West or Mike Rathke) player, matching Hunter every step of the way. Hunter's tribute to Mick Ronson, "Michael Picasso", is really moving, and the sense of community between him and his fans something to feel.

MIKE "PAPA NEZ" NESMITH, 70, hasn't played in London

since 1975, and makes a rather terrible decision. Sold to the audience as cutting-edge technology by Nesmith, the three musicians onstage play along with prerecorded tracks (mostly triggered by the keyboardist), which (a) makes the sound terrible, all clunky Casio drums and booming sound effects, and (b) forces everyone into a rather tight and metronomic way of playing – an already fairly predictable bass player becomes almost immobile, and the music has no sway or grace. This seems a real shame, as Nesmith's use of soundscapes on tracks like "Nevada Fighter", "Bonaparte's Retreat" or "Beyond the Blue Horizon" was really innovative, especially in a country rock context.

There are some beautiful songs here, from "Joanne" to "Grand Ennui" to "Rio", and Nesmith has the fine idea of setting up each song with a short piece of fiction contextualising the events that have (supposedly) led up to the song. But the bad sound, the gloopy, excessive synth string playing, the hopeless limping beats and Nesmith's out-of-practice and strained voice leaves us feeling somewhat underwhelmed.

FIVE NOT SO LUCKY, LUCKY, LUCKY

"I love all the PWL stuff slowed down, it sounds great," says Kylie talking about *The Abbey Road Sessions*, where she re-records her pop hits of the eighties. I remember when the band I was part of (who *NME* saw as the antithesis of Stock Aitken Waterman's PWL stuff – Rick Astley, Kylie, Jason Donovan) decided to record a slow version of Kylie's "I Should Be So Lucky" for a radio session. Sounded great when Mark roughed it out on piano with Heather, but someone somewhere in RCA Records hit the Irony Alert! button and thought better of it...

Wednesday, November 7

ONE BEST MUSIC-RELATED TOK PISIN PHRASE

"The Prince of Wales spoke in the local language called Tok Pisin as he introduced himself as the 'nambawan pikinini bilong Misis Kwin' – the number one child belonging to Mrs Queen... Tok Pisin is a creole language and is the most widely spoken in Papua New Guinea... Tok is derived from the English word talk and Pisin from pidgin." Much of its vocabulary has a special charm. For instance, "liklik box you pull him he cry you push him he cry" is an accordion.

TWO THE VIDEO THAT KILLED A CAREER

Alexis Petridis wrote an interesting piece about the new book *I Want My MTV* a few weeks back, and he mentioned eighties arena rock star Billy Squier and the video for the track "Rock Me Tonite", directed by Kenny Ortega. I finally got around to watching it, and it is quite the most deranged and strange video ever made (it often makes lists of the worst videos of all time), after which Billy's career tanked.

As I watched it I felt sad for Billy, and I perused the usual sidebar links to other Billy Squier videos. I alighted on one where he's sitting on a high stool in a lecture theatre, alone except for a blonde Telecaster capo'd at A. I clicked the link. He's playing a smallish fundraiser, fairly recently. He has a suit jacket on and looks like a better-preserved Joe Perry. The guitar is powerfully amped, and he starts a strutting riff as he plays "In the Dark". It's terrific. It's a fairly generic eighties rock number, but he gives it 110%, wailing and bending strings like a man possessed, and for as long as it plays you want to be driving down a road, really fast, at night.

THREE NAIL. HEAD. LADIES & GENTLEMEN, MR. ROBBIE FULKS

On sifting and sorting and downsizing his CD collection: "Scrapping fat glossy packages by the likes of Timbaland, Nelly, Luke Bryan, and T. G. Sheppard (to be clear, and not to inflame everyone, I like a few songs by all these guys okay, but can't justify the permanent storage of dozens of them) reminds me of the passing nature of fashionable taste and the extravagance of the moneyed sector of the music industry in satisfying it.

"The photography on the Timbaland record that has somehow come into my possession looks like it cost a hundred thousand dollars. The booklet is so thick you can hardly coax it from the jewel case. If some dude turns a goofball idea into a popular hit and everyone dances around and enjoys the summer more, it doesn't seem very objectionable.

"But when you give a moment's thought to the year-of-vaccines-for-Bangladeshis' worth of art design, the carbon footprint of multiple buses crisscrossing the country for years

on end, and the transfer of millions upon millions of dollars from work-weary parents to summer-enjoying kids... you almost have to weep."

FIVE WHAT HAS HAPPENED DOWN HERE IS THE WINDS HAVE CHANGED

Listening to jazz clarinettist Sammy Rimington sing "River Stay Away from My Door" on Saturday night, I'm put in mind of the

effects of Hurricane Sandy on friends on the East Coast. Rick in NYC: "It's weird and slightly creepy walking back into the deep dark of lower Manhattan below 30th Street at night. I expect highwaymen with every breeze."

And John in Woodstock: "A bunch of big old trees came down, leaving us cold and dark and off the grid until early this morning. The soundtrack is chainsaws, nothing but chainsaws." As the song's lovely Carmichaelish melody unfolds, Sammy sings plaintively over the top: "Don't come up any higher / Cause I'm all so alone / Just stay away from my bed and my fire / Cause that's all I own..."

Wednesday, November 14

ONE OH, AND STEELY DAN SANG "CALL ME DEACON BLUE"

Steve Miller sang "Some people call me the Space Cowboy, some call me the Gangster of Love". Carly Rae Jepsen sang "Call Me Maybe". Blondie and Al Green just sang "Call Me..." Beth Orton, like JJ Cale before her, sings "Call Me the Breeze". It's on her new album, *Sugaring Time*, and it's wonderful.

It sits on a groove that doesn't quit – the great Brian Blade drums, with Sebastian Steinberg on bass, and a loopy Nick Drakesque folk guitar – and builds on the interplay between the dead-on bass pulse and Blade's drums skipping and punctuating the 4/4, keeping it off-kilter enough to really hook you in. Atop this sit wonderful entwining vocals and a glorious organ solo that creeps up out of the track, attempting to wrest it away from the massed ranks of Beth. Beth just about wins.

Interestingly, I can barely find a reference to this song in any review that I've read so far. It doesn't fall into the "mournful-serious-intense-lyrical thang" that all reviewers seem to need in female singer-songwriters, like only those type of songs have any heft. Go figure.

TWO NO "BOUTIQUE FESTIVAL" SETTING?

My brother-in-law has a brilliant new stereo set-up in his house, and his new Yamaha amp offers to model the sound for you – giving them the vibe and atmos of a Viennese Concert

Hall, say, or a Cellar Club. At the rock end it offers two clubs from the seventies, the Roxy in Los Angeles and The Bottom Line in New York. If you buy a more expensive model, it gives you the Village Vanguard (*"Nice!"*). Sadly, there's no Boutique Festival, where the music is drowned out by the clatter of glasses and middle-class chatter. In the end we decide the sound is great with no kind of modelling at all.

THREE SHAKEN, NOT STIRRED. CREDIT SEQUENCE, *SKYFALL*

Yes, Adele's song is very nice, all Bassey-isms present and correct, and it insinuates itself into your head really efficiently, but oh my, the film... Following an Istanbul-set opening sequence that isn't a patch on *Taken 2*'s Istanbul-set chase sequences (and let's not forget that *Taken 2* is a B-picture photocopied from another B-picture, albeit a great one), the credits are unbelievably cheesy. Incoherent, naff images glide by with no stylistic consistency at all, and it just makes you fearful of the next two hours. Rightly, as it turns out. Has Sam Mendes not seen *The Girl with the Dragon Tattoo*?

FOUR THE CROP MARKS & ARROWS OF OUTRAGEOUS FORTUNE

The International Herald Tribune, celebrating its 125th anni-

BOB DYLAN

photo will be cropped, focusing on who the editors deemed the important part of the story.

On the left we see Bennie Goodman clowning with Steve Allen; The Stones in Paris (only Brian Jones escapes a wax pencil cross); Dylan press-release shot for *The Times They Are A-Changin'*, which someone wants straightened up; Jane Birkin [x] with Serge Gainsbourg; Lionel Hampton clowning with Elsie Smith. Notice how jazz musicians always seem forced to "clown around"...

FIVE TREY SONGZ' RHYTHM SECTION
Trey sings his glassy, glossy pop hit "Simply Amazing", his schtick a little out of place on *Later*, and it's all pretty groovy and efficient enough until about a minute and a half in, when you're not listening to Trey at all, you're just listening for what Nate Jones on bass will do next – adding little filigree high-register melodies, dropping back to the root notes on his way-deep five-string, totally in the pocket of the groove.

About ninety seconds from the end they drop into a breakdown section, and that's when drummer Antwan "Amadeus" Thompson and Jones decide to get down and have a party on the tune. An outrageous series of rolls and hi-hat snaps are followed by Nate giving it the full Level 42, bass jutted out in front of him like he was Chuck Berry. At the

versary, has an auction of pictures from its archives on November 19. Looking through the catalogue, I'm mostly struck by the pictures of musicians, especially the ones that have compositors' marks and instructions and arrows on, showing how the

ONE EXCLUSIVE!

The headline for the *ShortList* Malibu Red advertorial: "It's a little bit more exclusive." Well, apart from the fact that something is exclusive or it isn't, the very word in the same sentence as the sickly coconut liqueur Malibu is a little, shall we say, rum.

TWO DON'T YOU JUST LOVE THOSE CREATIVE COLLABORATIONS?

I know that I do... "When Ne-Yo was appointed the creative director of Malibu Red [I know, who knew you could be?], he took the role seriously. Incredibly seriously, in fact. The Grammy-award-winning singer wasn't just involved with the design of the bottle of Malibu Red [It's brilliant. It looks like a bottle] – the new tequila-infused drink from Malibu [Hold on a moment. Let's process this. Ne-Yo. Rum. Coconut. Tequila. Yum!] – he also helped create the unique fusion, wrote an exclusive* track and shot a music video. Not only was his involvement hands-on [I know, again. It makes it sound like

Ne-Yo is doing this as a favour rather than being paid nightclubs-full-of-cash], he's the embodiment of Malibu Red [whatever that is]."

THREE NE-YO, TELL US ABOUT YOUR VIDEO

"The concept of the video is taking the smooth of Malibu rum and the fire of silver tequila. It's the smooth mixing with the fire. In the video, I turn the smooth and fire into a person..." Ne-Yo! Ne-Yo! Enough Smooth 'n' Fire, already!

FOUR NE-YO! LET'S SEE IT!

It's... it's hopelessly, hopelessly dull. Ne-Yo is the "Smooth," a Latina everywoman the "Fire." It takes place in a disco. It's every bit as bad as that sounds. The song? Like a Forever 21 or Primark version of Nelly.

FIVE FYI

Malibu Red is available in supermarkets nationwide, now. That's a little bit more exclusive... no?

There's that word again.

{NELLY | "HOT IN HERRE"}

end Trey does a boxer's shuffle and feint to the bassist, which I fondly think is to honour an exceptional performance.

Wednesday, November 21

ONE COVER ME

Around the time of the singer-songwriter boom of the early seventies, cover versions used to be odd one-offs, musicians showing respect for their elders & forbears, and subsidiary to the act's own material. Then covers became cute – hipper bands would cover less-hip pop songs, thus hipping them up. Then it all seemed to go wrong when people started making tribute cover albums.

Steve McL, who posts interesting and entertaining covers, usually themed, at the excellent *Cover Freak* [COVERFREAK. COM], puts it pithily in his manifesto: "You should only cover a song if you have a reason for covering it. Financial considerations don't count. Bring something new to the song... you're a musician, interpret the music! It can be good or bad, just make it different from the original. Otherwise, what's the point?"

This is all a roundabout way of saying that Meshell Ndegeocello's album of songs associated with the late and certainly great *Nina Simone – Pour une âme souveraine ("For a sovereign soul")* – is terrific. So far, her reworkings of "Please Don't Let Me Be Misunderstood", "Feelin' Good" (I know, daunting to even attempt), "Don't Take All Night" with Sinead, and "To Be Young Gifted and Black" with Cody ChesnuTT are the ones

I keep going back to, but the whole album is a triumph, and in a week where I heard The Mumfords wanly strum through "The Boxer", a necessity.

TWO THE FIRST 30 SECONDS OF "JIVE TALKIN'"

Go on, listen to them. Chunks of muted guitar. Then a solar-plexus kick drum and a nasty, grungy synth bass. Then some sweetness with a little Chic-like rhythm guitar before the snare and a double-tracked Barry come strutting in. Actually the whole song is pretty wonderful, especially the great drumming of Dennis Bryon.

THREE SOUTHERN SOUL ODYSSEY ONE

An email with this attachment from my relative Brett, taking a break from touring and holidaying in Alabama: "Trip Down Memory Lane!" I'm put in mind of time spent in the Shoals. I found this scan the other day of Jimmy Johnson's pick, which later served time as the *Rock's Back Pages* logo.

FOUR SOUTHERN SOUL ODYSSEY TWO

Coincidentally, we were talking about artworks where someone instructs others to do the work, with the visiting Bob and Sam Gumpert. I was obsessed at one time with letterpress printing and sourced an order form for a great print shop in the eighties called Tribune Showprint, out of Earl Park, Indiana.

I had seen a fantastic poster that they'd printed for the Mighty Clouds of Joy when we were at Muscle Shoals – they printed posters for the Chitlin' Circuit and soul shows, often on hand-screenprinted "rainbow" cards.

Mark and I immediately got them to do posters and covers for Hot House, our band. How great – typing out the wording and enclosing a glossy 10x8, posting the order off airmail, and three weeks later getting twenty-five cardboard posters back. And a few months after we released our cover of Willie Nelson's "Crazy" using the poster on the cover, Tom Petty's *Full Moon Fever* was released...

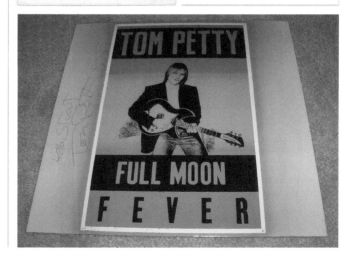

FIVE BORIS VIAN, MAN OF VISION

From the *International Herald Tribune* auction catalogue (see last week). "The Pianoctail is a strange instrument, imagined by Boris Vian in his novel *L'Écume des jours* (literally, 'The scum of days'). The renowned writer, who died in 1959, conceived this cocktail-making piano which would make a drink according to the notes played. An Americano is made when a major chord is played, and when a triad or tonic chord is played,

you get a gin fizz. The instrument was displayed this morning in a Parisian cinema, where the film is being shown tonight [March 20, 1968].

Vian described the Pianocktail in *L'Écume des jours* (this is Stanley Chapman's translation): "For each note there's a corresponding drink – either a wine, spirit, liqueur or fruit juice. The loud pedal puts in egg flip and the soft pedal adds ice. For soda you play a cadenza in F sharp. The quantities depend on how long a note is held – you get the sixteenth of a measure for a hemidemisemiquaver; a whole measure for a black note; and four measures for a semibreve.

"When you play a slow tune, then tone comes into control too to prevent the amounts growing too large and the drink getting too big for a cocktail – but the alcoholic content remains unchanged. And, depending on the length of the tune, you can, if you like, vary the measures used, reducing them, say, to a hundredth in order to get a drink taking advantage of all the harmonics, by means of an adjustment on the side."

Wednesday, November 28

ONE **THE RETURN OF SCOTT WALKER**

Exciting news for us Scott fans! In a relatively revealing *Guardian* interview as his new album, *Bish Bosch*, is launched, Scott talks about his fear of performing, as well as saying that no promoter would put him on anyway, as they're only interested in money. But Scott could tour cultural festivals, not rock arenas, if he chose.

In 2008, for instance, the Barbican put on *Drifting and Tilting: The Songs of Scott Walker*. It was more opera than rock. Scott, eyes hidden beneath baseball cap, stood at the mixing desk conducting his collaborator Peter Walsh. It was all I could do to drag my eyes away and back to the stage, which teemed with extraordinary visions.

The most arresting image? Possibly a boxer using a pig's carcass as a percussion instrument. Or maybe Gavin Friday as Elvis ("It casts its ruins in shadows / Under Memphis moonlight"), perched on a stool, singing to his stillborn twin Jesse, while a bequiffed and backlit figure strode from the backdrop of the stage until he assumed gigantic proportions, looming over the whole theatre. Whichever, it was an evening that lives on in the memory. Long may Scott run.

TWO **AMY'S BLUES**

The National Portrait Gallery in London buys a portrait by Marlene Dumas of the late Amy Winehouse. Dumas said "she

{GOOGLE | "BORIS VIAN PIANOCKTAIL" *to find Michel Gondry's film* MOOD INDIGO, *based on a Vian story*}

had been very moved by the news of Winehouse's death." Which sort of begs the question: why not be moved by something useful like her talent or her voice – while she was alive? What's "moving" about her death? "Dumas, who is based in Amsterdam, sought out images of Winehouse online for the work, which draws the viewer in to the singer's distinctive eyes and eyeliner."

Yes, you read that right. In "Art Speak", she Googled images of Amy online. And then copied some of the photos she found, quite badly. So, basically, this mediocre fan painting was co-created by GOOGLE IMAGE SEARCH (79,600,000 results).

THREE KERMIT THE FROG, MEET MILES DAVIS & JEANNE MOREAU

Genius overlay of Davis' session (filmed by Louis Malle) recording the soundtrack to *Lift to the Scaffold*, the great French noir from '58, with LCD Soundsystem's "New York, I Love You but You're Bringing Me Down". The film of Davis playing to a huge projection of Moreau walking the streets of Paris at night is just stunning. That's cut with Kermit on a rock across the river from Midtown Manhattan, and in Times Square.

Hats off to Alessandro Grespan for his inspired and crazy jamming together of these two videos. The despairing mood of both pieces is eloquently summed up in James Murphy's brilliant couplet: "There's a ton of the twist / but we're fresh out of shout..."

FOUR IS IT ROLLING, KEITH?

My favourite moment so far in *Crossfire Hurricane*, the Stones documentary, is the extraordinary stage-invasion footage. Keith: "It started, man, on the first tour. Halfway through, things started to get crazy [here the onstage cameras filming the concert record a group of young besuited guys pushing the Stones over, singing into Jagger's mike, attempting to pull Brian Jones' guitar off, as the soundtrack becomes phased and fragmented]... We didn't play a show after that, that was completed, for two or three years... We'd take bets on how long a show would last – You're on, 10 minutes..."

FIVE CHRISTIE'S POP CULTURE AUCTION PREVIEW, SOUTH KEN

A random sampling of the 20th century, from chairs that were part of the set of Rick's Café in *Casablanca*, via Harrison Ford's bullwhip from Raiders, to the "Iron Maiden" from Ken Russell's *Tommy* (a snip if it goes for its estimate of £1,000). I was there to gaze upon Mitch Mitchell's snare drum

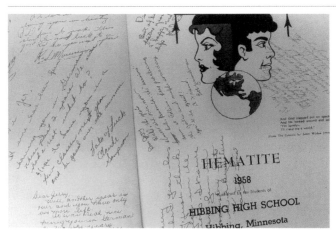

(as featured on "Purple Haze", "The Wind Cries Mary", "Hey Joe" etc) and Andy Warhol's mock-up of an unpublished book of the Stones' '75 tour. Favourite item? Hibbing High School Yearbook, 1958, signed: "Dear Jerry, Well the year's almost all over now, huh. Remember the 'sessions' down at Colliers. Keep practicing the guitar and maybe someday you'll be great! A friend, Bob Zimmerman."

Wednesday, December 5

ONE "THIS IS THE WEST, SIR. WHEN THE LEGEND BECOMES FACT, PRINT THE LEGEND."
Carleton Young as Maxwell Scott, in *The Man Who Shot Lib-erty Valance*. As I read *Mojo*'s obit of Terry Callier, the folk-jazz-soul singer-songwriter, my heart sinks as the oft-retold story of his first album is reprinted. Lois Wilson writes: "The following year saw him team with Prestige producer Samuel Charters. *The New Folk Sound* should have seated him next to Gil Scott-Heron and Nina Simone, such was its innovative cross-fertilization of jazz, folk, soul, blues and civil rights, but it finally arrived without fanfare in 1968, after Charters went AWOL with the tapes to Mexico."

And *Wikipedia*: "He met Samuel Charters of Prestige Records in 1964, and the following year they recorded his debut album. Charters then took the tapes with him into the Mexican desert, and the album was eventually released in 1968 as *The New Folk Sound of Terry Callier*."

From *The Guardian*, Will Hodgkinson: "He recorded his album, *The New Folk Sound*, under the influence of Coltrane, using two upright basses and two acoustic guitars to create a unique sound. The record would probably have been a hit but for the fact that its producer, Samuel Charters, took the tapes on a voyage of self-discovery into the North American desert, where he lived with the Yaki Indians for the next three years."

I decide to do the journalistic thing and ask someone who was there. The villain. Sam Charters. Here's Sam on the whole sorry tale: "There's been so much confusion that there's no quick answer. I was doing a lot of Chicago folk artists for Prestige, and I heard Terry at a folk club. I talked to him about recording and then I went to his family's apartment in one of the project buildings one evening and he sang his songs. Sweet family, and he was a very pleasant young guy.

"When we came to the studio he had new ideas, and there were two bass players – one on either side of him but with wide distances between. Then he wanted to record in the dark. When we had to turn on the lights between takes to do adjustments I was sure the basses were creeping up on me.

"Then I did the usual editing and we had the usual Friday afternoon sales meeting at Prestige – the only time we saw Bob Weinstock [owner of Prestige], if he even turned up – and the sales manager said we had to sell it as a protest album, since he was a black folk singer. So that was the promotion pitch, but

otherwise it was just another of the Chicago albums I did that didn't sell a lot, because he didn't have much of a club audience.

"I didn't think about it again until the stories began circulating that I'd stolen the tapes and taken them to Mexico and that was why the album didn't come out for two years and was a flop. I was fired about the time the record came out and Annie and I did drive to Mexico and California, but we were back in New York in April for the world premiere of Ives' Fourth Symphony, with Stokowski conducting. [He conducted it with the American Symphony Orchestra at Carnegie Hall on April 26, 1965.]

"When the stories started about me and the stolen tapes in Terry's interviews I regarded it as just one of those weird things. I tried to correct it when there was an article in *The New York Times*, but the journalist was in love with the story and wouldn't give it up. Fantasy had the old Prestige album and some sort of recording rights, and Bill Belmont called and asked if I'd like to produce a new album and I said very quickly no.

"Terry did appear in Stockholm a year later and told the same story and I thought of calling him and then I decided – why? His story was much better and he felt good with it and it didn't matter to me one way or another. I'd produced a lot of records for Prestige that didn't sell, and I'm sure all the artists have some equally colourful story."

TWO QUOTE OF THE WEEK!
Peter Doherty interview, Angelique Chrisafis, *The Guardian*. "Another French royal whose path he crossed was Carla Bruni, when he was invited to some music sessions at the house she shared with Nicolas Sarkozy, then president... Her house was 'a really strange scene, where you've got a guy with a submachine gun on each door.' Did he meet Sarkozy? 'You're joking, aren't you?' he laughs, blaming his bad reputation. 'She told me she took him to see Bob Dylan. She had the harmonica that Dylan gave her, and apparently he was like: I don't want to meet this guy, who is he anyway?'"

THREE BOLD AS JOAN OSBORNE

Another Day, Another Cover, but a sweet one: from Joan Osborne's album earlier this year, mostly singing songs written by black songwriters, her cover of Jimi's "Bold as Love" stands out. Hendrix is rarely covered, especially by non-guitarists, with the notable exception of Emmylou Harris and Daniel Lanois ("May This Be Love" on *Wrecking Ball*). Hendrix had a lot going for him as a songwriter – an ear for great melodies, wonderful chord changes and sweet, tremulous, touching lyrics are all present in a joyous stew. Osborne's a great singer – check out her performance of "What Becomes of the Brokenhearted" in *Standing in the Shadows of Motown*, especially the breakdown halfway through when the *Tell Me!* call and response starts happening.

FOUR TITLE FIGHT

Adam Ant's new album title – *Adam Ant Is the Blueblack Hussar in Marrying the Gunner's Daughter* – made me vaguely curious as to who holds the record for the longest album title ever. It turns out to be this 865-character cracker from Chumbawamba in 2008: *The Boy Bands Have Won, and All the Copyists and the Tribute Bands and the TV Talent Show Producers Have Won, If We Allow Our Culture to Be Shaped by Mimicry, Whether from Lack of Ideas or from Exaggerated Respect. You Should Never Try to Freeze Culture. What You Can Do Is Recycle That Culture. Take Your Older Brother's Hand-Me-Down Jacket and Re-Style It, Re-Fashion It to the Point Where It Becomes Your Own. But Don't Just Regurgitate Creative History, or Hold Art and Music and Literature as Fixed, Untouchable and Kept Under Glass. The People Who Try to "Guard" Any Particular Form of Music Are, Like the Copyists and Manufactured Bands, Doing It the Worst Disservice, Because the Only Thing That You Can Do to Music That Will Damage It Is Not Change It, Not Make It Your Own. Because Then It Dies, Then It's Over, Then It's Done, and the Boy Bands Have Won.*

Soon to be re-released on Syco Records, apparently.

FIVE LIOOEL RIIHIE?

Found during an iPhoto cull. Travelling in California last year, and accidentally turning the TV's subtitles on during Lionel Richie's *Who Do You Think You Are?* programme.

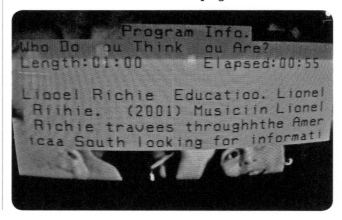

Wednesday, December 12

ONE DAVE BRUBECK, TALKING TO MARIAN MCPARTLAND

…on her wonderful series *Piano Jazz*, for NPR, about his great collaborator, Paul Desmond.

"I loved listening to him, every night, and the humour – if he wanted to say something funny through the horn – would just break me up… If I did something wrong, that he didn't like, he'd usually play 'I'm an Old Cowhand (From the Rio Grande)' because I was raised on a cattle ranch and he'd bring that up, musically. Or 'Don't Fence Me In'. He'd play a quote to get you back in line.

It was something that was always so funny, you'd laugh – you'd never take it too badly. He could tell a complete story in quotes of what just happened, his mind was so quick… [One night they had been] arrested for speeding on the Pennsylvania Turnpike, he did the whole story – of the arrest, where they went – all in tune titles. It was amazing."

Dave, talking about playing a Country Fair and Horse Show: "A guy came up on the stand with spurs on and he drug them across the stage and he walked up to me and he said, 'Tell the guy playing the traps [drums] that he's spookin' the horses…' and Paul was in hysterics, and when he started playing, he hit some high notes and all the chickens went crazy and started cackling… Paul was going to write a book [about all these tours] called *How Many of You Are There in the Quartet?*"

TWO WHAT? WHAT AM I NOT GETTING HERE?

Mumford & Sons, *Babel*. Big Boi (of Outkast) responds to a fan enquiring after his favourite non-hip-hop album of the year.

THREE RICHARD THOMPSON, NEW ALBUM, GREAT QUOTE

Electric is produced by Buddy Miller at his home studio in Nashville, TN. "We did it ridiculously quickly. It was just stupid. But it sounds great. It turned out surprisingly funky, sort of a new genre – folk-funk. It's quite snappy, somewhere between Judy Collins and Bootsy Collins."

FOUR TOM WAITS LETTER TO *THE NATION*, 2002, FROM *LETTERS OF NOTE*:

"Thank you for your eloquent 'rant' by John Densmore of The Doors on the subject of artists allowing their songs to be used in commercials. I spoke out whenever possible on the topic even before the Frito Lay case (*Waits v. Frito Lay*), where they used a sound-alike version of my song 'Step Right Up' so convincingly that I thought it was me. Ultimately, after much trial and tribulation, we prevailed and the court determined that my voice is my property.

"Songs carry emotional information and some transport us back to a poignant time, place or event in our lives. It's no wonder a corporation would want to hitch a ride on the spell these songs cast and encourage you to buy soft drinks, underwear or automobiles while you're in the trance. Artists who take money for ads poison and pervert their songs. It reduces them to the level of a jingle, a word that describes the sound of change in your pocket, which is what your songs become. Remember, when you sell your songs for commercials, you are selling your audience as well...

"Eventually, artists will be going onstage like race-car drivers covered in hundreds of logos. John, stay pure. Your credibility, your integrity and your honor are things no company should be able to buy."

Wednesday, December 19

ONE "DARK WAS THE NIGHT, COLD WAS THE GROUND..."

As we drove along Spain's Costa Tropical, past the last remaining sugar cane factory in Europe, the sky turned orange and Blind Willie Johnson came on the CD player. I don't really have the words to describe this performance, but it may be the loneliest sound ever committed to shellac. As the sun fell, it stilled the conversation. Ry Cooder's soundtrack to *Paris, Texas* is pretty much based around it.

From *Wikipedia*: "In 1977 Carl Sagan and a team of researchers were tasked with collecting a representation of Earth and the human experience for sending on the Voyager probe to other life forms in the universe. They collected sounds of frogs, crickets, volcanoes, a human heartbeat, laughter, greetings in 55 languages, and 27 pieces of music on the Voyager Golden Record. 'Dark Was the Night, Cold Was the Ground' was included, according to Sagan, because 'Johnson's song concerns a situation he faced many times: nightfall with no place to sleep. Since humans appeared on Earth, the shroud of night has yet to fall without touching a man or woman in the same plight.'"

TWO LETTER TO THE EDITOR, *THE GUARDIAN*

From Tony Staveacre: "Ravi Shankar did a great kindness to a young television director in November 1968. The great man was performing a raga in the BBC Riverside Studios (behind the Hammersmith Odeon) to be broadcast as part of the trendy BBC1 pop series *How It Is*. The trainee director had told the recording engineer to load a 20-minute videotape – 'that'll be long enough'. But it wasn't. A raga is an improvisation, unpredictable in content and length. So the tape ran out while the maestro was still playing.

The director, close to tears, had to go down to the studio floor, apologise for his incompetence, and plead with the musicians, 'Would you mind doing it again?' The response was a shrug, a beatific smile and: 'Of course we can – and it will probably be better this time.' And it was. The director was fired shortly after that, by telegram. I've still got it."

THREE WAYNE SHORTER ON MILES

In A Silent Way Recording Session, *Mojo* magazine. "When we recorded it [in February 1969] there were no written-out parts. Miles didn't want to know what you were going to play. 'Play music that doesn't sound like music,' he once told me. It was to get you out of your comfort zone... If he heard someone practicing, he'd say, 'Don't practice!' He told John [McLaughlin], 'Play the guitar like you don't know how to play the guitar.'"

FOUR IN PRAISE OF SINEAD

Clearing the hard drive, I watch an episode of *Later* from a few weeks ago. Among the dreary hipsters (yes Foals, that's you – the world doesn't need a Prog-Rock-Slash-Funkapolitan in 2012 – songs that want to be instrumentals but still seem to have words) and the old soulsters (Graham Central Station – Where's Sly? We need Sly! Larry has a microphone attached to his bass by a gooseneck. We can see why this has never caught on. Awful bass sound. They forgot to bring a song) and the Primark Bonnie Tyler that is Ellie Goulding, there is Sinead O'Connor. She is singing "Nothing Compares to You".

She has a flaccid band (imagine her backed on this song by Marc Ribot and Jay Bellerose instead, for instance) and by rights the song should have been consigned to the *"I've heard it too many times, it has no power left"* pile in the corner. But. But. She is one of the great natural singers of our age. There's not an unmelodic note. Hell, there's not an unmelodic breath between the notes...

She rips the bloody guts out of the song and leaves them on the studio floor, focused on extracting everything it has to give. And, even when it's just her breath you're listening to, she sounds like no one else on earth, and that's a rare, rare thing.

{SINEAD O'CONNOR | "4TH AND VINE"}

FIVE BLUE NOTE? IS THAT A CODE NAME?

You know when you see something that you wish you'd thought of? And it's something that you know how hard it is to do well? Take a bow, Ty Mattson at Mattson Creative.

2013

HITTING A STRIDE, AND TAKING UP TRANSCRIBING, TRYING TO PRESERVE EPHEMERAL WORDS

Wednesday, January 2, 2013

ONE POP MUSIC LIVES!

The Graham Norton Show. Girls Aloud. New Single. "Love Machine". I roll my eyes at the title. But it's great, a cracking pop single, with hints of Sweet's "Ballroom Blitz". And as the chorus powers into view, at the back of my mind, a nagging *What Else Does This Sound Like?* It only takes a few demented minutes of humming. Step forward The Butterfield Blues Band…

TWO "OK! HEP, TWO, THREE, FOUR…"

Woodstock Soundtrack, original vinyl, side six. The Butterfield Blues Band. Featuring saxophonist "Brother" Gene Dinwiddie. "I got a little somethin' I'd like to lay on y'all, if you'll bear with me a minute… please. We're gonna do a little March right along thru now… It's a Love March. We don't carry no guns and things in this army we got. Don't nobody have to be worried about keepin' in step, and we ain't even got no uniforms – we're a poor army. In order to keep our heads above the water and whatnot, we sing to one another, and we play to one another, and we trying to make each other feel good. OK! Hep, two, three, four…"

On the back of a great Rod Hicks bassline and Phillip Wilson's martial drumming, Dinwiddie gives his all to the uber-hippie lyrics of "Love March". As feedback crackles around Buzzy Feiten's guitar, the horn section (featuring David Sanborn) riff like the most soulful Marching Band ever. And it cer-tainly could be the inspiration for the Girls' songwriting team, although I doubt it.

THREE JOHN BARRY: *LICENCE TO THRILL* (BBC FOUR DOC WITH A ROTTEN TITLE)

I'd totally forgotten his great score for *The Ipcress File*. It uses one of my favourite instruments, a cimbalom (a hammered dulcimer). One night I was in Budapest at a conference and we were all taken to a Hungarian Folk Dance dinner. It was, hands down, the loudest thing I've ever witnessed. The stage floorboards were percussively assaulted by the dancers' boots and our insides were assaulted by the unholy bass vibrations that this set off. There were two cimbalom players at either side of the stage, hitting seven shades out of their instruments. The pitch of the treble strings as they were struck by the hammers was enough to take the top of your head off. Instant migraine. Brilliant. I bought a souvenir CD.

FOUR "TIS THE SONG, THE SIGH OF THE WEARY, HARD TIMES COME AGAIN NO MORE…"

Laura Barton's wonderful *Guardian* column, Hail, Hail, Rock'n'Roll, was one of the inspirations for me to do this blog, so I was sad to read of her hard year in the round-up of favourite moments by the paper's music writers. Here, she talked honestly about the past twelve months, and a rare bright moment.

"This was not the happiest of years for me; all through January, on into spring and the summer, I took a slow lesson in falling apart. I could no longer see the beauty in anything – days stood grey and flat, food was flavourless, even music seemed muffled and blunt.

"By the first Tuesday in March I was experiencing daily panic attacks, and often felt too fearful to leave the house. But that evening Future Islands were playing the Scala in London... They played my favourites of course, and it was one of the finest gigs of my life, but what really made it was the stage invasion – a sudden surge of excitement at the beginning of, I think, "Heart Grows Old", and suddenly we were all up there, dancing among the cables and the synths.

"And I remember in that moment looking down from the edge of the stage, out at all the bright faces and euphoria and glee, and feeling my chest swell with a brief, sweet gulp of long-lost joy."

FIVE R.I.P. FONTELLA BASS

"Rescue Me". The best Motown song that was never on Motown, and the best Motown bassline that wasn't a Motown bassline (it's played by Louis Satterfield). Fontella Bass was a powerful singer who made some wonderful gospel albums. The one I could find this morning was *From the Root to the Source*. It has Phillip Wilson, co-writer of "Love March" (see above) on drums. To further cement the Butterfield link, I found a YouTube clip of Fontella in the 80s, singing "Rescue Me" on Dave Sanborn and Jools Holland's fabulous *Sunday Night*, with Sanborn on sax. In memory, we'll play some Fontella tonight.

Wednesday, January 9

TWO ON THE ROAD AGAIN

FACT OF THE WEEK: At number 17 in the Highest Earning World Tours last year, Leonard Cohen is ahead (at £28.4 million) of Justin Bieber... and at number 27, The Black Keys are ahead of Celine Dion, having grossed $23.5 million. The Black Keys. $23.5 million. Wow...

THREE EMUSIC FIND OF THE MONTH: MENAHAN STREET BAND, *THE CROSSING*

Recorded in a studio paid for by a Jay-Z sample by some of the musicians behind Sharon Jones and Charles Bradley's sound, mostly during the night, this instrumental album is wonderful. Some of it is Spaghetti Western, some a kind of handicraft Portishead – try "Ivory and Blue": jazz horns, soulful wah-wah guitar, funky seventies pop drumming. Just the right amount of loose, just the right amount of tight, exactly the right amount of great.

FIVE BOWIE'S BACK, NILE RODGERS' BIO

On the evening before David Bowie's return to PopWorld™ I was reading Nile Rodgers' very entertaining biography *Le Freak*, and had reached the part where he talks about recording "Let's Dance" with the label-less Bowie. "As I say to vocalists who are singing a little flat, sharp, or out-of-the-pocket, 'We're in the neighborhood, but we haven't found the house yet.' David Bowie helped me find the house…

"Not long after I arrived in Switzerland, Bowie strolled into my bedroom with a guitar. 'Hey, Nile, listen to this… I think it could be a hit.' What followed was a folksy sketch of a composition with a solid melody: the only problem was it sounded to me like 'Donovan meets Anthony Newley'. And I don't mean that as a compliment… I'd been mandated to make hits, and could only hear what was missing… I started reworking the song. I soon discovered the diamond in the rough.

"[We asked] Claude Nobs, creator of the Montreux Jazz Festival, to round up a handful of local musicians… Gone were the strummy chords… I'd replaced them with staccato stabs and a strict harmonic interpretation. I used silence and big open spaces to create the groove and kept rearranging it on the spot, like I always did with Chic. David quickly got down with the reshaping of his song. We had a lot of fun and laughter in that studio with those terrific musicians… Laughter is the key to my sessions – the unconditionally loving parent in the room."

Wednesday, January 16

ONE MARIANNE FAITHFULL INTERVIEW

The Guardian: There's a fantastic YouTube clip of you in 1973, wearing a nun's outfit, singing with David Bowie at the Marquee club. It's like watching an early Lady Gaga.

Marianne Faithfull: "I've known that ever since Lady Gaga came along – I did it much better and long before you! Working with David Bowie was very interesting, but I couldn't surrender to it. I should have let him produce a record for me, but I'm very perverse in some ways. He's brilliant, but the entourage were rather daunting."

It's amazing how large the Marquee looks in this clip. It was a tiny place, but the US TV crew filming this special in '73 have made it seem much more expansive. I remember the band looming over the audience. And the costumes. I remember the costumes. But very little else, so it was great to see the space-rock Sonny & Cher again, singing "I Got You, Babe" †, and to hear the lovely guitar obbligato from Mick Ronson.

THREE EXCELLENT DAVID BAILEY QUOTE

I once saw the world's grumpiest photographer give a lecture at the Marble Arch Odeon in London. Everyone before him (all well known shooters) had done lavish slide shows with overviews of their entire oeuvre. Bailey did not do this. He merely handed a Polaroid print to a person in the first row and asked them to pass it along. So it was passed along, row by row, as he talked brilliantly about his career, cameras, lenses, models…

In the *Guardian* Weekend Q&A he was asked, "Which living person do you most admire and why?" and answered: "Bob Dylan, because he is like a singing Picasso."

FOUR MOTÖRHEAD: "DOWN. DOWN. STOP! UP. UP. A LITTLE BIT MORE – GREAT, THAT'S IT!"

Lemmy has launched a line of Motörhead branded headphones

in the United States. Specifically made for listening to rock music, the all-metal headphones are called Motörheadphönes. "People say we've never sold out. No one ever approached us," said Lemmy at the US launch earlier this week.

I didn't realise until recently that I saw a very early Motörhead gig (their eleventh), supporting Blue Öyster Cult at the Hammersmith [remember *No Sleep 'til Hammersmith?*] Odeon. We had gone because BÖC had a kind of rock-crit cachet as being "intelligent" hard rock. My lasting memory was of Larry Wallis trying to tune his guitar between songs without turning off his fuzz box [ah, loved those pre-electric tuner days!] and getting helped by the audience, as illustrated by the headline...

Wednesday, January 23

ONE DAUGHTER REVIEWS *LES MIS*

Running time: 2.5 hours
Spoken word count: 17
Number of times Hugh J cries: 6
Most used facial expression: anguish mixed with constipation
Most enhanced facial feature: lines around the mouth
Number of times stolen bread is mentioned: 12
Laugh-out-loud moments: Sacha B-C and Helena B-C as pickpocketing innkeepers
Time it takes Cosette and Marius to fall head over heels in love: 4 seconds

TWO REASONS THAT AWARDS ARE STUPID

Choose between these acts for Best International Male Solo Artist at the Brits: **(a) Bruce Springsteen (b) Frank Ocean (c) Gotye (d) Jack White (e) Michael Bublé**. So that's Rock v Hip-Hop v Club DJ v Roots v Light Jazz. Bizarre.

THREE AMAZING FACTS FROM PATRICK HUMPHRIES' EXCELLENT BIOGRAPHY OF LONNIE DONEGAN, *KING OF SKIFFLE*

"The first record Art Garfunkel remembers buying for himself was Lonnie's 'Rock Island Line'; and in Fairfax, California, that same Lonnie song was the very first tune that a shy 17-year-old Harvey Phillip Spector learned to play on the guitar.

"In New Orleans, the young Dr John – Malcolm 'Mac' Rebennack – was another who remembers being inspired by the Donegan hit. And way, way down in Texas, Jerry Allison and his buddy, Buddy Holly, were so captivated by Donegan's 'Rock Island Line' that they began incorporating it into the shows they played around Lubbock."

And when the Everly Brothers made their British debut they described themselves as an "an American skiffle group"!

FOUR "CAN YOU DANCE TO IT?"

Listening to a CD lovingly compiled by my friend Tim, of African singles [*African Serenades 44: Kenyan Singles*] and finding Tim's quote on the back: "I taught near Eldoret for two years in the early 1980s, fell in love with the music and then found that my ZigZag-reading, album-sleeve-obsessive completist's mindset was completely turned upside down because, of course, none of the friends I made cared about who was responsible for that amazing guitar solo or impassioned vocal. All they were concerned about was, 'Can you dance to it?' Which isn't a bad take on things when it comes down to it..."

Wednesday, January 30

**ONE WHAT IN MUSIC'S NAME IS THIS?
MARCEL'S MILLER/MOPTOPS MAYHEM**

A small package arrived in the mail. A CD covered in writing. There was no mystery who it was from, as it was signed, but it had an air of mystery around it, and these instructions: "Martin, follow these five simple steps to nausea and amazement. **1** Log on to FORGOTTENALBUMS.COM/albums/?p=59. It's this LP –*Dance To Beatles Hits In The Glenn Miller Sound with The Big Band Beat Of The Hiltonaires*. **2** Bask in a warm nostalgic glow as you enjoy the album cover. **3** Read the blog, remembering that this guy is not making this album up. **4** Play the CD. **5** Ask yourself "Why?" P.S. The guitar solo on "Let It Be" is THE FINEST thing I've ever heard. x Marcel."

From	Martin Colyer
Date	24 January 2013
To	Marcel Ashby
Subject	Has a song *not* benefited from the Glenn Miller treatment more than "Something"? God Almighty, that's horrific! Oh, hold on, I've just listened to "Michelle". Still trying to locate the original

melody. "Let It Be"? Let It Stop, more like. I'm thinking you shortened it by one track from the original disc – the great lost Beatles classic "Bird Cage Walk" – just out of the kindness of your heart. I must lie down now.

Oh, and don't get me started on that guitar solo in "Let It Be", which seems to be playing a different song, as if there was a surf guitarist walking past the studio door, playing, and they grabbed him, hit record and didn't miss a beat. The fact it has nothing to do with "Let It Be", or, indeed, any tune, is neither here nor there. And the last two notes are to die for. Or something.

TWO IN BOB NEWS THIS WEEK

First impressions, *Inside Llewyn Davis* trailer.
1 They've captured the look of 1962 New York rather well. **2** It's nice that a lesser-known Bobsong, "Farewell", from 1963 soundtracks this teaser. **3** It looks like Carey Mulligan has some strong lines. **4** Bob-strokes-cat a little earlier (1962) than

Guy Peellaert would have us believe in *Rock Dreams*. **5** John Goodman will have plenty of raucous lines, and his will be the haircut of the film. **6** Fresh from *Homeland*, F. Murray Abraham features as the owner of the Gate of Horn nightclub in Chicago. Which makes him Albert Grossman in this scenario. **7** Oscar Isaac's teeth look way-too-good for 1962.

THREE UH-HUH—IT WAS THE MANFREDS

From Tom McGuinness' sleeve notes for the Manfred Mann compilation CD, *Ages of Mann*: "Bob Dylan's "Mighty Quinn" was our third number One. Al Grossman, Dylan's manager, played it to us. 'Why does Dylan get such a useless vocalist to sing his demos?' Manfred asked. 'That's Bob singing', said Al."

Oh, and I never knew that Jack Bruce was in Manfred Mann. He plays bass on the great "Pretty Flamingo". Or, indeed, that Klaus Voormann replaced Bruce when he left.

FOUR AIMEE MANN, "GHOST WORLD", RFH, JAN 28

My favourite moment at Aimee's concert (thanks for the ticket, Barney!) was her performance of the best post-school/pre-life song ever written. Prompted by a Twitter request, this rarely played (and unknown by the rest of the band) gem stood out. Named for, and inspired by, Daniel Clowes' great graphic novel, every glorious line rang clear, sat on the cushion of Aimee's patented J-45 strum. "Finals blew, I barely knew / My graduation speech / And with college out of reach / If I don't find a job it's down to dad / And Myrtle Beach" – joined by bassist Paul

(Mountain Man) Bryan's harmonies and the trippy off-the-cuff keys of Jebin (Freak Flag) Bruni, all carnival swirl and hum.

And by coincidence, watching *Community* on tv the following night (your next must-rent box set) and having Jeff and Pierce's hysterical Spanish Project performance acted out to Aimee's "Wise Up".

FIVE DATELINE: NEW ORLEANS. BRETT MIELKE REPORTING...

"Well, the record shop I first went to and bought Ken's records back in 2003 survived Katrina and the slow death of record stores! Had a visit and bought a wealth of KC music. Also had a long chat with the clerk, who was about my age and knew an unbelievable amount about the music. Fear not, relatives of all generations, the Ken Colyer legacy is still alive and well in the Crescent City."

Wednesday, February 6

ONE FROM THE BLOG OF PHOTOGRAPHER HEATHER HARRIS

"The first four words of vocabulary we learned in Synthesizer 101 class at UCLA (circa 1972, so we're talking monophonic ARP 2600s) were the descriptions of all musical sound notes: attack, sustain, decay, release. How fitting to the lifeworks of creative types." Wow. Attack. Sustain. Decay. Release. That's a manifesto right there, and a great title for a project...

TWO MARTIN CARTHY ON BOB DYLAN ON *DESERT ISLAND DISCS*

"The influence of British folk music shows in his later work – he started writing these really anthemic tunes... He was a wonderful performer. I don't believe that anybody who saw his first performance at the King & Queen down in Foley Street would be able to say he gave a bad performance. He stood up, did three songs, absolutely knocked everybody flat. People loved him."

Host Kirsty Young asked him, "Is it right that you used to share a flat together?"

"No [exasperated exhale]. This story started going round that he stayed with me when he came to London – no, he didn't. But we did actually chop up a piano. The piano was a wreck, half the keys were missing, and it was a very, very cold winter, and my wife and I decided to chop up the piano, so we took it bit by bit. And by the time Bob came along we were down to the frame. And I'd been given, for my birthday, a samurai sword, and Bob came round to have a cup of tea, and Dorothy – my then wife – said, 'Make a fire, Mart,' so I got the sword, and he stood between me and the piano and said, 'You can't do that, it's a musical instrument!' I said 'It's a piece of junk' and went to swing at it, and before I could swing at it he was whispering in my ear, 'Can I have a go?'"

THREE THE LONDONJAZZCOLLECTOR THINKS...

"A bent piece of metal pipe with holes in it, called a saxophone, transforms human breath into a voice; drums extend the pulse of the heartbeat; a piano exchanges ten for eighty-eight fingers, while the bass is the feet on which music walks. Instruments are physical extensions of human form and function that transform man into musician, the ultimate analogue source, flesh into vinyl.

Whilst a singing voice can be beautiful, how often does it compare with a stream of triplets and sixteenths soaring from Charlie Parker's alto?

It strikes me that not only are records the new antiques, they are works of art, the equal of art framed on gallery walls. You are not just a mere record collector, a figure of fun and pity, poking around in dusty crates. You are, in that immortal expression of Charles Saatchi, an art-oholic, in need of a life-sustaining drink."

FOUR THIS FABULOUS PHOTOGRAPH OF JOHN LEE HOOKER EXPLAINING IT ALL

"Not getting any younger, but I'm not feeling very old / And I'm not shoppin' for my cemetery tomb soon / I'm gonna wait 'til John Lee Hooker makes room..."

That's Garland Jeffreys singing "'Til John Lee Hooker Calls Me", from his latest album [can we still say that?] *The King of In Between*, where, with the help of the great stringed instrument player, Larry Campbell, he continues to plow a furrow of his own making, never beaten down, a streetwise NYC poet, part Lou Reed, part Doo-Wop, part John Lee, still a ghostwriter with 35mm dreams.

Wednesday, February 13

ONE *DOWN TERRACE*

The music track for Ben Wheatley's first film (from 2009), an in-your-face saga of the spiralling disintegration of a Brighton criminal clan, is a fascinating mix of transatlantic rural music. The none-more-English folk music of The Copper Family sits happily next to Robert Johnson's "Little Queen of Spades". Sea shanties segue into acts of appalling violence, while the plaintive, pain-wracked "Are You Leaving for the Country?" by Karen Dalton soundtracks the disposal of a body. And as terrible as that sounds, the music acts as a kind of "life goes on" comfort, especially in the scenes where the father, played by Robert Hill, sits playing guitar with his band of friends in the living room at the house in Down Terrace.

TWO B. KLIBAN, LADY GAGA'S STYLIST...

... just about 30 years too early. Talking to friend and fellow B. Kliban fan Adam Roberts, about the singular genius of the Canadian cartoonist, and – looking out one of his books – finding this great cartoon.

THREE THOUGHTS WHILE RUNNING WITH "KID CHARLEMAGNE" BY STEELY DAN IN MY HEADPHONES

I'm struck by how this seventies classic would work as *Breaking Bad*'s theme tune:

> "On the hill the stuff was laced with kerosene
> But yours was kitchen-clean
> Everyone stopped to stare
> at your Technicolor motor home...
> Clean this mess up else we'll all end up in jail
> Those test tubes and the scale
> Just get it all out of here
> Is there gas in the car?
> Yes, there's gas in the car
> I think the people down the hall
> Know who you are..."

I don't listen to Larry Carlton's fantastic shape-shifting guitar solo, I don't listen to Bernard Purdie's lickety-split drumming, I don't even listen to Paul Griffin's funky Clavinet. I just listen to Chuck Rainey's sublime bass, pumping and prodding and pushing and powering the song along.

FIVE *FLIGHT* (CASSETTE?) DECK

With The Cowboy Junkies' version of "Sweet Jane", Bill Withers' "Ain't No Sunshine", The Red Hot Chili Peppers' "Under the Bridge", and Marvin's "What's Going On", *Flight* is a film about alcoholism and addiction masquerading as a legal/action thriller – with a terrific soundtrack and a nicely indie feel for a mainstream Hollywood production.

Wednesday, February 20

ONE WHAT I'VE LEARNED, THOM YORKE, U.S. *ESQUIRE*

"My grandfather would come to our house in the countryside, borrow one of our bikes, and disappear. He'd come back after dark and we had no idea where he'd been. If he ran into anybody, he'd just ask where the good nightclub was. He did that right up into his nineties."

TWO THE DISARRAY OF STAFF BENDA BILILI

Sad news that Congolese wonders Staff Benda Bilili are no more. Last year, Marcel and I went to see a preview of the documentary film telling their story, *Benda Bilili!*, followed by the band in concert, and both were wonderful.

The film's an uplifting piece of work full of great scenes (my favourite being when teen genius Roger – player of self-invented tin-can-and-wire instrument, having just been found downriver and asked to join the band – is given a stern talking-to by his mother and sister). The show was as riotous as a concert in a chapel can be, and finished with some of the finest dancing I've ever seen, especially as most of it was done – by men who had suffered polio as children – either on crutches or in wheelchairs.

THREE *MR HYDE* MAILOUT, EXTOLLING VIRTUES OF "THE BIRMINGHAM SCENE"

IS THIS THE NEXT BIG MUSIC SCENE? shouts the headline [MRHYDE.COM]. "What do you know about Digbeth? It's been lazily dubbed the 'Shoreditch of Birmingham' thanks to three young bands who are rising to prominence after spending their formative years hanging out there. Is 'B-Town' 2013's version of Madchester? Meet the major players and decide…"

So I do. I SoundCloud them all. Three bands from the, uh, West Midz. First up is Swim Deep: According to *Mr Hyde*, "producing ethereal, synth-heavy music that's unashamedly poppy, yet also soulful and endearingly rough." The band's vocalist says "[Birmingham bands] are making the UK's best music. It's not all the same like in other scenes – it's a really varied sound." Mmmm. I say: Ordinary boy vocals. Ordinary melodies. Tinny beats.

Let's try number two. Jaws. "Their fuzzed-out shoegaze-indebted sound can't remain in the shadows for long in any era that sees a new My Bloody Valentine album so warmly received." The vocalist says: "I heard someone describe us as Ian Curtis in LA, which is pretty cool." Right. Ordinary boy vocals. Ordinary melodies. Tinny beats.

Sensing a pattern, I move to number three, Peace. Mr Jekyll (sorry, I mean Mr Hyde): "Their gift is writing complex, Foals-esque tracks but with huge, sing-along choruses." The vocalist says: "Our music should make you want to shake and cry at the same time. And sometimes it should make you want to party." Ordinary boy vocals, more guitars than the others, slightly less tinny beats.

I've got to say, five minutes in the company of each of these bands only made me think, Where's the new here? Why are they all so satisfied with replicating what's gone before? Why are all the vocals so… dull? And how desperate are journalists to discover a new "scene"?

FOUR LATELY, A KEN COLYER STATE OF MIND

Before filming an interview with John Williamson and his charming crew for a BBC Four documentary, I had looked out some hopefully useful material. Among my favourite finds was this picture, taken by the Brighton *Evening Argus*, of Doug Dobell's first shop, shopfitted by my dad, in 1956. The programme, to be shown in late May, focuses on the British Jazz Revival of the late forties and early fifties. My job was to help illuminate the extraordinary trip Ken made to New Orleans in 1952, jumping ship in Mobile to play with some of his heroes, breaking the law in several ways to do so. I also recently compiled a piece for THE STANSBURY FORUM about Ken's pilgrimage, based on reminiscences and letters from *Goin' Home: The Uncompromising Life and Music of Ken Colyer*.

FIVE **THE MAD OPENING SONG OF** *A CHORUS LINE*

My mother's birthday. A show. The pre-opening night, the last of the previews, where the audience seems packed with the cast's relations, which gives a peculiarly heightened air to the whole performance. It's actually pretty great – in some ways a weirdly prescient view of Reality TV's audition process – but my favourite musical moment comes right at the beginning. The opening number, "I Hope I Get It", pits frenzied seventies Lalo Schifrin wah-wah disco, all tom rolls and rim shots, against the Tin Pan Alley tune of the refrain, "I really need this job / Please, God, I need this job / I've got to ge—t this jo—b." Cue massed jazz hands and that particularly Michael Bennett style of angular shock dancing. Magic!

Wednesday, February 27

ONE **"PSYCHIC CITY" BY YACHT**

I can't even remember what this song was used for this week – an advert or a programme segment... or something. All I knew was that it hit all those Blondie / ZE Records / Waitresses buttons. Great – almost dumb, possibly smart – pop.

> "I used to live in a voodoo city
> Where every little thing had its own secret life.
> I might be washing up the dishes
> And the kitchen might say
> 'Hang around baby baby, hang around baby baby
> Hang around baby, we'll be baking a cake for you...'"

TWO **FOR WHEN YOU HAVE A FEW MINUTES TO SPARE, SAYS STEVE CAPLIN, AND DIRECTS ME TO...**

FACEBOOK.COM/AwkwardBandAndMusicianPhotos. My favourites from a quick browse are the first two. The third? In the week that Heino releases a new album and it shoots to the top of the German charts, here's one he made earlier. As *The Guardian* reports: "The album contains cover versions of punk, hip-hop and hard-rock hits – to the disgust of many of the bands who originally performed them [this in reference to Heino's alleged far-right views]." Let's call him Heinous, no? Nevertheless, *Made Parole, Will Travel!* may just be the finest album title ever, and over-charging the lawmen (look closely) is just the icing on the cake!

FIVE **"AND THE SUN DON'T SHINE ANYMORE / AND THE RAINS FALL DOWN ON MY DOOR..."**

From *Rolling Stone*: "The Band's Garth Hudson saw some of his belongings sold off this weekend by his landlord in a Kingston, New York, garage sale after failing to pay rent on his loft space for about seven years... The multi-instrumentalist, kept the space for storage. He stored everything from personal possessions and household items to handwritten sheet music, and among the goodies are uncashed checks, including one issued from EMI in 1979 for $26,000...

Hudson's Facebook page had a note to fans encouraging them to attend the garage sale and purchase items to allow Hudson to buy them back. 'We were told everything there was sold,' read the note. 'We were not seeking funds, but were asking purchasers to allow us to reimburse them for what they bought as we were not on premises ourselves.' [The owner of the space] has already made an agreement with an online auction company to sell off the music-related items on April 1st. As for the fans, they're already on it: one woman bought Hudson's household items and personal belongings for a few thousand dollars with the apparent intention to return them to him."

Wednesday, March 6

ONE **BRUNO MARS, THE JONATHAN ROSS SHOW**

I started this blog after I watched Bruno Mars at the Brits a year ago and loved the performance of his bass player so much that I wanted to write about it. It was these non-headline moments that I found interesting, and no one seemed to be writing about them. This week Bruno does the promo round for his next tour and turns up at Jonathan's with a piano player, an organist and a pretty good gospel/R&B song. He's very slick and can really sing, but what's great is the interplay between his voice and the stripped-back accompaniment, and it makes a change from the usual banal "just like the record" performance.

TWO **ALMOST FINISHING MICHAEL GRAY'S FINE *HAND ME MY TRAVELIN' SHOES: IN SEARCH OF BLIND WILLIE MCTELL***

"McTell comes storming through here, fusing great feeling with an intimate looseness of delivery that he has never captured on record before. It is thrilling to hear – and this is what he keeps up as he moves on to the marvellous 'Savannah Mama', where, right from the magnificent opening moments, his guitar work is so concentrated and precise, so felt and so assertive (*this* is what inspired The Allman Brothers' slide style), while his vocal lines flow across all this precision with the grace of heartfelt risk-taking. He sings with an experimental mannered fluidity somehow freed from artifice by open ardor."

FOUR **WEST OF EDEN?**

Kanye West, speaking to Paris' Le Zenith crowd: "There's no motherfucking awards or sponsorships or none of that shit that can stop the dedication to bringing y'all that real shit."

He continued: "No matter how they try to control you, or the motherfucker next to you tries to peer-pressure you, you can do what you motherfucking want. I am Picasso. I'm Walt Disney, I'm Steve Jobs."

Wednesday, March 13

ONE ALABAMA SHAKES, "ALWAYS ALRIGHT"

Best moment in the very ho-hum *Silver Linings Playbook* (a film fatally scuppered by having Robert De Niro play the father, so the whole thing just reminds you of *Meet the Whatevers* but with a less likeable male lead). Jennifer Lawrence is great – the Juliette Lewis de nos jours, but the film less than the sum of its parts. "Always Alright", however, is a keeper. Great lyrics, great vocal, and a driving Stax-like beat topped with a bendy guitar riff.

TWO BILL FRISELL: TWO HANDS, A GUITAR, MINIMAL AMPLIFICATION, "JUST LIKE A WOMAN"

Don't you wish that you could play guitar like Bill Frisell? I know I do, every time I see him. There's just something so *human* about his playing. I always think of him halfway along a scale from Joe Pass to Derek Bailey. Here he is, on a small platform, could be an arts centre. There's the door to the toilets just behind him. The crowd sounds small, maybe fifty people. Cars go by outside on rainy streets. He plays the song, taking his time, leading the melody through a series of thoughtful stages. There's always a little Reggie Young in his playing, rooting him in the Southern musics – here there's a little Wayne Moss or Joe South, too, whichever of the two *Blonde on Blonde* guitarists it was that invented the lovely filigreed guitar figure that features between the verses of the Nashville original of "Just Like a Woman".

THREE ONE NIGHT IN NASHVILLE (JUST OFF CARNABY STREET)

Two hours in the company of some great folks from Nashville, promoting the Opry and the Country Music Hall of Fame, one of my *most* favourite museums. Steve and I learn that there are few country songs about cats (unless you count "Nashville Cats" and Kitty Wells, of course), that the glorious "Don't It Make My Brown Eyes Blue" was inspired by songwriter Richard Leigh's dog, and that Vince Gill is officially the nicest man in Nashville, as well as a killer musician and singer.

FOUR REICH & GLASS REMOVALS

Steve Reich talking to Alexis Petridis, *The Guardian*: "Well, I take the Chuck Berry approach," he smiles. "Any old way you use it. In other words, music has to have legs. You could walk into a coffee shop and hear the Fifth Brandenburg Concerto. Well, it's perfect for just sitting down and having your coffee and making the atmosphere more pleasant. But you could take that same music home and play it on your headphones and take out your score and say: 'My God, this is the most unbelievable counterpoint I've ever seen in my life.' Anywhere you put it, any way you orchestrate it – Wendy Carlos, Glenn Gould, you name it – if the notes are right, the rhythms are right, it works."

Petridis reveals that "After completing his studies in composition at Juilliard in his native New York and then at California's Mills College, Reich famously declined to continue in academia, preferring to support himself via a series of blue-collar jobs: at one point, he and Philip Glass started their own furniture removal business, which these days sounds less like something that might actually have happened than the basis of a particularly weird Vic Reeves sketch."

FIVE JUST AS WE MOVE OUR OFFICE FROM EDGWARE ROAD...

An interesting-looking exhibition about to open around the

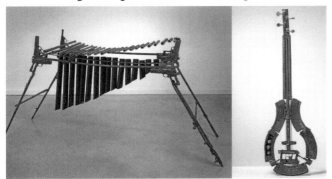

corner at Lisson Grove. Pedro Reyes. Musical instruments made from illegal weaponry.

Wednesday, March 20

ONE SOUTHLAND

The fever dream that was *Beasts of the Southern Wild* led me back to Kate Campbell's "When Panthers Roamed in Arkansas" – first heard on a CD accompanying the wonderful *Oxford American* magazine's Music Issue, years ago. The small girl at the centre of the film sees giant aurochs – ancestors of domestic cattle – astride the landscape, a result of the ecological disaster that's befalling them. Campbell, with a Nashville twang but a Memphis musical sensibility, kicks off the song with a fast "Ode to Billy Joe" vamp, before the horns storm in:

"I miss Elvis in the movies / With his dyed black hair...
Wish that I could find an ice-cold / Double Cola somewhere,
If I had a time machine I'd go back...
When panthers roamed in Arkansas / And buffalo made their
home in Tennessee"

And the great last verse tips its hat to ecological disaster, too:

"Frogs are disappearing / Through the ozone hole,
I can't find one song I like / On the radio...

TWO FROM MICK BROWN'S GREAT PIECE ABOUT THE DISCREET CHARM OF NANDO'S IN THE *SUNDAY TELEGRAPH* MAGAZINE

"The most tireless contributor to *Rate Your Nando's* [a website for devoted fans of the Chicken chain] is Ryan Wilson, who has eaten more than 1,000 meals in 139 branches across the country. Wilson lost his Nando's virginity, so to speak ('Actually it was more enjoyable than losing my virginity. There was some conversation at least'), about 11 years ago at the Birmingham Broad Street branch… He had been taken there by a friend from work named Dylan Wesleyharding. 'I think,' Wilson said, 'his dad got a bit carried away in the 1960s.'"

THREE AT ONE POINT, FIVE COWBELLS

Trouble Funk, Islington Assembly Hall. The DJ plays go-go. As Mark says, we're about to see ninety minutes of go-go, PLAY SOMETHING ELSE! Big Tony on Earthquake Bass. A beat so relentless it shakes the beer in your glass into a flat, flavourless liquid. "Uptown, Downtown, Around Town, All Aboard!" They do, indeed, "Drop the Bomb".

HE'S WAITED OVER 20 YEARS FOR THIS… A HAPPY, HAPPY FAN

FOUR WHATEVER HAPPENED TO SHEA SEGER?

Watching Cameron Crowe's *We Bought a Zoo* (yes, yes, I knew it wouldn't be up to much) I noticed a familiar name in the credits. The name was Shea Seger, a Texan who – transplanted to London – made a great album, *The May Street Project*, in 2001, featuring a great single, "The Last Time". I went online to see if anyone else had spotted it. And of course someone had.

Kristian Lin in the *Fort Worth Weekly*, last April: "Even though I didn't care for the movie when it hit theaters last December, I was intrigued by a minor mystery about it involving Fort Worth singer-songwriter and recent *Weekly* cover subject Shea Seger. [Early in the movie a woman hits on Matt Damon. She's played by] an actress named Desi Lydic. This character is never named in the film (and indeed never appears on screen again), but in the closing credits, she's identified as 'Shea Seger (Lasagna Mom)'. Given how knowledgeable Cameron Crowe is about music, it seemed inconceivable that this could have been a coincidence.

"I sent inquiries about this to 20th Century Fox, but nobody there seemed to know. This week, we got an answer from the filmmaker himself. The writer-director of *Say Anything…* and *Almost Famous* tweeted back: 'may street project… truly great album. there was an outtake from our elton john doc where he was raving about her too.' No word yet from Shea Seger herself about Crowe associating her with sex-hungry moms, crushes on Matt Damon, or lasagna, but if she gets back to me, I'll let you all know."

FIVE **NIGEL KENNEDY INTERVIEW, LINDA BARNETT, *THE GUARDIAN***

Do you care about fame? "It's useful: it's given me choice about what music I play. And of course it's more heartwarming to play to a full concert hall. I remember one concert in Dublin, when I was 19 and completely unknown. About 50 people turned up to a hall that could hold 5,000. I said, 'Look, come round the pub, I'll do it there.' So that's where we all went."

Is there anything about your career you regret? "Not getting a band of my own together earlier. When I started playing my own stuff, people in the classical world would say: "Who does he think he is, writing his own music when he could be playing Beethoven?" I should have realised sooner that that's not the point. No one has to be Beethoven: he's been dead a fair amount of time now."

Wednesday, March 27

ONE **POLIÇA**

If Rooney Mara was the lead singer of a band, it would be Minnesota's Poliça. With her alt-Dusty Springfield arm gestures, Channy Leaneagh seems – in the words of Daughter – to be the flamboyant conductor of this little orchestra that consists of a bassist and two drummers (*The Independent*'s critic thought the same). Joe Cocker's *Mad Dogs and Englishmen* tour had two drummers, as did Steely Dan's '73 road trip, and there's something wonderful and thrilling about the thump and para-diddle of synchro'd drum sets, especially when they control the beat as much as Ben Ivascu and Drew Christopherson.

Chris Bierden's bass half holds the bottom end, half dances around the ghostly, swooning melodies of Leaneagh's auto-tuned, layered and reverbed vocals. Though she seems out of sorts for the first half of the set, the sounds coming off the stage are monstrous. The third number's juxtaposition of solo vocals and pulverising drum breaks is nothing short of astonishing. Their set is a perfect length – 60 minutes – and for an encore there's a eerie solo version of the old folk song "When I Was a Young Girl" followed by a new roller-coaster thumper. Fabulous!

TWO **THE LAST SENTENCE IS NOT MADE UP**

Metro newspaper tells us that… "British rap star Professor Green refused to let sub-zero temperatures freeze his secret gig at a bus depot on Saturday night. The star raised the temperature by ordering fans to thrash around to his tracks in order to beat the big chill. Meanwhile Pro's stunning girlfriend, *Made in Chelsea* star Millie Mackintosh, was also in attendance to see her beau on stage… She was also seen enjoying a greasy pizza and bottle of beer to help keep warm at the exclusive gig.

Professor Green was performing in celebration of **Barclaycard Contactless** now being accepted on all Transport for London buses."

THREE ARTHUR ROTHSTEIN, DUST STORM IN CIMARRON COUNTY, OKLAHOMA, 1936

Snowbound at my friend Kwok's. We're talking about Elliott Erwitt and his photos of Yukio Mishima, when he pulls this beautiful print out to show me. I know it as the cover to Folkways' *Dust Bowl Ballads* Sung by Woody Guthrie. Arthur had wanted Kwok to have it – he was given it by Eve Rothstein, Arthur's daughter, on November 11, 1985, the day that Arthur passed away.

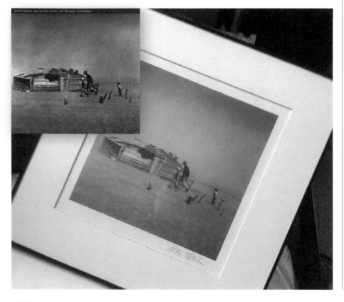

FIVE PHILIP LARKIN, GARRISON KEILLOR & BOB DYLAN GO ANTIQUING

I loved this drawing [right] when John Cuneo did it in 2011, and this week it gets blown up and put over a whole wall at the Delaware Art Museum. Roll On, John!

Wednesday, April 3

ONE "JANUARY 26, 1962: PASSED DYLAN ON THE STREET, HE SAID THAT HE 'DIDN'T KNOW WHY WHY SO MANY THINGS ARE HAPPENING TO ME.' I SAID THAT HE DID."

Michael Gray writes a very nice piece on Izzy Young on the occasion of his 85th birthday. A couple of years ago in Stockholm we sat with Izzy outside his office, the Folklore Centrum, having tea with Sarah Blasko (Izzy is a magnet for any musician  of a certain bent who is in town).

After we leave, Sam Charters tells me that the last time Bob Dylan played in Stockholm, Bob's people arranged for Izzy to meet him, and he ended up having a chat to Bob by the side of the bus. As they said goodbye, Izzy grabbed Dylan's cheeks and waggled them, like a Jewish grandfather would do to his grandson. *Security!* Nobody touches Bob! Bob, however, burst out laughing… Sam said that Bob's road manager told him it was the only time he saw Bob laugh on the whole tour…

TWO BP GARAGE, CLAPHAM COMMON NORTHSIDE, THURSDAY

A man in front of me is slowly paying for petrol and weird "garage" shopping: a bottle of wine, jelly babies, screen wash, iced buns... so I idly pick up the new Bowie CD. He looks at me and says, "Dreadful cover," about Jonathan Barnbrook's white square over *Heroes*. I disagree and say that the fact that it created thousands of memes proves that it worked as one part of Bowie's brilliant stealth marketing for *The Next Day*'s release. Who's been that excited about an album launch in years? He smiles, says "Fair point", and Exits Garage Left.

THREE LOVIN' SITE-SPECIFIC SIGNS & SLANG!

"Artist Jay Shells channelled his love of hip-hop music and his uncanny sign-making skills towards a brand-new project: Rap Quotes. For this ongoing project, Shells created official-looking street signs quoting famous rap lyrics that shout out specific street corners and locations. He then installed them at those specific street corners and locations."

FOUR eMUSIC FIND OF THE MONTH

Marnie Stern, downloaded for the title alone: *The Chronicles of Marnia*. She's a really talented guitarist who "shreds" (ask the kids) and seems to have made an album that references Math Rock and electronica. It's manic and great and slightly odd – fretboard squalling, swooping vocal whoops and wild drumming. Somehow I was disappointed that the cover wasn't more like this, *The Voyage of the Dawn Shredder*...

Wednesday, April 10

THREE THE ART OF LISTENING TO RECORDS

I listened to two fantastic stereo systems this week, Alex's and George's. My neighbour Alex put Eric Clapton's "The Core" from *Slowhand* on his Technics deck and it felt like being in the studio. After listening to George's – driven by a Garrard deck set in concrete – it seemed like Taj Mahal and the Pointer Sisters were actually in the room as we listened to "Sweet Home Chicago", a wonderful performance I had forgotten all about. I always appreciate amazing stereos when I hear them, and am in awe of the lengths people go to – steam-cleaning records, adding AC/DC converters, setting decks in concrete and the like.

The Voyage of the
DAWN TREADER
C.S. LEWIS

A Puffin Book

Later that week, George responded with this...

"Just to set the record straight, so to speak, my turntable is a 50-year-old Garrard 301 from the days of British precision engineering. It is set into a plinth made of layers of lead sheet and MDF bolted together. The whole is supported on a slate slab, which in turn is floated on 2 layers of air-filled BMX inner tubes for complete isolation from vibration. (The turntable in the Dobell's exhibition was also a Garrard but made 25 years later, when the company had been sold to new owners who took it downmarket.)

The converter you refer to is a DAC (Digital to Analogue Converter), which is usually incorporated into CD players. Digital players only produce a series of signals which are either "on" or "off", expressed as 1 or 0. They produce these at very high speeds, and the DAC decodes them and turns them into waveforms which amplifiers understand. At these ultra-high speeds accuracy can be a problem. The more accurate the decoding, the better the music will sound."

FOUR THEN I SAW THIS...

on *LondonJazzCollector*: "I read something recently on the subject of record and hi-fi reviews which struck a chord. It was this. No one really knows what anyone else hears. Thinking about it, it's true. I only really know what I hear, and sometimes I'm not even sure of that. Sometimes I am only remembering what I thought about what I heard, which is not the same thing. I am remembering an opinion, not a sound...

Every now and then I put on a record I haven't played for a while, but remember thinking at the time was one of the best pressings I had ever heard, only to find it rather ordinary. It hasn't changed, I have. Or the system has. Or something I am not aware of has. Worse, I recently upgraded a copy of a record I can remember really liking. Only to find, on playing, I no longer like it at all..."

Actually, worse is my admission that my favourite place of all to listen to music is one that any self-respecting audiophile absolutely scorns: the car.

FIVE SPRING ARRIVES, CALYPSO TIME!

As if to prove my point, no sooner has the sun come out (after what seems like an eternity) when "Lorraine" by Explainer bursts into life on the iPhone as I'm driving around town. Truly, one of the great intros: a bouncing bass, a chattering guitar, tss-tss hi-hat and the Explainer shouting: "Taxi! Taxi! Airport Kennedy!" And it sounds fantastic in the car...

MORE ROCK 'N' ROLL. PHEW!

My friend Pal Hansen had this to say about photographing people whose work you know: "Sometimes you get that com-

mission to photograph someone whose work you admire and who you think is genuinely interesting. Many times, you walk away disappointed and with a distaste for whatever you did admire them for in the first place."*

It's a little like that with most rock biographies, I find. And, my God, books written by musicians are seriously depressing, no? I've barely recovered from the ghastly sleazefest that was Warren Zevon's *I'll Sleep When I'm Dead* when I pick up Dallas Taylor's *Prisoner of Woodstock*. Taylor – Crosby, Stills, Nash & Young's drummer in the late sixties – is a favourite of mine, but this terrible tale of abuse, insecurity, drugs, surgery and ego was almost too awful to read.

*Pal then went on to say: "However, once in a while, someone who comes across as truly talented and nice is actually just that. One of my favourite actors, Forest Whitaker, is as nice as they come."

Wednesday, April 17

ONE WORDS FAIL, PT 73

From the *Evening Standard*: The soundtrack to [Prime Minister] David and Samantha Cameron's marriage is an album of Depression-era US folk music, the PM's wife has disclosed. *Time (The Revelator)* is a 2001 collection of austere narratives by Nashville singer Gillian Welch. Peter Mensch, manager of

The Dobell's exhibition at my old alma mater, Chelsea School of Art (now relocated in the shadow of Tate Britain and renamed University of the Arts London, Chelsea), was a Proustian rush – who knew that the Museum of London had collected parts of the original shop when the Tower Street branch finally closed in 1992? The "drum" sign, the record bags, the cover artworks, an original record rack built by my dad – they all filled in a picture of what it was like to be there, at a time when record shops were part business, part clubhouse, and part preacher's pulpit.

I met two of my old bosses, Les and Gerry, caught up with Leon Parker – whose hard work had made the exhibition happen – and ended up between Donald Smith (the curator) and Jona ("You'll Always Find Me in the Kitchen at Parties") Lewie as they both reminisced about Anthony Newley and sang snatches of his songs back and forth, which seemed a strangely appropriate end to the evening.

{DICK FARINA, RIC VON SCHMIDT & BLIND BOY GRUNT (BOB DYLAN) | "GLORY, GLORY", *recorded at Dobell's*}

Richard Williams was there, too, and writes about the story of Dobell's in a typically astute post on his blog [*link below*]. Below, a few photos of life in the shop in Kemptown, Brighton. On the left, the opening ceremony, Bill second left, Doug in the centre, the svelte John Jack on the right. In the middle is one of the shopwindows dreamed up by my dad, centering on his dislike of Elvis, not shared by me, and on the right, a visit to the shop by Sonny Terry and Brownie McGhee.

rock stars such as Metallica and husband of ex-Tory MP Louise, discussed the Camerons' tastes at a Tory function. "I asked Samantha Cameron, 'Why Gillian Welch?'," said Mensch, who manages the singer and invited the couple to her Hammersmith concert in 2011. "She said, 'There was a record store in Notting Hill where David and I used to live. I would say to the guy with the purple mohawk: "What should I be listening to?" He sold me *Time (The Revelator)*. For the past 10 years David and I listened to it all the time'."

TWO LANA DEL REY, "CHELSEA HOTEL NO. 2"

A simple and atmospheric version of a song its author has often felt uneasy about. I'm not even sure *anyone* but Leonard Cohen should sing this, but the solemn and melancholy tune is a draw to a certain type of singer.

I think my favourite version is actually Meshell Ndegeocello's, where she creates such a slowed-down, sultry arrangement that it seems that she's only singing the song for one person to hear, not an audience. I don't think it'll be on the set list next week at Ronnie Scott's.

THREE FROM OUR WOODSTOCK CORRESPONDENT

"The road from Rt 28 to W'stock, formerly Rt 375, will be officially renamed Levon Helm Memorial Boulevard. Meanwhile, all Robbie has named after him is the house next door, and that's not even official. (But a couple has moved in and are doing a nice job renovating...) As ever, john c"

FOUR WHAT I SAY
Yeah Yeah Yeahs' excellent notice, posted on the doors of Webster Hall, New York.

FIVE *KILLING THEM SOFTLY*
The soundscape of this beautifully photographed film based on George V. Higgins' fine book *Cogan's Trade*, and recently released on DVD, is fantastic. It's worth watching just for that. It starts with the opening credits – crunching footsteps underneath a voiceover of Obama on the election trail. The election is a presence throughout the film, playing on TVs in bars and on car radios. From the creak of car seats and the roar of throaty engines to the rain on windshields and the echoing hallways, real care is taken. Music supervisor is Rachel Fox, piano pieces and musical ambiences by Marc Streitenfeld. Take a bow.

Wednesday, April 22

ONE THINKING ABOUT RICHIE HAVENS
Introduced to him by Don Sollash, manager of Dobell's record shop ("I listened to jazz all day – the last thing I wanted to listen to at home was more jazz…"), I bought all of the late 60s–early 70s Havens LPs and loved them. I re-bought some of them last year on iTunes and gloried again to "I Started a Joke", "It Could Be the First Day", "Handsome Johnny" and their like.

PLEASE DO NOT WATCH THE SHOW THROUGH A SCREEN ON YOUR SMART DEVICE/CAMERA.

PUT THAT SHIT AWAY as a courtesy to the person behind you and to Nick, Karen and Brian.

MUCH LOVE AND MANY THANKS! YEAH YEAH YEAHS

Marcel called when the BBC showed a programme of Beatles cover versions, saying how great Richie's strummed version of "Here Comes the Sun" was. It's true. His second guitarist and conga player have the damnedest time trying to keep up…

And this is lovely, from Richard Williams' THEBLUEMOMENT: "I interviewed Havens once, for the *Melody Maker*, and it gave me a good story to tell. It was at a hotel on Park Lane, in 1970 or 71. I went up to his room at the appointed time, knocked on the door, and was shown in. He greeted me with great warmth, and looked me straight in the eye. 'Aquarius,' he declared. Er, sorry, I said, but no. Still that piercing look. 'Sagittarius!' No, wrong again. 'Capricorn!' Look, sorry about this, but… 'Taurus!' You can guess the rest: he ran through the whole card before a process of elimination gave him the right answer. He didn't appear at all embarrassed, and it certainly amused me. Then we got to talk. He seemed like one of the good guys."

I also like Havens' story of walking on Hampstead Heath in 1974 and spotting Ray Charles from a distance, sitting on a park bench. "Suddenly I heard, 'Hey, Richie. Get over here!' And it was Ray. He had extraordinary senses…"

THREE "PUT A LITTLE LOVE IN YOUR HEART"
Used in a cholesterol spread advert, this, (probably Jackie DeShannon's biggest hit, from 1969) popped on TV the night

before her cover of Neil Young's "Only Love Can Break Your Heart" came on my iPhone. Now most versions of this, even by good people, are dull and lugubrious. This one, in the hands of the estimable Jackie, is different. It starts straight, then an accordion enters and gets a Bacharach/Butch Cassidy feel going. It takes a left turn with the entrance of a pedal steel into a Bones Howe/5th Dimension groove, and DeShannon pushes the vocal line away from the original, but in a good way. Oh, and it has an accordion. Did I mention that?

FOUR "YOUR MAMA WAS A TENT SHOW QUEEN!"
Bob Gumpert sends a link to a fascinating piece by Carl Wilson (not the Beach Boy) on the Random House Canada blog. It's the strange story of, to quote the intro, "a gay, cross-dressing, black singer named Jackie Shane, who scored a surprise radio hit in what was then staid and uptight Toronto." His only surviving TV clip can be seen on YouTube, a compellingly diffident performance of Rufus Thomas' "Walking the Dog".

ONE THE *MUSCLE SHOALS* FILM
I'm really looking forward to this documentary, showing at the Sundance Festival in London this week. I wrote about the time that our band, Hot House, went there to record [*link below*]. Incidentally, the Rock's Back Pages logo is the legendary Jimmy Johnson's guitar pick [*see page 77*]. A gentleman, he lent us his car as well, which I promptly reversed into a telegraph pole.

On her blog, PRETTYCLEVERFILMGAL writes: "Have you ever heard of Muscle Shoals, Alabama? Let me rephrase the question – have you heard an Aretha Franklin song? Have you ever grooved to Wilson Pickett's 'Land of 1000 Dances'? Have you ever thought, 'Yes, Percy Sledge, that is EXACTLY what happens when a man loves a woman!' Have you ever driven way too fast while the Rolling Stones' 'Brown Sugar' blasted through your speakers?

If you answered yes to any of those questions, then you've heard the Shoals sound, subject of this documentary from Greg 'Freddy' Camalier. In the interest of full disclosure, these are my people y'all! I grew up just east of Muscle Shoals, also on the banks of the Tennessee River – 'The Singing River' to the Native Americans who made their home there for millennia before Rick Hall founded FAME studios. Driven by a need to escape the crushing poverty and overwhelming tragedy that befalls him, Hall is the central figure in the story of the famed 'Muscle Shoals sound' – well, him and a group of homegrown, white-as-cotton studio musicians known as the 'Swampers'. These men shaped what ultimately proved to be some of the finest rock, soul, and R&B America would ever produce."

FIVE MESHELL NDEGEOCELLO: RONNIE SCOTT'S
The drummer, Earl Harvin, sits on the left, his kit pointing across the stage. His mallets are at the ready. Chris Bruce, the guitarist, playing a modded Tele Custom from the seventies, crouches at his pedalboard. Meshell Ndegeocello, her angular bass worn high, counts the song down. And, like setting out a

manifesto, they start playing "Tomorrow Never Knows"...

> *"Turn off your mind relax and float downstream*
> *It is not dying, it is not dying*
> *Lay down all thoughts, surrender to the void*
> *It is shining, it is shining.*
> *Yet you may see the meaning of within*
> *It is being, it is being..."*

and underneath it all creep the contorted keys of Jebin Bruni, wrenching decayed and tweaked noises from his banks of vintage organs and synths and laptop screens.

There is, in her music, enough of the familiar to feel comforted. Often the songs are known – tonight derives mostly from her album in tribute to Nina Simone – but the constituent parts are roughly handled. They keep you on the edge of your seat: how far will they push before it all collapses? Great holes appear, to be suddenly filled by the rolling thunder of the drums or a shard of guitar or a sliver of keyboard or the clanging slap of Ndegeocello's bass.

It's as if all the comforting sureties of the songs have been stripped away – but it's music of beauty. It's just that it's not afraid to be ugly, too, like it wants to encompass the whole experience of life.

It's really hard to do it justice: my hastily scribbled notes in the darkness have phrases like "ghostly martial doo-wop" liberally sprinkled. But I'm making it sound doomy and it wasn't at all. There's such joy in hearing these musicians play. The metal freak-out that ends "Feeling Good", the girls at the bar providing the backing vocals for "See Line Woman", the stunning bass solo that brings a double-time "Suzanne" to an end – this is all wonderful, wonderful stuff. A version of "Pink Moon" in honour of London and Nick Drake, and the stark and short "Oysters" are the icing on the cake. If she plays your town, go.

Wednesday, May 1

ONE A RAINY NIGHT IN BOURGES-AH...

The annual Le Printemps festival brings a platter of bands to almost every bar in this Loire town. Trying to decide where to go and who to see brings the following descriptions from the programme: Superhero Big Beat Surf / Pop Art Punk / Reggae Occitan / Black Death / House Celt Rock Experimental, and my favourite – Rock Noise Folk Blues. This poster [*below*] in a nearby town would have had me putting money down for tickets, but it was in the past...

Best music we saw was a cracking band called Minou, consisting of Pierre Simon and Sabine Quinet, plus a bald percussionist on electric pads. They play guitars and keyboards, both

well, and their oeuvre is some unholy mixture of Kraftwerk, Nirvana and Talking Heads, put over with personality and pizazz and great timing. They were playing in a plastic garden tent, set up in the street, with a pop-up bar serving beer and lethal rum punch, and gave it their all – a welcome relief from the sub-Punk Rock being played in most bars, that the French seem, unaccountably, to be in love with.

TWO BOB GUMPERT APPALLED BY RICIN SUSPECT

Josh Marshall, TPM [TALKINGPOINTSMEMO.COM]: "We had the first court appearance this morning for James Everett Dutschke... Unlike his predecessor, a flat claim of true innocence does not seem to be in the cards. More shocking, it's now alleged Dutschke is a *Wayne Newton* impersonator."

Bob says: "Perhaps only in Mississippi – the first guy arrested for poison letters was an Elvis impersonator. He was turned loose. The new person arrested is a Wayne Newton impersonator and that is just plain offensive." To make it even worse for Bob, the *Daily Mail* reports that "the FBI searched his home, vehicles and former studio last week, after dropping charges against an Elvis impersonator who says he had feuded with Dutschke in the past." You couldn't make that up – feudin' poison-letter-writing impersonators: Elvis vs Wayne...

THREE *THE THICK OF IT* WRITER IAN MARTIN'S 60 THOUGHTS ABOUT TURNING 60

My favourites from this article in *The Guardian*:

4 It was 1968. Early summer evening, a Saturday. My mate and I were hitching home in the Essex countryside. We got a lift from a happy couple in a boaty car that smelled of leather and engine oil. We were 15, they were proper old, 20-ish. Relaxed and so very much in love. They treated us as equals, laughed at our jokes, we smoked their cigarettes. "Walk Away Renee" by the Four Tops came on the radio. We all sang along to the chorus. I felt a blissful certainty that life as an adult might genuinely be a laugh. The entire encounter lasted no more than 10 minutes. I have thought about that couple every day since. Every day, for 45 years. Imagine that. A Belisha Beacon of kindness pulsing through the murk of a whole life.

58 "Nice snare sound." Always say this to someone you like when they are playing you terrible music, especially if it's their demo. This insincere but specific observation allows both parties to sidestep more general, and potentially cruel, discussion. If the person insists, they deserve everything they get, starting with "shit snare sound".

FOUR PORTRAIT OF THE ARTIST, *THE GUARDIAN*: MADELEINE PEYROUX, SINGER

What work of art would you most like to own? "I hate the idea of owning a work of art. But I do own a guitar that I consider a work of art. It's a 1943 Martin 0-17. I took it on tour with me for 16 years, but I've just had to put it back in the closet. It was made in the United States during the second world war, when metal was rationed – there's no metal in the neck, which means it's constantly going out of tune."

FIVE RADIO DJ EDITH BOWMAN'S 10 BEST SONGS EVER WRITTEN, *STYLIST* MAGAZINE

Marvin Gaye, "What's Going On": "To be honest, I don't feel there's a lot I can say about the song itself. Just listening to it says it all. It's the perfect tonic. It brings out the sunshine. The horn section at the start of the song, coupled with the melodies, makes you want to groove from the first few bars. Instant smiles from the get-go."

Marvin would be pleased, I'm sure, that his agonised plea for peace and understanding (opening lines "Mother, mother, there's too many of you crying / Brother, brother, brother, there's far too many of you dying...") soundtracks Edith's brain-dead summer picnics. And she actually says, about Joni Mitchell's "River", "she sings it in a way that makes her feel totally accessible, the fragility in her voice encouraging you to sing along. This is probably quite a 'girl's choice' to be honest..."

In what world is choosing a song by one of the greatest songwriters ever to have graced pop music girly? Not a lot of fragility in Joni. Bare, naked honesty, yes. Fragility? I don't think so. This is a woman who got totally pissed off when she played acetates of *Court and Spark* at a party after Dylan had played acetates of *Planet Waves*, and having no one listen. And know-

{MADELEINE PEYROUX | "WEARY BLUES (FROM WAITIN')"}

ing that it was a better record. To whom Dylan whispered, after they shared a bill together in the early 2000s, "Joni, you make me sound like a hillbilly." Oh, Edith. Behave.

Wednesday, May 8

ONE **TONY, TONY, TONY**

Following on from the despair of a couple of weeks ago at depressing rock reads, this rebalanced everything: Eamonn Forde's brilliant abbreviation of Tony Blackburn's hysterical, self-regarding autobiography, *Poptastic!* Two examples, the first about Gary Glitter. Read it and weep. With laughter.

> looked. Some years later, I had him on as a guest on my Radio One children's show, and he came in blind drunk wearing a sailor's cap. Later still, at a Children In Need event, he was doing the old act, yelling "Come on, come on!" at the top of his failing voice. By the end of the show, he was in a dreadful state, perspiring badly and needing to be helped into a chair.
>
> Of course, that was nothing compared to the tattered state of his reputation now. None of us had any idea what he was up to. I met his son once and even he told me his dad was a bit weird. I don't think we'll ever be seeing Gary Glitter on a stage again, let alone at another Children In Need concert.
>
> The Radio London Soul Night Out probably did more for bringing Londoners together than anything that ever appeared on the statute book during that period. Apart from one ugly night, when we took over this club in Leicester Square and the evening ended in murder, the Soul Night Out was a joy-filled weekly event where everyone, black, white and all shades between, united around a shared love for the music.

TWO **ELTON DOCUMENTARY, BBC**

I caught the last quarter of the Elton doc, which seemed to compress the past thirty years of his career into ten minutes, and was struck by this: why, if you've got an interview with Terry O'Neill, and he says, "Elton rang me up and said we're doing a show at Dodger Stadium, it's gonna be great, get over here and take some pictures," do you not show any of Terry's now-iconic shots, just some fairly run-of-the-mill video?

THREE *ORPHEUS*, **BATTERSEA ARTS CENTRE**

Amidst the wonderfully mad recreation of Hades and the beautifully evoked Parisian nightclub of this Django-ised retelling of the Orpheus myth by Little Bulb Theatre, a truly stunning moment. Tom Penn, who plays The Drummer/Stage Hand/Dancing Bear/Too Many Parts to Mention, sits down and, as Persephone (the Queen of the Underworld) plucks the opening notes on a harp of a beautiful ballad, "La Chanson de Persephone", written by the company. From his mouth issues a falsetto that is extraordinary – part Bon Iver, part Antony – and in a production filled to the brim with indelible music – "Minor Swing", Saint-Saëns, Debussy, Piaf's "Hymne à l'amour" – brings the house down. A song you wanted to hear again the second it finished.

FOUR **"I ANALYSE LEADERS FOR A LIVING, AND NONE ARE AS GREAT AS ALEX FERGUSON"**

Nick Robinson, the BBC's political editor: "Like the impresario of a great opera company or the chief executive of a mighty corporation he succeeded so much and survived for so long because he understood people – how to motivate them, how to discipline them and how to inspire them. When this year Harvard Business School asked Fergie to share some of his secrets, he explained how as a young manager he studied and learned from leaders in other walks of life: 'I had never been to a classical concert in my life. But I am watching this and thinking about the coordination and the teamwork – one starts and one stops, just fantastic. So I spoke to my players about the orchestra – how they are a perfect team.' He didn't merely manage teams – he created them."

FIVE TRIBECA FILM LOGO SCREEN

I'm not even sure what those quick pre-credit sequences that show the production company of the film are even called. Splashes? You know – the Lion of MGM, the Searchlight of Fox, the Calder Mobile thing for Pathé? Whatever, check out this little beauty from Tribeca Film at the head of the two-minute preview for *Greetings from Tim Buckley*. Using a lighthouse sweep, it's just gorgeous.

Wednesday, May 15

ONE BOWIE WALK

After I helped the V&A with a photo of Dobell's, they're kind enough to send me this Jonathan Barnbrook–designed pamphlet, *David Bowie Is Walking in Soho*. The tour starts here.

TWO RIDERS OF THE STARS

FRANK SINATRA: One bottle each: Absolut, Jack Daniel's, Chivas Regal, Courvoisier, Beefeater Gin, white wine, red wine. Twenty-four chilled jumbo shrimp, Life Savers, cough drops. [*No mixers?*]

BRITNEY SPEARS: Fish and chips, McDonald's cheeseburgers without the buns, 100 prunes and figs, a framed photo of Princess Diana. [*Britney, as always, touched by genius!*]

AL GREEN: Twenty-four long-stem red roses (dethorned). [*Having seen Rev. Green present these in the flesh to his adoring audience, I'm touched by the thoughtfulness.*]

THREE BATHROOMS & BULLIES

On *Woman's Hour* [BBC Radio 4] I catch Chan Marshall talking about the best places she found to sing as a teenager, and she talks of

{BRITNEY SPEARS | "PIECE OF ME"}

school bathrooms when no one was in them, singing to the walls, and the echo – and when she's on *Later* that night, you can see how her voice now has those reflections and deflections built into it. With a haircut borrowed from Nick Lowe and her hands jerking in and out of her jean shirt, her performance of "Bully" was twitchy and vulnerable, but beautifully *her* – she doesn't sound much like anybody else (the same is true of Laura Mvula, also on the show, who – making a nod to Nina Simone – is refreshingly different from her peer group).

FOUR FOUND WHILE GOOGLING WHO WROTE "WALKING TO NEW ORLEANS"?

On the website BESTOFNEWORLEANS.COM: *Well Composed: Bobby Charles Tells How He Wrote Three of His Classic Songs*
"WALKING TO NEW ORLEANS"
"I had sent Fats a copy of 'Before I Grow Too Old', and he had

recorded it, but I didn't know. The next night he was playing in Lafayette, and I went to see him play. He told me, 'I cut your song last night – I wish I'd brought a copy of it for you to listen to'. And he said, 'You gotta come to New Orleans to see me and hang out with me'.

I said, 'I'd love to, but right now I'm really on my butt and got no money and no way to get over there'. He said, 'Take a bus or something'. I told him, 'The only way I'd be able to get there would be to walk to New Orleans'. As soon as I said that, I said, 'I gotta go'. I jumped in the car and wrote the song on the way back home from Lafayette to Abbeville." [I'm appalled that I'd never known that Bobby Charles wrote one of my all-time favourite songs – *ed*]
"SEE YOU LATER ALLIGATOR"
"I used to say to the band or friends, 'See you later alligator'. One night after a dance, I was walking out the door, and my piano player was sitting down in a back booth, and there were two drunk couples in the booths in front of him. I said, 'See you later alligator' to him as I was walking out, and it was one of those doors that closed real slow. I heard a girl say something about 'crocodile'. I walked back in and said, 'I don't mean to bother you, but I just told him, "See you later, alligator."

What did you say?' She said, 'After a while, crocodile'. I said,

'Thank you' and went home and wrote the song in 20 minutes. My daddy was screaming at me to turn out the lights, because he had to get up and go to work at 5 o'clock in the morning. I said, 'Give me five more minutes'. I had to sing it to myself over and over so I wouldn't forget it."

"THE JEALOUS KIND"

"I was married at the time, and I was in the bathtub. My wife was fussing and hollering at me while I was taking a bath. I said, 'Why don't you bring me paper and a pencil and just leave me alone for 30 minutes'. She said, 'You and your damn paper and pencil'. I wrote it right there in the bathtub. Same thing with 'Before I Grow Too Old'. She said, 'You gonna be like this for the rest of your life?' I said, 'I'm gonna try and hurry up and do as much as I can before I get too old'. Bam! Bring me a paper and pencil!".

FIVE AND MORE FROM THE BIG EASY...

...in the shape of another Hugh Laurie documentary. He's dry and funny, has great taste in producers and musicians, and plays pretty good piano. I just never want to hear him sing again, if that can be arranged. Best bit: the amazing Jon Cleary, an Englishman in New Orleans, doing a staggering take on James Booker and Professor Longhair. He rips through a sonic wonderworld of rhumba rhythms and tumbling blues, then turns to Laurie and says, "New Orleans comes into fashion, goes out of fashion. They don't stop playing here just because no one's looking."

AND... PROFESSOR LONGHAIR'S HOUSE, 2010

Longhair had my favourite band name ever: Professor Longhair and His Shuffling Hungarians [called that, as Wikipedia says, for reasons lost to time. As far as I can ascertain, there were no Hungarians in the band]. I do remember going with Mark to see James Booker at the 100 Club. As we came down the stairs to the basement room, we heard the sound of a New Orleans band pounding out "Junco Partner", the bass shaking the walls, what sounded like a horn section high-stepping the accents. We stepped through the door to find Booker alone at the piano, committing his mischief, conjuring up an orchestra's worth of accompaniment with just two hands...

{JAMES BOOKER | "TIPITINA/THE GRASS LOOKS GREENER" *from* Live at Montreux}

Wednesday, May 22

ONE **R.I.P. GEORGE JONES: A MEMORY OF THE WEMBLEY COUNTRY FESTIVAL, 1981**

Simon and I loved the Killer, Jerry Lee Lewis, and were prepared to endure any amount of maudlin production-line Nashville filler to see him. However, the bill at the 1981 International Festival of Country Music (© Mervyn Conn) at the Empire Pool was pretty good, and Carl Perkins' set led into Jerry's, the highlight of which was a staggeringly over-the-top rendition of "Somewhere Over the Rainbow".

The icing on the cake, however, was the towering (but pretty short, if memory serves me well) performance by the legendary George. I had inveigled a press pass and snuck into the VIP section to take photos, and found myself next to Elvis Costello, who was there to pay homage, I'm guessing. Two frames, a rather evil-eyed look from one of Elvis's companions, and I concentrated on the stage. My favourite shot, though, is of Simon, resplendent in bootlace tie and Jim Reeves badge...

TWO **MICHAEL HANN VS GINGER BAKER**

I'm with Ginger on this video press conference. Hann should have realised from question one that he needed to be a bit less rock-writerly. The business of being a working musician is often about money and survival, not art, so asking him questions like "Your time in Africa – it seems from the film to be very, very important to you, was that the time when you felt

most musically fulfilled?" may not be the best starting point, especially as it implies that anything post that period was a letdown...

FOUR **A WEEK OF GIFTS...**

Lloyd gives me Imelda May's plectrum: "Hubbard, my oldest friend from Hull, is mad about Imelda. He went to see her and after the gig got chatting and she gave it to him – it's the one she used."

And Weston kindly gives me these cigarette cards of guitarists, part of a set issued by Polydor in the seventies. It reminds me that I need to download the Shuggie Otis outtakes that Richard Williams writes so well about here [*link below*].

FIVE **LADIES & GENTLEMEN, HENRY DILTZ**

I'm introduced to Henry, legendary lensman of Laurel Canyon, whose iconic pictures of The Doors, Buffalo Springfield, The Eagles, Joni Mitchell and CSN&Y were the visual soundtrack to my adolescence. I ask him when he switched his focus from musician (he was a member of The Modern Folk Quartet, playing banjo) to photographer. He tells me that Steve Stills mentioned that the Springfield were going to do a gig at Redondo Beach, so he tagged along to take pictures for the slide show that he would do for his friends every weekend, showing pictures of LA itself and sometimes its musicians, who were often among those gathered in Henry's house. (Then, the only way to see the colour photographs that you'd taken was to buy a Kodak Carousel to project them onto a white wall or sheet.)

The Springfield came outside from their sound check and he asked if they'd pose in front of a large mural. A magazine heard that he had some shots and paid him $100. Realising he could make this photography thing work, he started taking more and more and, often with designer Gary Burden, photographed his friends' album covers.

I loved hearing about his time playing banjo for Phil Spector: Spector was interested in the nascent folk-rock scene

and took The Modern Folk Quartet into the studio, where they recorded a Harry Nilsson song, "This Could Be the Night". Brian Wilson dropped by while they were recording it, in his pajamas and dressing gown, and sat there with the song on repeat, mesmerized. Spector, very paranoid about any song he released, afraid that it wouldn't scale the heights of his previous successes and would therefore damage his reputation, never put it out. But Henry did get to play banjo sitting next to Barney Kessel in the guitar section of the Wall of Sound, on the Righteous Brothers' "Ebb Tide" among others...

Wednesday, May 29

ONE **WAYNE MILLER DIED LAST WEEK**

Wayne Miller was one of the less famous names at the legendary photo agency Magnum. When we were looking for a cover for the debut Hot House album in 1986, to be called *South*, we were determined not to have ourselves in the frame. Our first single had used a Weegee photo of a burning building, and we liked the anti-80s feel of black and white photography – in the mid-80s every cover seemed to have sharp pinks and hard yellows and glossy, overlit faces shining out.

We were looking for a photo that summed up the feel of a record recorded partly in the Alabama heat of Muscle Shoals, and found it in the book that accompanied Ed Steichen's famous *Family of Man* exhibition at the Museum of Modern Art in 1955. The photo we fell in love with was of a couple in a clinch. It was part of a series taken in 1949 of migrant workers – cotton pickers – in California. We thought that the intensity and intimacy was something to behold. There's another wonderful image in this series of the same couple, the man sitting disconsolately on the bed, with the woman lazily fiddling with her nails.

I'm still not sure how we convinced anyone to go with this approach, but we did. Of course, the record company could probably point to the cover having something to do with the paltry sales of the album... The type is cut out of the posters that we had printed by Tribune Showprint, of Earl Park, Indiana.

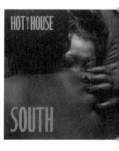

TWO **THE CLASH INTERVIEWED,** *THE GUARDIAN*

Paul Simonon on musicianship: "I'd become musically more capable. I could take off the notes that were painted on the neck of my guitar. But then I did make a mistake in being really confident: I went for one of those jazz basses that didn't have frets... And when it goes really dark, and you can't quite hear what you're playing, it suddenly sounds like you're drunk. So I said: 'You know what? I think I'll have the frets put back on.' I got a bit carried away. I thought I was getting quite good, but I got a big slap in the face."

...and on presentation: "A lot of the looks were down to financial problems. Everyone in those days wore flares and had long hair. So if you went into secondhand stores, there'd be so many straight-legged trousers because everyone wanted flares. That instantly set you apart from everybody else. And also there was another place called Laurence Corner, selling army surplus..."

At the moment I work along the road from where Laurence Corner was, and still fondly remember the green army jacket I bought there. Now there's a chemist in its place, but they've put a little plaque in the window...

THREE **THAT DIFFICULT SECOND ALBUM**

Sexual Healing, Pamela Stephenson Connolly's sex therapy column in *The Guardian*: "My boyfriend talks too much during sex. We've been together for a year and recently he's started talking to me while we're intimate. At first it was everyday stuff like what he wants for dinner but then essentially he began ranting. Do you know how hard it is to climax while listening to someone talk about how many bands have produced 'disappointing second albums'? I don't know if I can go on like this."

FOUR **ROLLING STONE'S BOB DYLAN SPECIAL**

No professional manicures for Bob, no sir...

Wednesday, June 5

ONE **DAFT. NOT PUNK.**

So I ask Mark what he thinks of the new Daft Punk album and

he says "Rubbish", and I think 50 million people and all the broadsheet critics can't be wrong. So I listen. I put it on Spotify when summer arrives for a day and we have a barbecue. I play it when I'm walking around the house or making tea. And guess what. Mark is right. Everyone else is wrong. And I love disco, and I love session musicians, but this is just... For instance, one track sounds like a wonky, rubbish version of a Police song. The nadir is reached with the Paul Williams tune, which sounds like a lame copy of something from Joss Whedon's genius *Buffy* musical. It's a cute idea to work with Williams (who wrote some of the Carpenters hits) but it just sounds... rubbish.

So why is everyone so invested in saying it's great? Is it because half of them seem to be creative partners in some promotional campaign (stand up, Pitchfork), or have got special access and an interview? The sell is clever, and it's smart to get their collaborators to act as shills for them, but I'll leave you with three words: *Emperor's New Clothes* (or in this case, *Motorbike Helmets*).

TWO *THE BLUES*, A FILM

Sam Charters showed us this, his brilliant, little-seen, 1962 film, as he was on his way to Scotland to spend time with Document Records remastering it. Shot as he and Ann Charters travelled through the South recording bluesmen who had had their moment in the sun in the twenties and thirties, it is twenty-two minutes of poetry and poverty. From a host of riv-

eting performances, a favourite moment: Pink Anderson and his sweet-faced boy, Little Pink, playing Leadbelly's "Cotton Fields". Pink was the inspiration, along with another Georgia bluesman, Floyd Council, for the name of Syd Barrett's new band in 1966. Hopefully the DVD will see the light of day later in the year.

THREE **GO AWAY YOU BOMB?**

"Hand-typed [as opposed to...?] lyrics to a Bob Dylan song which he never recorded are expected to sell for £35,000 when they go up for auction at Christie's in London next month. Dylan's lyric sheet for 'Go Away You Bomb' will go under the hammer at Christie's in London on June 26." – *NME*

Israel "Izzy" Young: "I was compiling a book of songs against the atom bomb and asked Dylan to contribute; he gave me this

1963

Bob Dylan wrote this when I booked him to do a gig

bomb song book

```
Go away you Bomb get away go away
Fast right now fast quick you get me sick
My good gal don' lx like you none an' the kids on my corner are scared a' you
An' my friends 're gettin xxxxxxxx headaches that split an' spit an'
That kind a feelin' is rubbin' off on me an' I don' like it none too good
I hate the letters in yer word - B that' means bad yer so bad that even
A dead hog in the sun would get up an' run O that stands for xxxx orrible
Yer so orrible that the word drops it's first letter and runs xxxxx H
That stands for morgue an' all them folks in it 're feelin' lucky an' I don'
Mind folks feelin' lucky but I hate that feelin' of envy an' sometimes when
I get to thinkin' bout how lucky they are I get xxxxxxxx xxxxxx envious
of 'm an' that's a bad lonesome feelin' too B- that means bad but that's
The secondx time so it's twice as bad
```

song the very next day. I have never sold anything important to me until now, and the funds raised will help to keep the Folklore Center in Stockholm going.

"I have always had a passion for folk music and I have collected books and music since I was a kid. I produced my first catalogue of folk books in 1955, comprised of books that nobody had ever heard of – this was the beginning of the interest in American folk music. Bob Dylan used to hang around the store and would look through every single book and listen to every single record I had."

FOUR **CERYS MATTHEWS ON BOB**
From *The Guardian*: "By 2008, her marriage was over and she was back in the UK. By now, she had a low-key solo career up and running, made an unexpected appearance on *I'm a Celeb-rity... Get Me Out of Here!* and was starting to present shows on BBC 6 MUSIC. A year later, she married her manager, Steve Abbott. The couple met when she recorded a duet with one of Abbott's other clients, Aled Jones. 'We just clicked. We had very similar taste in music, right down to the line between liking Bob Dylan and not really liking Tom Petty.' She smiles. 'That kind of thing is important to me. I'm very opinionated about music. So is he.'" Exactly right, Cerys! People always assume that you'll like Tom Petty because you like Bob. And it's just not true.

FIVE **YOU REALLY COULDN'T MAKE THIS UP**
The sisters Mamet [daughters of David, band name The Cabin Sisters] introduce their (in their own words) unique brand of folk via body percussion, banjo and harmonies. "This music video for 'Bleak Love' is our chance to realize through the visual artistry of some very talented people the universal feeling of un-requited love. Your support for this project will be the backbone to a body of excited filmmakers, producers and musicians all making something from nothing. We have a wonderful concept from a bright young director that includes, beautiful gowns, statues, a large opulent loft space, extensive make-up, saturated tones needing anamorphic lens.

Pledge $8,000 or more

0 backers Limited (1 of 1 left)

Zosia Mamet's (director styled) set chair, from season 2, signed by the GIRLS! with Shoshanna embroidered in its back you could have a piece of television memorabilia and help the cause! plus a t-Shirt, signed vinyl and digital download

Estimated delivery: Aug 2013
Add $100 to ship outside the US

"We also have those folks who are good enough to work for free that we are trying to travel and feed. It is an expensive proposition when all is said and done, but we have a realistic budget that we know we can make work. So, please please join us in the fight against heartbreak!"

Apart from the hazy punctuation – wtf? Listen to Zosia's stumbling and half-assed reasons why you should back her in the begging video. Well-paid, well-connected actresses using Kickstarter for vanity projects? I'm betting that, for your $8,000, the director-styled chair is not cutting it.

Wednesday, June 12

ONE OTIS BLACK
Talking about the Otis Redding documentary last week, Hugh told us: "I was in the art class at Dunfermline High when I heard that Otis had died. My fellow Mods and I gathered together at lunchtime to discuss the sad news and it was agreed that we would all wear black ties the next day. So I borrowed (or nicked) my dad's funeral tie and duly turned up at school – to find that I was the only one who had remembered or, to be more accurate, bothered – Mods could be a fickle bunch, with a bit more style than substance."

TWO FOUR-HOUR FLIGHT OF "THE EAGLES"
Possibly too long, not enough peyote, or grumpiness with CS&N. Too much "how we got back together after sacking everyone…" But an awesome level of ability and professionalism, some great singing and guitar slinging, the right amount of indebtedness to Jackson, JD Souther and – most especially – Linda Ronstadt, and a fair sampling of the treasurable Joe Walsh, a true one-off.

My favourite moment is when Glenn Frey is talking about how being on the road so much makes you go a little crazy and the camera pans across to Joe, wearing (of course) a fly's head made of aluminium foil, and he nods. But the silver-foil head is lovingly crafted. It has antennae and a proboscis, and the longer he nods the funnier it becomes. Richard Williams recently told me to listen to "I'll Tell the World About You" from Walsh's *Barnstorm*. You are advised to track it down post-haste. It's a truly gorgeous meld of Southern Soul and Southern California.

THREE "MARNIE STERN, HERE'S IMELDA'S PICK"
Talking of one-offs, after Marnie's blistering screamfest of an opening number, Marcel turns to me and says, "Well, at least she's not copying anyone". Cartoon-voiced, foul-mouthed, with two burly men on bass and drums, she thrashes out one short sharp song after another, filled with firecracker guitar and lots of shouting. It's exhilarating. The melodies are jagged and the riffs punchy – like a slightly more benign thrash metal. Marnie looks like Cameron Diaz playing the role of AC/DC's Angus Young. The person I've seen recently with the same quality of intensity and humour is Este Haim, the bassist with Haim, whose gurning and whirling are a sight to see. At one

point Marnie's bassist shoots a film of the audience clapping and cheering to prove, Marnie says, "that people love me", as her mother is convinced they don't…

Just before the last song she drops her plectrum and can't find it. I'm kind of stunned she doesn't have a gaggle of picks taped to her mike – this must be a regular occurrence. I remember I have Imelda May's pick in my jeans [*why? see May 22*] and proffer it to Marnie, getting a warm clap on the back from a fellow audience member. The show goes on to climax in a number

where the drummer gets louder and faster, the bassist is all over the frets and Marnie is spinning and playing a raucous off-kilter riff, combining John Bonham with Philip Glass, and, oh I don't know… Yngwie Malmsteen? Whatever, its pummelling intensity for six minutes gives the following minute a blissful sense of headiness, as if you'd been holding your breath and suddenly let go. Marcel gets a CD signed: "Thanks for the pick!!! It was great heartxo".

FOUR CALLING BILL HICKS

I'm always at a loss why already-rich people are shills for the likes of watch and perfume companies, but I guess jazz musicians don't take home the money that film stars do. So the appearance, only a few pages apart, of two advertisements featuring Wynton Marsalis in the new edition of American *Esquire* shouldn't surprise me.

Mind you, it pales in comparison to this: Jermaine Jackson says, "Being involved in the hospitality business is a dream I shared with my brother Michael, and Jermajesty Hotels and Resorts is named after my son [that's right – his son is called Jermajesty]. I am absolutely delighted to have GoConnect joining us in this emotional journey [!]. Rarely is there an opportunity for an upscale hospitality business to be able to capitalize on the success of a global entertainment brand… that opportunity has now finally arrived."

FIVE ON THE DIGITISING OF MUSIC

A Sophie Heawood article about disposing of all digitised music from her life in *The Guardian* prompted this nice letter the next day: "I was pleased to read that Sophie Heawood (G2, 5 June) has rediscovered the pleasure of listening to good music on a decent stereo. As Alex said in *A Clockwork Orange*: 'What you got back home, little sister, to play your fuzzy warbles on? I bet you got little save pitiful, portable picnic players. Come with uncle and hear all proper! Hear angel trumpets and devil trombones. You are invited.'" – Ralph Jones

Wednesday, June 19

TWO I RESCUE SON AND SEB FROM DOWNLOAD

... after they had the car key stolen. They are at the edge of a massive event that stretches for miles, but considering that it only finished the night before, the clean-up and dismantling that's taken place is majorly impressive.

THREE I LOVE THE SOUNDTRACK...

by Mogwai for eerie French drama *The Returned*. Its crepuscular, Lynchian feel is given extra heft by the almost constant musical backdrop, sometimes a spindly xx-y kind of guitar track, sometimes a curdled piano and spooky xylophone. I came across this interview with Fabrice Gobert, who wrote and directed the series, and Dominic Aitchison, from Mogwai.

FABRICE GOBERT: "Six months before filming, we were casting the actors and I thought it was very important to cast the music too, as it would be a main character in the drama. I love what Mogwai do in general, but especially the film about Zinedine Zidane [Mogwai wrote the soundtrack for *Zidane: A 21st Century Portrait*]. It was a strange movie and the music was spectacular. When I was writing the scripts I was listening to that music a lot. I thought it would be strange to imagine that a band like Mogwai would agree to work on a French drama, but we tried it. And they were interested. I don't know why.

"I talked to them about a Swedish film, *Let the Right One In*, a film with vampires rather than zombies, but it was very realistic, and a good influence for what we wanted to do. We don't want to make *The Walking Dead*; we wanted to make a French fantasy drama where dead people come back.

"I gave them some photographs from Gregory Crewdson, an American who photographs the American suburbs and makes the spectator feel very uncomfortable with something very familiar and very strange. And I gave them music from films that I like. The sort of thing musicians make with movies when they are free, such as Neil Young for *Dead Man*, and Miles Davis for Louis Malle's *Elevator to the Gallows*."

DOMINIC AITCHISON: "We received the basic synopsis, plus a list of films and books that might influence the tone of the programme. We've always wanted to do more soundtracks. The Zidane film was the only chance we'd really had to do something like that. It was great fun and quite different from writing a normal record – you have to try not to have obvious effects that would really ramp up the tension. You have to keep it really simple, and try to keep the dynamics quite flat; not having it jump up, and not having the big scares."

FIVE I FINALLY TAKE THE PLUNGE

This week, after four years' prevarication, I finally take the plunge and order one of these... Yes, it's an Ampeg Scroll Bass,

as played by one of my heroes, Rick Danko. I first saw one on the *Rock of Ages* sleeve in 1972, and I have wanted one ever since. I once met a jazz bassist with one, and I saw a picture of

Brian Eno playing one that I clipped out of *The Guardian* years ago (see left), but four years ago I found that Bruce Johnson – a retired Disney thrill-ride engineer – had set up shop and was loving recreating (while considerably improving) Ampeg basses.

Every piece of the body and neck, virtually every part of the hardware, made by hand, on turn-of-the-century lathes that Bruce has overhauled. On holiday in LA we made a midnight visit to Bruce's workshop in Burbank and spent a fascinating hour with him and his dog.

Check out YouTube for a video of Rick (a man who, in Ralph J. Gleason's wonderful line, "looked like he could swing Coit Tower", so muscular was his playing, so lurching his stage movements) with his fretless at Brooklyn's Academy of Music, New Year's Eve, 1971, with "W.S. Walcott's Medicine Show". Watch for the excellent lurching at 2:30.

Wednesday, June 26

ONE L. RON MELLOTRON

On a walking tour of Fitzrovia, a whole host of music references, from the squat where Boy George and Jon Moss wrote "Do You Really Want to Hurt Me?" to the mansion flat that Robert Nesta Marley lived in for a year in 1972. Bob's flat was in the rectangular block of streets between Tottenham Court Road and Gower Street, which is technically Fitzrovia but in a no-man's-land between it and Bloomsbury known as the Gower Peninsula. We proceed to the original location of Cranks, first organic café in London, where Johnny Rotten and Sid Vicious worked – washing up – for a short time.

My favourite moment comes as we pass a large, grand house on Fitzroy Street, and someone says, "That's where L. Ron Hubbard lived". And I overhear a man talking to his partner, saying "I was down in East Grinstead for work and we passed Saint Hill Manor [Scientology's national headquarters, a huge brick temple with visitors centre] and we were given a tour by a slightly scary woman, and I got to play L. Ron Hubbard's mellotron." I ask him what he played, as the mellotron songbook is not huge. "Strawberry Fields Forever", he says.

TWO **I LOVED THIS PHOTO**

…of jazz guitarist Johnny Smith, playing in a Tucson music store in the late 1970s. It ran with the *New York Times* obit. It's partly for the faded Kodachrome, partly for the light, partly for the clothes, partly for the wonderful selection of guitars. A lovely quote stood out: "He accomplished everything he ever wanted," his daughter, Kim Smith Stewart, said. "He played with the best musicians in the world, he went deep sea fishing in the Gulf of Mexico, he was a great father."

THREE **GEORGE LEWIS WITH ACKER BILK'S BAND, THE MARQUEE**

Caught on *Jazz 625* from the early sixties. At the end of the song, Humphrey Lyttelton says: "Every great jazz musician has one number which is his one-way ticket to immortality, and that surely is George Lewis's – 'Burgundy Street Blues'." Simon emails: "It may have been the extra-wide-screen TV I was watching on, but George Lewis, in the *625* film, had the longest ET-like fingers, specially designed for the clarinet – I'm still reeling…" George's performance is lovely, swooping and poised. As he and the band finish, Acker says *Yeah…* softly and touches him on the arm.

FOUR **MORE JAZZ**

Reviewing *Jazz: New York in the Roaring Twenties* by Robert Nippoldt and Hans-Jürgen Schaal, for *eye* magazine. My favourite brace of spreads are these, featuring the waveforms of the twenty songs from the enclosed CD, along with a timing graph. Only "Rhapsody in Blue", commissioned by Paul White-

man from George Gershwin, is over 3 minutes 20 seconds, and continues by itself onto the second spread.

Wednesday, July 3

TWO **KENNY ROGERS, QUESTIONED BY ALEXIS PETRIDIS IN** *THE GUARDIAN*

I found an old newspaper story online about you beginning a parallel career in professional tennis in the late 70s. What was that all about?

"I'm kind of an impulsive obsessive, I don't know if there's a category like that. I get impulsively involved in something and I get obsessed with it. I did that with tennis. I didn't start playing until I was 35 years old, and then I got obsessed with it and I played eight hours a day. I played in professional matches. I had a national ranking. I was one spot above Björn Borg in doubles."

You're joking!

"No! That's just my nature. Then I couldn't physically play ten-

nis any more, so I took up photography. I studied for four years under a guy who'd been Ansel Adams' assistant..." [describes photographer Adams' "zone system" codification of the principles of sensitometry in mind-boggling depth].

THREE **BUSKER, NORTHERN LINE TO OLD STREET**

As he tried to pick up a Polish girl ("Sorry, love, thought you said Portuguese..."), he starts playing Marley's "Three Little Birds", all Glasto peace & love, but failing to feel any enthusiasm from a listless Tube carriage, takes a weird right turn into "Blue Suede Shoes" – *One for the money / Two for the show...*

FIVE **FAVOURITE LETTER OF THE WEEK**

"Marie Paterson bemoans the coverage of classical as opposed to pop music (Letters, 1 July) but at least 'pop' music is performed by the composers, whereas classical music, with some exceptions, is usually performed by a tribute band, often known as an orchestra." – Derek Middlemiss, Notts, in *The Guardian*

Wednesday, July 10

ONE **ROBERT CHRISTGAU ON THE LOUIS ARMSTRONG HOUSE MUSEUM,** *MSN.COM*

"Armstrong never made the money he should have – [his manager, Joe] Glaser kept most of it. But he could have afforded a far grander place, and that he chose not to says something telling about a genius who never aspired to rise above a common station except in the notes he played. Within the limits he laid out for himself, however, Armstrong didn't stint.

"Reading about the mirrored bathroom, gold-plated toilet fixtures, cheetah-print stair carpet, and aquamarine everything, you may fear the house is pretentious or embarrassing, but it's not at all, at least not to someone who grew up in Queens when Armstrong lived there. On the contrary, it's an object lesson in limited luxury. With its careful period authenticity –

even the air-conditioners are very 1970, although their guts have been replaced – the museum is a vivid reminder of how much more acquisitive, pretentious, and would-be hip wealth has become since the days of the affluent society."

This reminded me of something that Rupert Everett, the actor, said in an interview to coincide with the release of his second book, the brittle and fascinating *Vanished Years*. "If you look at books of Hollywood homes in the 70s, it's just amazing how humble they are; they're like little beach shanty houses with bric-a-brac furniture. Now the smallest fucking brainless Hollywood producer lives in an Earth Wind & Fire Egyptian Palace. It's just... It's become so tasteless, I suppose."

TWO **STARRY-EYED AN' LAUGHING**

I swear I don't try to shoehorn Bob into every post, but when I visited Mayfair's (and, quite possibly, the world's) greatest

wine store, Hedonism, the record on the deck (they have a ridiculously high-end system, somewhat matching the drink selection) is *Another Side Of...* and track four, side one plays as I wander around, window shopping. Later, around the corner, I pass this plaque on the wall of the building that used to be home to the Robert Stigwood Organisation...

THREE **TWO LETTERS ABOUT THE STONES,** *THE GUARDIAN*

¶ In 1962 or 1963 I went to Ken Colyer's jazz club with other members of High Wycombe YCND [Youth Campaign for Nuclear Disarmament]. A note on the door said that the usual Dixieland wouldn't be playing: instead, "a young rhythm and blues band, the Rolling Stones". Not impressed, we spent the evening in the pub. – Jo Russell, Stoke-on-Trent

¶ I remember seeing the Stones about 1964 at the Empress

Ballroom in Wigan (later to become the Wigan Casino, home of Northern Soul). During their performance, Jagger threw his sweaty shirt into the audience. I and another girl caught it. She ended up with one sleeve and I won the rest of it. I stored it carefully in one of my drawers at home, where my mother found it and, seeing it was damaged, tore it up and used it for dusters. – Marie Blundell, Wigan

FOUR BUSKER, EUSTON STATION

The summer heat brings an unusual sight and sound: a black guy, possibly blind, Bizet's *Carmen* blasted through an amp hanging from his neck, playing the top line (tone courtesy of Paul Butterfield) on a crunchily amplified harmonica. Orchestral Harp vs Blues Harp. No contest.

FIVE RICKIE LEE JONES, *ON MY PLAYLIST*, METRO. ELOQUENT.

¶ "On the Road Again" CANNED HEAT
Alan "Blind Owl" Wilson, the harmonica player, plays so lyrically, I often quip and hoot to myself as I listen.
¶ "Linden Arden Stole the Highlights" VAN MORRISON
The lyric on this is so wild. Van is a master. This is timeless, uplifting and healing, and is a transporter to some other realm. [Helped along by a stunning piece of bass playing by David Hayes – Ed]
¶ "John Barleycorn Must Die" TRAFFIC
This song was very influential: the sound of the recording, the

sweet voices and the English accents were all very interesting to me when I was 16.
¶ "Into White" CAT STEVENS
Like Van, Cat seemed to be familiar to me, as if his musical language emanated from a home I shared.
¶ "Voodoo Chile" JIMI HENDRIX
This is live and crazy good. Avoid the new remastering – it's like a graffiti artist smudging the Mona Lisa. The original mixes were perfect. Delicate, loud, sexy and otherworldly.
– As told to Zena Alkayat

Wednesday, July 17

ONE OH, *YEEZUS*...

You know when pop stars used to re-record their latest hits in the language of another market – say, Germany or France – before the world was totally consumed by the language of Amerenglish pop? Bowie did it, Dusty did it. I wish we could bring it back, and Kanye West would re-record *Yeezus* in a language I don't understand. Then I'd be happier when I listened to it.

Because the words on *Yeezus* are f***ing unlistenable. As if written by a seriously misogynistic asshole with self-aggrandisement issues. You wouldn't want to be his wife. And it's a drag, because the music, the beats, the soundscape, the whatever... is utterly, utterly great. Just out-of-the-park brilliant.

Here's Laughing Lou Reed on *Talkhouse*: "The guy really, really, really is talented. He's really trying to raise the bar. No one's near doing what he's doing, it's not even on the same planet... If you like sound, listen to what he's giving you. Majestic and inspiring." Lou also had an issue with the words and talks interestingly about that – it's worth checking the full review out.

TWO AND THE HITS JUST KEEP ON COMIN'
Bob Dylan, *The Bootleg Series Vol. 10 – Another Self Portrait (1969–1971)* is set to cover some interesting, if maligned, years. The complete Isle of Wight Festival performance from August 31, 1969, a personal favourite (even in really bad audience-taped bootleg quality) with Dylan and The Band alternating a sweet, woody country sound with ragged roadhouse rip-'em-ups. Also some great *New Morning* alternate versions (a piano-based "Went to See the Gypsy" and "Sign on the Window" with a string section should be particularly good if real bootlegs from the past are anything to go by). And finally, some cleaned-up/stripped-down *Self Portrait* tracks accompanied (amusingly) by liner notes courtesy of Greil Marcus, writer of the famous *SP* review in *Rolling Stone* with the deathly opening line, "What is this shit?"

THREE MAY NEED TO START A KEN COLYER CORNER IN FIVE THINGS
Two more letters about The Stones, *The Guardian*:
¶ Messrs Gilbert and Blundell, prepare to eat dirt (Letters, 6 July). I saw the Stones at the Ken Colyer Jazz Club (It was actually called Studio 51, but was generally known as Ken's

Club) in Leicester Square in June 1963. "Come On" was slowly climbing the charts. It was the first date I ever went on. I was 16. The cellar venue was stifling with condensation and we drew CND signs in it on the low ceiling. The Stones looked like cavemen and sang every great rock number, including "Poison Ivy", "Johnny B Goode" and "Route 66".

My date and I caught the last train back – the 12:42 from Victoria to Bromley South. When we arrived at Shortlands Station, my father was on the platform to meet us. "Just checking," he said and walked off. My boyfriend lasted less than 50 days, but the Stones – well, you all know the rest. – Susan Castles, Wem, Shropshire
¶ How about 1962 in the small cellar Studio 51, Great Newport Street, W1? Chatting with all of them every Sunday at the bar during the break. Two sessions, 4pm and 6pm. Signed pre-first record release photo to prove it, with a note from Bill on the back apologising for no news of first "disc". Anybody else who was there? – Gerry Montague, Berkhamsted, Hertfordshire

FOUR *THE AMERICANS* AWAKENS A LONG-BURIED LOVE FOR POST–PETER GREEN MAC
The 80s-tastic Russian/US spy series features a cracking soundtrack from my least-liked decade. "Tusk" by Fleetwood Mac in episode 1 sends me to the remastered album – as recommended, months ago, by Tom at work. It's amazingly odd for a mainstream Californian rock record (and amazingly good, though I didn't listen in 1979), and nothing's stranger than

Extra: Loft Farewell

Consumed by moving house, saying goodbye to the loft, some nostalgia, so only this picture this week, if you'll indulge me.

ONE OUT OF LEFT FIELD

Ken [Colyer] at the 51; Skiffle Group – Ken, Alexis, Lonnie, Chris, Bill [Colyer]; a ticket for the Rock Island Line; Bill's old mucker, stride great Ralph Sutton; Ken with Sister Rosetta, photographed by Terry Cryer; Me on the beach at Malibu and on Jimmy Johnson's car, Muscle Shoals; Bob Mitchum and Jane Greer movie still from *Out Of The Past*.

TWO STUCK IN THE MIDDLE

MLK glasses, watch and radio; Bob in studio, 1965, by Daniel Kramer; Sonny Terry & Brownie McGhee, signed to my dad, Bill; Buddy Guy & Junior Wells, 1970; Wayne Miller photo of couple, as used on Hot House *South* cover; George Lewis applauds, by Terry Cryer; my photo of Joni Mitchell watching Neil Young at Mariposa Folk Fest, Toronto, 1972, 100 Club matches, Armstrong and Django memorabilia.

THREE RIGHT IN TIME

Mr Leonard Cohen by Mr Antonio Olmos; Muscle Shoals sign; Mark at the Wurli in the studio in the Shoals; Bill in Hamburg, 1955; Motor racing at Crystal Palace, early 60s; reprint of *Monterey Pop* poster.

"Tusk" itself, with the tribal percussion, the mumbling/chanting and the most eccentric drum rolls in pop's history.

FIVE BOB GUMPERT SENDS ME THIS, AN ALAN LOMAX GALLERY

...with this sensational contact sheet. This is Stavin' Chain playing guitar, Lafayette, Louisiana, 1934. The movement in that top triptych is just stunning.

Wednesday, July 31

ONE EVERY DAY I HAVE THE BLUES...

Or every day that Richard posts, anyway. And in a good way. Not to be bossy or anything, but you really should all be following THEBLUEMOMENT, for the way Richard Williams illuminates popular (and some other kinds of) music with a lucidity that shines out of the computer screen. This week, one of the things that propelled him to the keys was *Frances Ha*. "It's not often I want to get up and dance in the aisles of a cinema, but that's how I felt halfway through Noah Baumbach's *Frances Ha* the other night, when David Bowie's 'Modern Love' erupted out of the speakers. I've never been keen on Bowie (although I admire the stuff from his Berlin period), but 'Modern Love' is one of those tracks – like Boffalongo's 'Dancing in the Moonlight', Danny Wilson's 'Mary's Prayer' or the New Radicals' 'You Get What You Give' – that automatically quicken the heartbeat and turn the world's colours up a shade. It doesn't matter who it's by. Listen without prejudice, as someone once suggested."

TWO LAST NIGHT I HAD A DREAM...

...in which Bill Nighy suggests I listen to the music of G.T. Moore and The Reggae Guitars. Strange.

THREE NEIL, HUNG

Hanging Henry Diltz's beautiful photo of NY at Balboa Stadium in 1969 (bought at a strikingly strange auction after a

live at the Police Academy, Chavez Ravine, June 28, 1955, Los Angeles, CA. Look up a copy of Ry Cooder's *Chavez Ravine*, a concept album telling the story of the Mexican-American community demolished in the 1950s in order to build public housing, which, this being LA, was never built. Eventually the Brooklyn Dodgers built a stadium on the site as part of their move to Los Angeles.

Fantastic music, especially good on hot summer days, with fine guest vocalists and astonishing percussion.

showing of *Legends of the Canyon*), I put iTunes on a random Neil Young playlist and it threw up something I had never heard (let alone knowingly owned). It's from the *Citizen Kane Junior Blues* bootleg recorded at The Bottom Line in New York in May 1974. Young was there to see Ry Cooder – and was so inspired that, when Ry had finished, he got up on the stage and played for an hour. Most of the material was unknown to the audience, being from the as-yet unreleased *On the Beach*. "Greensleeves was my heart of gold" sings Neil, before talking amusingly about depressing folk singers...

FOUR NOW THAT'S A RECORD COVER
From the blog LONDONJAZZCOLLECTOR, the moody Hampton Hawes, caught in a great sepia mood. Its recording venue:

FIVE BEST. BUSKER. EVER.
Where folkster Donovan ("Sunny Goodge Street") meets The Strange World of Arthur Brown ("Fire") at twilight by the American Church, halfway up Tottenham Court Road. Every so often, he topped the tuba up with methylated spirits...

Wednesday, August 7

ONE SELFRIDGES SHOE DEPARTMENT
Blue suede shoes by Jeffery West, with the deathly "Please allow me to introduce myself…" line engraved on the sole. And don't you step on my blue leopard-skin shoes, either. (FYI: both remained unbought.)

TWO FAVOURITE SONG OF THE SUMMER (SO FAR)
Lana Del Rey has covered Nancy Sinatra and Lee Hazlewood's 1967 track "Summer Wine" ("Strawberries, cherries and an angel's kiss in spring / My summer wine is really made from all these things") with, appropriately, her boyfriend – Barrie-James O'Neill of Scottish rockers Kassidy – stepping into Lee Hazlewood's cowboy boots. It's bass-heavy and groovy, with gloriously woozy backing vox. It ends with a distant peal of thunder, a snatch of Billie Holiday, some chattering and some beachside noises.

In a great piece of iPhone synchronicity it merges into the start of Kevin Ayers' "Song from the Bottom of a Well" with its treated guitars and booming noises (sounding exactly like the song's title) static-ing between the speakers like some early version of Scott Walker's *The Drift*.

THREE UNDERNEATH PUTNEY BRIDGE, SUNDAY

Ukulele practising/busking. We do a quick duet on "I'll See You in My Dreams", the beautiful Isham Jones/ Gus Kahn tune from 1924 that Joe Brown played to close the George Harrison tribute concert in 2002.

FOUR MISSIVE FROM TIM, RE: THE ALLEYCAT
"Just to let you know the Iko's New Orleans Music Shop at the Alleycat is fab. The excellent house band played tunes by Champion Jack Dupree, Professor Longhair, Jelly Roll Morton, the Band ("Ophelia") and more. The jam session that followed was of an amazingly high standard and the vibe was all-inclusive, everyone from twentysomethings to pensioners, dreads to suits. I had to drag myself away at midnight to catch the tube, though apparently they carry on to 2am…"

From the Alleycat website: The club sits beneath the fabled Regent Sound Studios which was set up at 4 Denmark Street in 1963. With The Rolling Stones recording their first album here, The Kinks recording "You Really Got Me", Black Sabbath recording "Paranoid", the studio took off as the place to be seen to be making music.

FIVE **LATE AFTERNOON, TOTTENHAM COURT RD.**

Taxi advertising my friend MJ Paranzino's choir, quite possibly a first in choral advertising, swiftly followed by a roller-derby flash mob gyrating to "Disco Inferno", blasting from a tricycle with giant speakers. We once worked with the co-writer of "DI", Ron "Have Mercy" Kersey, cutting a version of Willie Nelson's "Crazy" in LA. Ron was fabulously louche, feet on the control board as he lazily played the bassline on a synthesiser, gassing and joking with his engineer, the wonderfully named Hill Swimmer.

My memories of the session are of Mark playing the most gorgeous Reggie Young–like parallel fourths to the general amazement of the studio gatherees, and Ron asking where the hell he'd learned to play like that and if he was available for sessions. And of sitting against the wall of the recording room as Alex Brown (Ron's partner and genius vocal arranger/songwriter for the likes of Anita Baker and Whitney) and her girls sang the backing vocals. What on the record sounds sweet and swooping was delivered to the microphones at an ear-bending volume and hair-raising power. Heather and I stepped back into the control room, emotional and speechless.

Ron then had an acetate cut and took us to his local bar, where he would play stuff he was working on to the patrons, for feedback! I can see him there, sipping a gin and tonic through a thin black straw, laughing, enjoying their bemused reaction.

Wednesday, August 14

ONE **NICE PROMO, THE BLIND BOYS OF ALABAMA**
Their new album, produced by Justin Vernon (Bon Iver) sounds pretty good from the clips. Listen out for Shara Worden singing "I'll Find a Way", written by Motown guitarist Ted Lucas (no, me neither), that in the short clip sounds just great. Vernon has taste in female singers – his cover of Bonnie Raitt's

"I Can't Make You Love Me" testifies to that – and I'll give him the benefit on his hyperbole about Worden. There's a touching moment where Shara plays the finished item for Ted's widow and rushes for the tissue box.

TWO TRUE SAY, WILL!

"Sometimes a band arrives and becomes extremely popular without good reason. Who are the million people who bought the debut album by White Lies, the trio from Ealing in West London? And who are the ever-growing hordes piling into arenas to hear their polished but unremarkable pop-rock? What do they hear in White Lies that can't be heard from any number of Eighties-influenced bands, or indeed on albums by actual bands from the Eighties?

Perhaps the answer is in White Lies' ability to make euphoric, reverb-drenched, large-scale music that hints at dark edges but doesn't actually have any, thereby making the listener feel they might be exploring hidden depths without running the risk of being exposed to anything challenging or depressing..." – Will Hodgkinson, *The Times*.

THREE URBAN PROMS, BBC/COOLIO'S CASH

The *Urban Proms* was pretty good musically, although most of what I saw cleaved to the Coolio template of "Gangsta's Paradise", namely hip-hop/rap/grime/whatevs with, er, a string section playing the melody. But the between-songs links were crucifyingly embarrassing, so *I Name and Shame*... Sarah-Jane

Crawford (BBC Radio 3) and Charlie Sloth (BBC Radio 1Xtra). Unbelievably bad, with Sloth a kind of lightweight, unfunny James Corden. I know. Imagine that. By the way, if you want to profit from "Gangsta's Paradise", go to the Royalty Exchange, where $140,000 will get you a cut of Coolio's copyrights.

FOUR KAREN BLACK, R.I.P.

I'll always treasure her Rayette in *Five Easy Pieces*, loving Tammy Wynette with all her heart. First seen as a late teen in a Stockholm cinema in the afternoon, told by friends that it couldn't be missed, and they were dead-on.

Even now "Stand By Your Man" gets me, with its strangely **off-beat army of acoustic guitars punching home the chorus.**

Ryan Gilbey, in his *Guardian* obit, wrote well: "These parts were strikingly different from one another, but they had in common Black's knack for conveying her characters' rich and troubled inner lives, their cramped or thwarted dreams. The consummate example could be found in her Oscar-nominated performance as Rayette, the Tammy Wynette–loving girlfriend to Nicholson's discontented antihero Bobby Dupea, in *Five Easy Pieces*. There was a comical but achingly sad intellectual gap between the two. Bobby resented her. Crucially, the audience never did. 'I dig [Rayette], she's not dumb, she's just not into thinking,' said Black in 1970. 'I didn't have to know anybody like her to play her. I mean, I'm like her, in ways. Rayette enjoys things as she sees them, she doesn't have to add significances. She can just love the dog, love the cat. See? There are many things she does not know, but that's cool; she doesn't intrude on anybody else's trip. And she's going to survive.'"

FIVE *SOUTHCLIFFE*

Wonderfully nuanced use of sound in this slightly pointless mass-murderer tale. The amped-up folk band in the nighttime town square are all bass and a tiny bit of vocals, Otis and James Carr on the car stereo sound exactly right, the metal band in a bar is as muffled and chaotic as it would be in life. Bass thrash, guitar blur, gruff vox. The Pretenders' "Brass in Pocket" in the pub makes you remember what a great and unusual song that is:

> "Got brass in pocket / Got bottle, I'm gonna use it
> Intention, I feel inventive / Gonna make you, make you, make you notice
> Got motion, restrained emotion / Been driving, Detroit leaning
> No reason, just seems so pleasing, / Gonna make you, make you, make you notice"

Wednesday, August 21

ONE BOOKER T. JONES, RONNIE SCOTT'S Q&A, SATURDAY AFTERNOON

I ask how come Booker T. played bass on "Knocking on Heaven's Door". He replies (in the soft but strong voice of a man who thinks before he speaks): "In my community, out in Malibu, musicians would very often stop by, and one of them was Bob Dylan. He would come, and bring an acoustic guitar or play one of mine and play his songs... try out his songs on me. In my little studio. Bring his electric guitar, plug it into my tape recorder, which I never thought to turn on (as he says this his eyes widen slightly and he smiles to himself – the audience cracks up).

Anyway, he was working on this movie with Jason Robards and Sam Peckinpah and thought to ask me to come play bass with him on that song, late one... late... early one morning, so we went out to Burbank and recorded that. I was a bass player from the beginning – that was how I made my living. I started out at the Flamingo Rooms. I was known around Memphis as a bass player, just happened to play the Hammond because of 'Green Onions' at Stax. At heart, I still have my bass." And I was wrong about "KoHD" – Booker T. actually played on "Turkey Chase", but he kindly didn't correct me...

TWO BOB DYLAN, "WENT TO SEE THE GYPSY", *ANOTHER SELF PORTRAIT*

The only track I've heard so far, this demo version of an (imagined?) visit to see Elvis in Vegas is like a stunning precursor to "Blind Willie McTell". Dylan doesn't seem to have yet fixed the melody in his mind, but the passion of the performance carries it to a wonderful outro where the guitar accompaniment (David Bromberg, I'm guessing) is fantastic, like Robbie Robertson on "Dirge" or Mark Knopfler on "Blind Willie".

THREE THE CONVENTIONS WILL APPLY

That awful blight of current TV programmes – they spend the first ten minutes telling you what the other fifty will consist of – reached a nadir with the documentary on Fairport Convention. A series of talking heads said "they changed English Folk Music" fourteen different ways, as did Frank Skinner on the voiceover (and over). None of the unthrilling footage of the current band trundling around in coaches and playing was doing the job, so they must have figured we'd better tell the viewer how great and influential they were.

What turned out to be an interesting programme with some neat footage was ill-served by the turgid and off-putting start. Filmmakers don't do that kind of thing. They generally trust the audience. It has to be the dead hand of the commissioners.

FOUR AN OLYMPIC NIGHT

Evening Standard: "A former London recording studio where everyone from Jimi Hendrix to the Spice Girls made albums is to return to its original life as a cinema. Olympic Studios in Church Road, Barnes, will reopen with two screens, a café and dining room… after local businessman Stephen Burdge stepped in to save it. One recording studio will remain in the basement."

In the seventies, Tony's mum's friend says that he runs Olympic Studios. We're 16 years old. We believe him. Why would he say it if it wasn't true? So we go along one evening and he lets us in. I have a very vague recollection of creeping around on a balmy night, trying not to be conspicuous.

I email Tony and ask him who we saw recording and he says: "Colin Skeith let us in. He claimed he ran the place but was, in fact, merely the raging alcoholic janitor. We saw Rod Stewart, Pete Townshend and a very angry Leslie West!" Tony is unforthcoming on why Leslie West was so angry. If you don't remember Leslie West, he was a great "Rock Guitarist", most famously in Mountain, with Felix Pappalardi on Gibson EB-1 violin bass. Check out their version of Jack Bruce's "Theme for an Imaginary Western" on the *Woodstock Two* soundtrack. Still sounds great.

Wednesday, August 28

ONE SIMMY RICHMAN INTERVIEW WITH STEPHEN STILLS, *THE INDEPENDENT*

Is it true that you play percussion on the Bee Gees' 'You Should Be Dancing'?

"We were in the studio next door making a CSN album and David was all full of himself and saying this is going to be the album of the year. I went, 'No it's not, that's being recorded across the hall,' cos I'd heard some of that Saturday Night Fever stuff and I knew it was totally unique and going to be a monster. So I played timbales and for a long time that was my only platinum single".

You have a reputation for sometimes being short with journalists…

"I had a torturous day in New York one time where someone

had fed a writer this thing that I had tried out for the Monkees and failed. The truth was that I wanted to sell my songs to a hit TV show to make money. The thought of being a pretend Beatle on TV was so appalling that I couldn't imagine it, but I went down and said I know a kid, and I sent them Peter Tork.

"This journalist kept saying, 'But they turned you down, right?' I was like, 'You're not getting the point.' So I ended up going fuck you! Often the journalist has already written the piece and all they're looking for you to do is to confirm their obnoxious preconceptions. There's a point where you just go, fuck fame, fuck being famous, fuck being a celebrity, fuck this. I'm a fucking musician. Take my picture and make it up.
Thanks for not being like that with me. That was an absolute pleasure.
"It was. I love that I talked about all the things you were warned not to talk to me about. High fives on that!"

FOUR SEEN AND HEARD AT THE ZOOLOGICAL MUSEUM

Artists in museums. Not sure that they really work, and feel they're always overshadowed by the exhibits. So, poor Sam Risley Billingham is onto a hiding to nothing with his "Structurally amassed beat-mix soundscape" when up against A JAR OF MOLES.

FIVE *THE GUARDIAN*'S FASHION…

Can anyone explain this particular bit of fashion to me? And why poor Anastasia has been forced to (a) stand like that, and (b) wear "cute" animal ears. In the meantime, I'll look forward to the Gil Scott-Heron sweater.

Wednesday, September 4

ONE AEROPHONES & DRONES

Have you ever been in a small room with a bagpiper playing full blast? Actually, that may be the only way to play them – there's nothing tentative or half-throttle about the mechanics of the bagpipes. The noise is utterly overwhelming, a melodious fire alarm, a wailing mourner. At the funeral of a great friend

of my mother's – a proud Scotswoman – the piper played the most melancholy air, and it was startlingly moving. He walked up to the coffin, executed an about-turn, and headed out of the small chapel still playing, the pipes fading into the distance as he strode off…

TWO NUTTERS & JAZZERS

Asking for *The Bootleg Series Vol. 10 – Another Self Portrait* at HMV, I'm informed that they sold out as soon as they arrived. "All those Dylan Nutters", I'm informed by the friendly man at the desk, which I guess means that he [generously] doesn't number me among them. Reminds me of standing in the queue at Ronnie's for the Booker T. Q&A when a guy comes up and asks what the line is waiting for. When told, he says, "Thought it looked like a Jazz Queue".

THREE AND TALKING OF PORTRAITS: BOB DYLAN PASTELS, NATIONAL PORTRAIT GALLERY

Bob's strange jagged faces, rooted in the FSA photographs of the Depression, are mostly quite poor. A few have something more going on – but there's nothing, really nothing to get excited by. For that you have to see the other musician exhibited at the NPG. A room down from Dylan is a portrait series by Humphrey Ocean, who some may remember as the bass player in Kilburn and the High Roads, Ian Dury's first foray away from art and into rock. Ocean's paintings of friends, sloppy gouaches that somehow capture expression, tilt and attitude, are wonderful. This is a properly arrived-at style, whereas Bob's, one feels, is still on the road.

FOUR IN A SILENT WAY

My friend, photographer Bob Gumpert, gets a gig shooting 2 Chainz, a rapper, and finds he enjoys it. He sends the last paragraph of this piece – about crowded, loud clubs – by British poet, writer and explorer Robert Twigger (who lives in Cairo), in *Aeon* magazine. I look up the article [aeon.co/essays/how-the-sound-of-silence-rejuvenates-the-soul] and it's great. Some excerpts:

"A film director once told me that shooting exteriors in Cairo is a nightmare. Often they fake it, using Tunisian locations instead. The reason is the sound: the hum, they call it. You get it even if you shoot at 3 a.m. on Zamalek island, the wealthy garden district in the middle of the Nile. It's the aural equivalent of smog; hardly noticeable at first, not a problem for many, but insidious, worming its way inside you, rattling you, shaking you up like a cornflake packet. Your contents never settle…

"As you get older you value silence more. Your nerves get jangled more easily. Loud music becomes less and less attractive. Instead of wanting to rev up, you seek ways to calm down. But I suspect the search for real silence goes deeper than just a desire to relax. It's no accident that many religious orders have vows of silence. Only in silence can the soul unburden itself and then listen out for subtler signs, information from the unknown inner regions.

"How much silence does a person need? You can get greedy for it,

addicted to it. I know people who spend half their time in the desert and the other half working out how to get back to it. They are running away from life, some say; they are certainly running away from noise. Recent research suggests that long-term exposure to noise doesn't just damage hearing (and the average decibel level in Cairo is 85, often getting to 95 and higher, which is only slightly quieter than standing next to a jackhammer); it damages your heart. Continuous noise causes chronic stress. Stress hormones become your constant companion, circulating day and night, wearing out your heart. That must be why the first few days in the desert seem so wonderfully rejuvenating. I've seen an elderly man – a retired heart surgeon, coincidentally – go from doddering around the camp to springing along the edge of dunes and rocky cliffs. That's the power of silence.

"You know you're cured when you relish the sound of loud pop music again. Crowded clubs hold no fear; the pumping bass seems like a familiar friend, not a message from the Antichrist. You can 'take it'. Modern life is 'OK'. You've detoxed and the result is that you seem more youthful. Young people haven't filled themselves up with noise (yet), so they actively seek it out. For those who have had too much, then emptied it out, the glad return to a noisy world is invigorating. How long does the immunity last? About two weeks, if you're lucky."

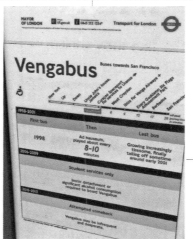

FIVE ALL ABOARD! IF YOU REMEMBER THE VENGABOYS, THAT IS...

The brilliant Tom Scott, web thinker with a comedic bent, defaces a London bus time-table in some style. I really want to visit the Curaçao Spaceport...

Wednesday, September 11

ONE *ANOTHER SELF PORTRAIT* DELUXE: AN ACCOUNTANCY ISSUE

I – yes, yes, a Dylan Nutter™ – have to go for the one with the extra two discs and a couple of books. But wait! A three-CD set of this ilk (we'll ignore the remastered "Original *Self Portrait*" disc) would probably retail at about £19.99, say £23.99 if we're being generous, with a fair-sized book and box. We have to ignore the fact that I'd lazily thought it included a film of the Isle of Wight performance (not sure where I got that idea – I do have some video somewhere of a few songs). So then I'm thinking, "Well, at least I have handsome books with wonderful liner notes and essays". And one of the books has those things, by Michael Simmonds and Greil Marcus, and it holds the discs as well.

But the other book is a bizarre hotchpotch of photo sessions from this period mixed with press clippings and foreign single covers. John Cohen is a good photographer (his *Young Bob* book is terrific, as is *There Is No Eye*), but his work is ill-served by reproducing repetitive and poorly focused shots of a one-expression Bob. The reproduction looks cheap – flat and badly balanced – and Al Clayton's Nashville black-and-whites really suffer. The proofreading is appalling – Jack Keroac, anyone?

The guilty man is Bob's house designer, Geoff Gans, who wouldn't know a smart quote if it hit him. The copyright reads: ©2013 PERCEIVED VALUE PUBLICATIONS. I feel wound up – it works out that this extra book has set me back around £55. "Can I have my money back, please sir?" as Billy Connolly and Gerry Rafferty once sang.

TWO **HURRY, HURRY, BUY YOUR BOB DYLAN '66 TOUR TREGGINGS NOW!**

Into Marks & Spencer, past the embalmed-looking Annie Leibovitz portraits of Britain's great and good women (someone should be reprimanded for making the riverboat Helen Mirren look like she's stepped out of *Are You Being Served?*, what with that jaunty cap and scarf). My gaze alights on a rack of these.

The Dylan '66 Houndstooth! As created by the Hawks' favourite tailor in Toronto! If only they were for men (and came with a jacket), then my fashion decisions for Bob at the RAH in November would be sorted... Oh, and Treggings? A cross between trousers and leggings, obviously.

THREE **KEN COLYER VISITS EDDIE CONDON'S CLUB, NYC, EARLY 1950s**

A great selection of Jazz photos from the fifties in colour, by Nat Singerman, runs in The New York Times Magazine. *One of them shows Eddie Condon's band. Around 1950, my uncle Ken was in the Merchant Navy and, when he landed in New York, visited Condon's club. He paints a vivid picture:*

I got washed and changed, once again forgetting that nightlife doesn't start 'til later this side of the ocean. I shined my shoes and I was ready to go with my sub in my pocket. There were still four dollars to the pound. I had read about Eddie Condon's club and heard their once-a-month town hall concerts on the BBC at home. I had no idea where the club was. New York is a big place.

I saw a newsstand and asked if they had a *Downbeat*. 'No, don't you know it's not due out 'til next week?' I didn't know about *The New Yorker* then, which has an excellent section devoted to nightlife with Whitney Balliett's pithy descriptions of each place and its style of entertainment. I walked on until I saw a cabby tinkering under the bonnet of his cab. 'Do you know Eddie Condon's club?'

LOOK

Images of Jazz Greats

EDDIE CONDON
presents Nightly
Bob Casey - Bass
Edmund Hall - Clarinet
John Windhurst - Trumpet
Cutty Cutshall - Trombone
Gene Schroeder - Piano
Buzzy Drootin - Drums
Eddie Condon - Guitar
INTERMISSION — RALPH SUTTON (at the piano)
JAM SESSIONS EVERY TUESDAY
Closed Sundays

Photograph by Nat Singerman/Joe Lauro Archive

Condon on guitar, George Brunis on trombone, Wild Bill Davison on cornet and Buzzy Drootin on drums

CONDON AND CREW; KEN'S AUTOGRAPHED PLACE CARD

'Hop in; I'll be with you in a minute.' He didn't want to lose a fare. I got in the cab. It had seen better days, in fact it was a wreck. But I didn't mind as long as it got me there. I was sure I would find the place like a homing pigeon finds his home. The cabbie finally got the engine going and we started cruising.

'What was the name of that place?' I told him. 'What sort of musicians play there?' 'Jazz musicians.' 'Who's playing beside Condon?' He'd got me there. I didn't know Eddie's present lineup. I mentioned a few names, then Pee Wee Russell. 'Pee Wee, he's a friend of mine, know him well. I took him for his medical when he got drafted. He told me to wait; he was only gone ten minutes. They threw him out because he was seventy proof. Now I've got an idea it might be the old Howdy Club. Used to be a burlesque joint. Want me to try there?' he asked, eyeing the clock.

'Go ahead,' I said. We drove into Greenwich Village, turned a corner and there was the 'mutton chop' sign David Stone Martin designed for Eddie hanging over the entrance. I was elated. I gave the cabbie a generous tip. He told me not to forget the address: West Third Street. Before he pulled away he called: 'Don't forget to tell Pee Wee his old friend Al brought you here. So long, pal.'

There was a commissionaire in livery standing by the door looking dignified. He saw me reading the board. 'Are all these people playing tonight?' 'Yes, but it's a little early yet... why don't you go to that little bar down the road and have a drink. Come back about eight-thirty and you'll get a seat right by the band.'

I said, 'Thanks, I will.' He was no hustler. I found out later that Eddie wouldn't allow it. He had played enough clip joints himself and also considered it was important to encourage youngsters to listen to the music. And they turned a blind eye if you were obviously under age.

On each table was a small green card. On one side it gave the personnel: Pee Wee Russell, clarinet; Wild Bill Davison, cornet; George Brunis, trombone; Gene Schroeder, piano; Sid Weiss, bass; Maurey Feld, drums; Eddie Condon, guitar, and Joe Sullivan, intermission piano. On the other it proclaimed: 'Jazz in its finest flower,' a quote from my favourite critic, Whitney Balliett.

As I sipped a beer the band turned up. George oiled his slide with an elaborate flourish, then the band kicked off. Within a couple of numbers they were playing with a power, swing and tonal quality I would not have believed possible.

It struck me for the first time that the gramophone record is badly misleading when it comes to jazz.

No recording could ever completely capture the greatness of this music.

As each number got rocking I seemed to be suspended, just sitting on air. And when the music finished I flopped back on my chair as though physically exhausted.

The sensation I got from hearing Wild Bill for the first time was a sort of numb joy that such a man lived and played. If Louis Armstrong was better in person, then it was beyond my imagination. His teaming with Brunis heightened this reaction. When Edmond Hall took over from Pee Wee, playing his cutting electric phrases, it was almost more than I could bear.

Brunis was entertaining to watch. While playing excellent trombone, he constantly screwed his body into the most awkward-looking positions, sometimes jamming one leg against the piano. If there was a drunk in the room he would play snatches of "I'm Forever Blowing Bubbles", or something equally appropriate, in the most syrupy manner, during the breaks, then crack back in with glorious golden-toned tail-gate.

Pee Wee, with his broken comb moustache and a slightly distant look in his eyes, was also entertaining. I was told he had a select band of fans, who follow him mainly to watch his weird expressions that contort his face while he plays. Also he is a little eccentric and difficult to get to know, but if you knew anything about poodles, he would open up and be friendly.

As nightclub prices go in New York, Eddie's were very reasonable. But I still had to make every beer last as long as I could. The waiters didn't like this too much. The first night I left comparatively early. I felt a little sick but hadn't drunk very much. It was the emotional impact that was making me feel groggy. The old Negro toilet attendant was sympathetic and understanding. 'That's OK, son, I know how it is.'

FOUR **DAVID BAILEY NAMES EXHIBITION AFTER HIS FAVOURITE SONG, "STARDUST"**

I work my way through all the versions I own. Top of the pops: Larry Adler's fabulous harmonica, alternately shuddering and gliding over the timeless Hoagy Carmichael melody. And of course, the fantastic scene in Woody Allen's *Stardust Memo-*

{BEN WEBSTER | "STARDUST", *from* Plays Ballads}

ries where he eats breakfast as Louis Armstrong plays his giddily great take.

As the instrumental first half unwinds, Sandy, (Allen), talks: "It was one of those great spring days, a Sunday, and you knew summer would be coming soon... We came back to the apartment. We were just sitting around and I put on a record of Louis Armstrong, which is music that I grew up loving, and it was very, very pretty, and I happened to glance over and I saw Dorrie sitting there...

And, I dunno, I guess it was the combination of everything – the sound of the music, and the breeze, and how beautiful Dorrie looked to me, and for one brief moment everything just seemed to come together perfectly and I felt happy. Almost indestructible, in a way..."

And Charlotte Rampling fixes the camera with one of cinema's greatest stares, as Armstrong's vocal comes in, singing and scatting Mitchell Parish's words, giving the merest approximation of the actual lyrics. And then it cuts to the cinema audience watching it, split between a woman saying, "That was so beautiful", and another shouting, "Why do all comedians turn out to be sentimental bores!"

Wednesday, September 18

ONE **AMY EXHIBITION, JEWISH MUSEUM**
A touching collection of the memorabilia of someone who died

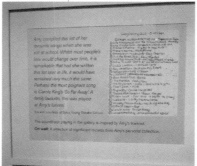

too young. One of the records displayed, Sarah Vaughan's *The Divine One*, still had its Record & Tape Exchange sticker. Starting at £10, by the time Amy bought it the price was a bargain £3.

THREE **ONE NIGHT IN SOHO: PART ONE**
It started with Barney's phone call to come see a screening of *Inside Llewyn Davis*, the Coens' take on a would-be Folk Star in Greenwich Village, '62. The night before, I'd watched a *Mastermind* contestant do his Two Minutes on "The Life and Work of Bob Dylan". He scores 13. I knew one he didn't – the studio in Minneapolis where Bob re-recorded *Blood on The Tracks* (that's Sound 80, pop pickers). He knew one I didn't – the two books of the Old Testament that feature in the lyrics of "Jokerman" (that's Deuteronomy and Leviticus, fact fans).

And I screwed up an easy one by interrupting and shouting "Robert Shelton!" when they asked about the night in the Village when Dylan was reviewed* in *The New York Times*, when the answer was the name of the club (the Gaslight).

And the Coens' film centres, dramatically, on that very night. Which made me wonder about the mainstream audience reaction to a film that turns on a concert review... The evocation of time and place is predictably good, and its sense of humour is not a million miles from *A Mighty Wind*, especially the hysterical recording session where Justin Timberlake (half of folk duo Jim and Jean with Carey Mulligan) is attempting to cash in with an assumed name (The John Glenn Singers) and a Space Race ditty ("Dear Mr Kennedy").

The supporting actor casting is worthy of *Broadway Danny Rose* or *Stardust Memories* – extraordinary faces, pungent performances. Carey Mulligan rocks an acerbic fringe, John Goodman is monstrously withering, and Oscar Isaac is really convincing as an almost-good-enough folk-boom troubadour. If you know your Greenwich Village in the early sixties, go see it. If not? Not so sure. I'd be interested to know what an impartial observer would make of it.

FOUR ONE NIGHT IN SOHO: PART TWO

The restaurants of Soho seem to be having a Boogie/Swamp moment. If it's not the Allmans and John Fogerty's "The Old Man Down the Road" (*ooo-eee* – remember that? Creedence in all but name?) playing in ramen joint Bone Daddies, it's Canned Heat at Pizza Pilgrims, which is where I found myself after the film. As I walked to meet Tim in St Giles, I passed this in Soho

Square, screening off the Crossrail development. It seems that Dobell's is unavoidable at the moment...

FIVE ONE NIGHT IN SOHO: PART THREE

Tim's spot, The Alleycat in Denmark Street, is a dive, in all the best senses of the word. Every other Tuesday, £4 on the door, and Paloma Faith's musical director, Dom Pipkin, playing excellent Longhair/Booker piano, his keyboard sonically split, with bass in the left hand and electric piano in the right. Along with a drummer doing the right thing (staying on the hi-hat, not much cymbal action) and a low-down trombonist, they make a holy noise.

Dom's dad is coaxed up for "Doctor Jazz", N.O. style, before he and his wife head off for Wales, a man in a cap adds fine accordion, the young dudes in the audience groove, and we're all happily transported to Claiborne Avenue and Rampart Street for a couple of hours. I tell my mother about it, and she says that's how it used to be, and so we make a date to hit The

Alleycat some future Tuesday. (Catch Dom and The Iko's on Sunday, when they are promoting and supporting the legendary Meter, Zigaboo Modeliste at the 100 Club.)

Wednesday, September 25

ONE I LIKED THIS PAINTING

Glanced through the window of the Riflemaker Gallery on Beak Street, a rather lovely painting with stylistic echoes of John Currin: *Take the Night off (Laura Marling)* by Stuart Pearson Wright [oil on canvas, 2013, 60 x 40 cm].

TWO I LIKED THIS EMAIL

From Our Woodstock Correspondent, John Cuneo: "I thought of you after reading about Springsteen on your blog, and then 20 minutes later when I went out for a walk and said hello to a passing David Sancious (he of the early E Street Band, and, I gather, just back from the road touring with Sting). We were about a mile from downtown, across the street from the Bear Cafe (the restaurant that Albert Grossman opened) and right at the bottom of Striebel Rd (where Dylan had his bike spill).

I've never spoken a word to the guy before, but there was no one else around and it would have been awkward to not acknowledge each other, so I smiled and blurted out a 'Hello David', as if we see each other every day. Being from Jersey, I feel it's my inherited geographical privilege to refer to all the E St. members by their first name (I plan to go with just 'Steve', not Little Steven, if the opportunity presents itself)."

THREE I LIKED THIS POEM

Producer Bob Johnston, at the end of the *Another Self Portrait* documentary short:

"Down the kerb and around the bend he came
and it'll never end now because he's been
on this roller coaster ride ever since he left
Minnesota.
He's been brutalised, sunrised, baptised in

the waters of the Village.
Still it goes on, from Soho to Moscow to Oslo.
They speak of this trip, this battleship, who sailed in the harbour of Tin Pan Alley and sank it with his Subterranean Homesick Blues.
There isn't but one Bob Dylan."

… and now Mr Dylan, Heavy Metalwork Artist, is COLD IRONS BOUND (or, as *The Guardian* would have it, singing "Ballad of a Tin Man").

FOUR I LIKED SEEING JIMMY NAIL ON *LATER*

Just after the Kings of Leon had vied for the title of WORLD'S MOST UNEXCITING ROCK BAND (they looked to be boring themselves to death with the sludge coming out of their amps), it was excellent to spy Jimmy Nail (*Spender*! *Crocodile Shoes*!) singing backing vox for Sting, looking in great shape.

I remember our friend Sarah doing the costumes on *Spender*, and saying that she was off to work with Jimmy again on a "Country-singing-Newcastle-Boy-goes-to-Nashville" story and that they were searching for an American actress who could sing. I remembered "Too Close", sung beautifully by Amy Madigan on Ry Cooder's *Alamo Bay* soundtrack, and I gave Sarah the record to play to the director and producer.

Lo, they hired her for *Crocodile Shoes*! I hadn't realised ('til a quick search told me) that Amy had form: throughout the late 1970s she played keyboard, percussion and vocals behind folk-singer Steve Goodman on tour.

Meanwhile, back on *Later*, Sting's luxury brand of Steely Dan Light™ came dripping with expensive guitar playing, like so many Swarovski crystals flung over a bolt of minor ninths and flattened fifths. It was the aural equivalent of a Gucci ad. For songs about the shipworkers of Newcastle, that's sort of weird.

FIVE I LIKED ZIGABOO AT THE 100 CLUB

A party in the summer of '75 in Kennington. My friend Mick Gardner commandeers the deck and puts on *Fire on the Bayou*, the newly released album by The Meters. The evening had been a whirl of great funk records, but this topped them all, and I recall thinking I would never in my life hear something funkier than this.

I thought of that night on Sunday, listening, or rather feeling, the viscerally thrilling drumming of Joseph Modeliste, the Meters drummer. It was a terrific show, presented with avuncular charm (should that be afunkular?) by a master. Mark pointed out that the band were obviously inspired by the girls joyfully dancing at the foot of the stage, rather than the less-well coordinated gaggle of middle-aged white men behind, offering a variety of dance styles that covered the waterfront.

To be fair, it was impossible not to dance, such was the floor-shaking power of Zig's snare and hi-hat. Most things that you wanted to hear were played ("Africa", "Just Kissed My Baby", "People Say", "Hey Pocky A-Way"), each better than the last.

{GOOGLE | "YOUTUBE COLD IRONS BOUND LIVE VIDEO"}

Wednesday, October 2

ONE LICK THE STAMP, JACK!

Seeing this just-released stamp of Ray, here paired with an earlier release of Johnny Cash, sent me back to a tape given to me by Bob Wray in Muscle Shoals. Bob (member of the THIRD GREAT RICK HALL RHYTHM SECTION, and a wonderful bassist) was playing on a Ray Charles album. Johnny Cash dropped by the studio and they started playing a Kris Kristofferson song that they both knew, "Why Me, Lord".

Bob described Ray getting so into it as he ripped out a solo on the old beige Wurlitzer that the piano started to jerk across the studio floor, almost crashing over. Just listen to Ray's stubby intro, heightened by the bass drum, followed by the band dropping right in behind JC. Off the cuff and probably better than anything that made the album.

{RAY CHARLES AND JOHNNY CASH | "WHY ME LORD" †}

TWO THERE'S AN OWL IN THE BACKGROUND

Neil Brand interviewing Angelo Badalamenti about David Lynch in the wonderful *Sound of Cinema: The Music that Made the Movies*. Badalamenti tells how, in 1989, he and Lynch sat down at Badalamenti's piano and, "in a single take, wrote the theme for a groundbreaking new television series:

'David comes in and says, "Angelo!" – now we're really pals, you know – and he says, "We're in a dark wood", and I'm going like... [plays a pulsing two-chord pattern on the keyboard].

"No, Angelo, those are beautiful notes, but can you do 'em slower?"

"Oh, OK." [It's starting to feel closer to the theme we know.]

"No, no, Angelo, slower."

"David, if I do 'em any slower I'm gonna play in reverse." (laughs) [He plays what is now recognisable as the opening to Twin Peaks.]

"OK, Angelo, now there's a girl named Laura Palmer. She's a very troubled teenager and she's in the dark woods, and she's coming out behind some trees.

She's very beautiful, too... give me something that's her." [The crepuscular sequence of climbing notes starts.]

"That's it, Angelo, now let it build... 'Cause she's coming close, and she's so troubled." [Badalamenti plays a string pad behind the piano melody.]

"She's got tears in her eyes, Angelo, it's so sad. Reach a climax… That's it, just keep it going… beautiful, beautiful.

Now start coming down, but fall slowly, come slowly, slowly, down, down that's it, that's it, quiet….

Now, Angelo, go back into the dark woods, and stay there. There's an owl in the background…" [The strings disappear and fade.]

He said, "Angelo – you just wrote Twin Peaks…"'*

THREE KANYE. BELIEVE IT.

On *Later*, Kanye West sings a song from his new album "Bound 2" with Charlie Wilson from The Gap Band. It's pretty great. I remember a time when people protested when pop stars compared themselves to God or Christ, but I guess there's so much stuff out there now that no one bothers. Kanye's crucified pose at the climax of this song was kind of stupid, but the song itself was fantastic.

Built on the back of a song called "Bound", by the sensationally named Ponderosa Twins Plus One – taking just the intro – and samples of Brenda Lee's "Sweet Nothin's", it's a highlight track of *Yeezus*, and could, quite possibly, be your entry point to this great album. He seems a miserable bugger, though.

Oh, and mention, too, of Lorde, New Zealand teen sensation! Precocious, or what? Mannered but mature, and a sure, sure sense of melody, pitching her sultry voice against a choir and a synth bass. The song is "Royals". Her actual name is Ella Yelich-O'Connor. As of July 2013, a Year Twelve student at Takapuna Grammar School. God knows how good she could get to be.

FOUR DIG/DEAD

The Artangel installation of Daniel Silver's *Dig* at the old Odeon site on Grafton Way, just off Tottenham Court Road, is fantastic. This musical set of dancing figures, amidst the "recovered' statues of Freud and Darwin, caught my eye. As, later that day, did this bottle of Grateful Dead wine. (Apparently the Rolling Stones *Forty Licks* offering is not up to much, but the guy at Gerry's told me this was a proper bottle of wine.)

Wednesday, October 9

ONE HOW WE MADE "BOOGIE WONDERLAND"

Allee Willis, songwriter, in *The Guardian*: "In the late 1970s, I teamed up with Jon Lind, who'd written 'Sun Goddess' for Earth, Wind & Fire. In the disco era, lots of songs contained the word 'boogie', but we didn't want to write just another dance song. I'd just seen *Looking for Mr Goodbar*, a harsh film starring Diane Keaton as a dissatisfied teacher, who takes drugs, goes out dancing every night and picks up a different guy. One night, she brings home a sexually confused Vietnam vet who beats, rapes and kills her. I wanted to write about the desperation some people feel – and how dancing can provide a release.

"The line, 'Midnight creeps so slowly into hearts of men who need more than they get / Daylight deals a bad hand to a woman who has laid too many bets" is so bleak. But the groove came first and – musically – it's uplifting, with a chorus that feels almost theatrical, like Broadway, like Mary Poppins."

I'd never noticed those lyrics (or their inspiration). The following lines aren't much brighter: "The mirror stares you in the face and says, 'Baby, uh, uh, it don't work' / You say your prayers though you don't care; you dance and shake the hurt". More ammunition for the Nile Rodgers take on disco: that the songs were often lyrically acute portraits of the society of the time.

TWO ON PHOTOGRAPHING RONNIE WOOD

From Chris Floyd's blog: The music of The Rolling Stones plays continuously. All the hits from the last half century...

I set up two different shots simultaneously, so that we can wheel Ronnie from one seamlessly to the next, without losing him to boredom somewhere in between... As one gilded Stones hit fades away and a new one immerses us in its familiar scent, a thought comes into my head. A question for Ronnie. Yes, can I ask you something, Ronnie?

"Yeah man, as long as it's not about The Faces."

I gesticulate to the speakers, to the music.

"Well, when you go somewhere, a bar, a pub, a restaurant, a shop, a cab, and you hear a Stones song on the stereo, the radio, well, what do you hear? What do you hear that we don't hear?" The opening bars of "Gimme Shelter" are washing down over us. Ronald David Wood cocks an ear, his body comes up on its haunches as he searches the spectrum for the signal. The only thing missing from this familiar posture is a guitar. The apocalyptic, heart of darkness groove of my favourite ever Stones song cascades down in a torrent over us: "Oh, a storm is threat'ning / My very life today..."

Ronald David Wood finds the signal or, more correctly, the signal finds him and his arm starts to move, followed quickly by his hips. He loses himself in it for five, maybe six seconds, locked inside. Then his head slowly comes up, he pulls his Ray-Bans down his nose an inch and his black, black eyes look at me for a second before his nineteen fifties, postwar, Hillingdon ration-boy face breaks into the slyest little smirk you've ever seen, and he says:

"Yeah... I like it."

FOUR JOURNEY THROUGH THE PAST NO. 1

I find some things while we're moving house. This letter [over page] is a favourite... sixteen years old and a winner. *Zachariah* turns out to be a Hippie Musical Western loosely based on Hermann Hesse's *Siddhartha*, adapted as a Musical Western by the Firesign Theatre comedy troupe. Country Joe and the Fish star as an inept gang of robbers called The Crackers. Wikipedia: "Underneath the gunplay, the jokes, and the music, an important message is delivered: a life of pacifism, quiet contemplation, male bonding and vegetarianism is preferable to a life of violence." I don't remember getting that at all. But Elvin Jones (!) is great as drumming gunslinger Job Cain, and Doug Kershaw plays a fantastic Cajun stomp, "Ballad of Job Cain", that I treasure to this day – my first exposure to Cajun music, before Charlie Gillett gave us all The Sundown Playboys on *Honky Tonk*. It gets better. Apparently Ginger Baker was originally going to play the part of Zachariah… and the film recorded a loss of $1,435,000 (impressive for 1971, no?).

FIVE CSN AT THE ALBERT HALL

It was almost worth it for Steve Stills' guitar playing in "Bluebird". Almost. Three hours of dodgy harmonies, the backing band churning it up like buttermilk and multiple pleas for peace were, frankly, a bit of a slog. Even for songs that feel part of one's DNA. It all started with the lights going down to Jeff Beck's version of "A Day in the Life" (a change from "Fanfare for the Common Man", say, and a neat reference to both the Albert Hall and Stills' debt to Beck in his soloing).

The sound was muggy for the first few songs – the drums in particular a horrible cardboard thump – but it gradually cleared. Unfortunately this revealed that Stills' voice is shot and that CSN's live harmonies haven't got any tighter since the late sixties. We're then on a merry-go-round. A couple of Crosby songs followed by a couple of Nash songs followed by a… you get the idea. Crosby comes out pretty well, always an interestingly different songwriter (apart from a dreadful reworking of "Triad", sounding not unlike a bad eighties cop-show theme). Nash, however (Brian Nash, according to *The Guardian*'s review), is just dreadful. Pompous, pretentious, unpleasantly nasal and off the cliché-ometer, lyrically. "Military Madness" and "Cathedral" haven't improved over the years. A new song, "Burning for the Buddha", is as dreadful as its title.

Pretty much all the fun comes from Stills, launching himself without a safety net into solo after solo.

{CROSBY STILLS & NASH | "WOODEN SHIPS"}

"Bluebird", the old Springfield chestnut, was dusted off and sent into the stratosphere, all trem-bar swoops and harmonics. It was outrageously good, Stills got a standing ovation, and I was given back the will to stay to the end. On "Treetop Flyer" he walked the stage playing the most beautifully liquid blues fills, nods to Chuck Berry's "Havana Moon" one minute, to BB King the next, before dashing back to the mike to sing another laconic verse of his paean to Vietnam Vets turned drug smugglers.

His solos in "Almost Cut My Hair" were equally good, spurred on by Crosby's impassioned singing. Finally came the encore of "Suite: Judy Blue Eyes" – all over the shop but made good by Stills' channelling Davy Graham for a raga-infused breakdown in the middle. I left the Hall strangely gloomy, wondering if I expected too much.

Wednesday, October 16

TWO HEADS UP: DEPRESSING RE-EMERGENCE OF BARRE-CHORD ROCK

The return of Kings of Leon seems to have presaged this dire turn of events. Now Jake Bugg is on *Later* doing Church Hall Rock (or Church Crypt Rock, or Scout Hut Rock, even) – that style of music beloved of those who picked up a guitar in the seventies and thrashed away in the nearest rehearsal space they could find, moving their hands up and down the neck, fingers locked into that one bloody shape. These people are too young for that. Surely we've come too far for this, lads?

FOUR FROM THE BIG BOX OF NONSENSE, CONINGSBY GALLERY W1

Lovely work by Andrew Baker, a series of woodcuts of nonsense poems by John Lennon, Ivor Cutler and Spike Milligan, among others.

FIVE PETER SERAFINOWICZ SINGS THE FIRST PAGE OF THE MORRISSEY BOOK

Just great. Comedian and writer Serafinowicz nails it. I'm with Richard Williams on this: "Morrissey's autobiography is to be published as a Penguin Classic: an effortless insult to every author in the series and every reader, too."

Wednesday, October 23

ONE 6 CITRONS, DU PARMESAN, ET UN POT DE CRÈME FRAÎCHE, MERCI…

A bizarre collection of Serge Gainsbourg's belongings are at auction on October 31. The list of items includes four cigarette butts in a cassette case (estimate £425–£600), a pair of his nail clippers (estimate £40–£70) and a telegram to his wife, Jane Birkin, of controversial Number One single "Je T'aime… Moi Non Plus" fame.

Last year his handwritten shopping lists were sold for £6,540. Said David Richard, a spokesperson for the auction house: "When we sold those we realised there was a great interest in items from his everyday life. Quite a lot of the bidders were women and they were prepared to go quite far, but it's always difficult to know how much people are prepared to pay for these things." Well, here's a few of my favourite things [left], but I think I'll pass on actually bidding.

TWO BLOOMFIELD AND BIG JOE

From Michael Gray's Outtakes *blog:* "In 1980 Mike Bloomfield published a short memoir, *Me and Big Joe,* [that's Williams] which not only portrayed the difficulties of their relationship very honestly but also, in Peter Narváez' phrase, illustrated 'the

"Joe was still there in the road, fumbling with his suitcase and equipment."

cross-cultural triumph of the blues tradition'. Bloomfield wrote: 'Joe's world wasn't my world, but his music was. It was my life; it would be my life. So playing on was all I could do, and I did it the best that I was able. And the music I played, I knew where it came from; and there was not any way I'd forget.'"

I really love that sentence, and reading more excerpts, discover that the book is compelling, well-written and illustrated by Robert Crumb.

THREE **FAVOURITE STORY OF THE WEEK**
Tony Bennett questionnaire, *The Guardian*:
You must have mixed with them all.
"I lived for 15 years in Los Angeles and I still can't believe that the handsomest man in the world, Cary Grant, and the greatest

performer in the world, Fred Astaire... [were] in my home... I celebrated my 50th birthday with them. Unforgettable."
Did any of them do anything in your home that you've had to keep secret?
"No. But once Dean Martin was in his home, having this mad party, and he was trying to study his lines for a television show so he called up the police and said: "I'm Dean Martin's neighbour and there's too much noise coming from his house. Have the police come and slow down the party." And the police came and broke the party up and he got rid of everybody in the house."

FOUR **A NOTE ON PACKAGING THE PAST**
I give in to temptation. I've bought this music on vinyl, in 1972. In its first digital form on CD in the late eighties. On remastered CD in 2000. And here we are, buying it again in 2013, remixed, reprogrammed, repackaged.

Rock of Ages by The Band, originally in a three-gatefold sleeve of purple with Bob Cato's enigmatic oriental statue on the front and mysterious pictures by Magnum's Ernst Haas (the impressionistic colour ones) and John Scheele (the beautiful B&Ws) on the inside. One of the great live albums of the rock era. As Allen Toussaint says: "They dance by a different drummer, all the time. There was nothing stock about them."

But I baulk at the stupidly priced Venal-Record-Company-

Death-Throes Box Set, with its 5.1 Surround Sound DVD version of the tracks and the Sebastian Robertson soundboard mix of the uncut New Year's Eve night. Come on. How many times can the people who love this music be ripped off? Yes, I know that everything in HERITAGE ROCK WORLD™ has to be a "production". And, yes, it sounds fantastic, remixed by Robertson and the brilliant Bob Clearmountain with a staggering degree of detail. But then, it always did sound fantastic, I just didn't know it could sound better, and may never have felt I was missing out...

FIVE AND ALSO...

From Robbie Robertson's liner notes. I love what he says about Rick Danko: "Rick showed something during this period that I still don't understand. While singing like a bird, he played

a fretless bass... in an unorthodox style that worked against reason and normality." Toussaint again: "Rick Danko – his approach, there's nothing like it. Some people, you can tell what school of thought they come from on the bass... I don't know where Rick Danko comes from. I don't know his source of reference... it was just his very own thing and I think it was perfect."

Wednesday, October 30

ONE **DOWN WITH THE COOL KIDS**

The disappointing lack of cool jazz in the new series of *Homeland* is more than balanced by its recent appearance in *Downton Abbey*, thanks to young Lady Rose. As an imported-from-London Jazz orchestra plays, Lady Grantham (Maggie Smith) is asked by a guest: "Is this your first experience of Jazz, Lady Grantham?" "Oh, is *that* what it is?" (*pregnant pause, looks at the band...*) "Do you think any of them know what the others are playing?"

TWO **VIRGIN 40TH ANNIVERSARY POP-UP (OR DOWN) EXHIBITION, BLOOMSBURY**

Deep in the basement of one of those extraordinarily grand "London Headquarters"-style buildings from the beginning of the 1900s that resemble landlocked battleships, a hollow hagiography of a label I always found slightly naff. I'd gone because I thought they had recreated the original Oxford

{NEIL YOUNG | "REVOLUTION BLUES", *with Rick Danko's fabulous yomping bass*}

Street shop, opened in 1971, where it had usurped Dobell's for me as a teenager as a place to buy music, because they sold bootlegs. Upstairs, under the counter. You had to get to know the guys in the shop, and you had to know what you were looking for. "Have you got, uh, *Wooden Nickel*? *Stealin'*? Oh, great, thanks, that's £3, right..."

However, they hadn't recreated Oxford Street, but the Notting Hill branch at the time of the Sex Pistols *NMTB* launch, which felt a bit lame.

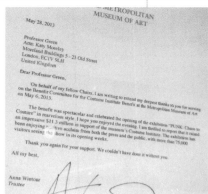

[Note: The word "bootleg" originates from the practice of smuggling illicit items in the legs of tall boots, particularly the smuggling of alcohol during the American Prohibition era. The word, over time, has come to refer to any illegal or illicit product and has become an umbrella term for unofficial, or unlicenced recordings. – Wikipedia]

This photo shows a ridiculous letter from Anna Wintour to Professor Green that is beyond comment, and a modified rusty Telecaster, one careful owner, as played on *Tubular Bells*.

THREE **REED BETWEEN THE LINES**

Watching the BBC video of "Perfect Day" as it ended another tribute to Lou Reed, I was struck by the less obvious artists who appeared in it: Emmylou Harris, Dr John, Robert Cray... did you remember Robert Cray singing a line? I listened to *New York* whole, top to bottom, as Lou wished. It's my favourite Reed album, and I remember boring friends in 1989, endlessly making them listen, saying it had the greatest guitar sound ever recorded (the chorus guitar of "Hold On"). It opens with the killer triple-whammy of "Romeo Had Juliette"/"Halloween Parade"/"Dirty Blvd". Sensational.

FOUR **VAN MORRISON, "INTO THE MYSTIC", TAKE 11**

Nothing will replace in your heart the *Moondance* version of a song Morrison first titled "Into the Misty", but try to hear this tracking session take. Van on intense, focused and dynamic rhythm guitar, possibly John Platania on second guitar, drummer Gary Mallaber and bassist John Klingberg playing off his lead... These guys are in the moment, in the mystic and it's glorious. As Lou would say, you can't beat two guitars, bass, drum.

FIVE RONNIE WOOD TICKET FOR SALE. STOP PUSHING AT THE BACK.

Someone included me in a round robin offering this for sale. £125? For Ronnie Wood playing three chords for two hours. I love Jimmy Reed, but there are limits. I saw a *Sky Arts* tribute to BB King the other day, where a large group of guitarists and singers added very little to B's show. In the thirty minutes I saw, Ron contributed the least, but was a jocular figure, happy to be there. Mick Hucknall sang, Susan Tedeschi barely got a look in on guitar but sang very nicely.

Slash was jarringly inconsistent – sometimes good, sometimes not. B was imperious when he played, which was not a lot of the time, but was always telling, which others weren't. But the man who was king was humble Derek Trucks, whose mix of slide and fingers pulled off a wonderful solo in the ol' slowie "Guess Who" and knocked everyone else into a cocked hat.

Wednesday, November 6

ONE JOURNEY THROUGH THE PAST NO. 2

Before the web, if you liked something, you ripped it out of the magazine and filed it away. And then twenty years later, you

find it again. Like this letter to *The New York Times* from the late, great Jerry Wexler.

TWO ALWAYS FUN TO HEAR HOW THINGS GET NAMED

Fun fact: How did *Just Seventeen* get its name? Founding editor David Hepworth says: "It's always funny to reflect on the names that magazines could have had. Steve Bush, the art director, wanted to call it *Sasha*. We had to call it *Seventeen* because that was the right title for a magazine for 14-year-olds. The publishers of the American magazine of the same name made legal noises and so we had to come up with an alternative. Peter Strong, the publisher, suggested adding the word 'just'. It wasn't until years later I realised he must have got that idea from the Beatles song 'I Saw Her Standing There'."

THREE A COUPLE OF THINGS I READ THIS WEEK CONCERNING JOHN COLTRANE 1

Recalling the year he turned 20 in *Mojo*'s 20th Anniversary issue, David Crosby tells of his time as an itinerant troubadour: "During my Chicago stint, I had one of the best experiences I ever had in my life! I was living in an apartment with an English guy... One day [his girlfriend] said to us, 'Do you wanna hear some real music? John Coltrane is playing on the South Side.' So this attractive little German girl took us down to McKee's—163rd and Cottage Grove, way South. We were the only white people in the room.

"The way 'Trane played then was that the band would come out and the set was one song which would start out with ensemble playing. 'Trane would warm up by blowing a little to get going, and they all took their time because they figured their set would be an hour long so they had time [to stretch out]. He'd play for a bit and walk off still blowing. Then McCoy Tyner would play...

"Now, I will admit to being higher than three kites hooked up in series. I was blitzed. Elvin Jones is a pretty intense drummer. [His playing] pushed me up from the table and up against the back wall of the room! I'm standing there trying to hold on and I ducked into the men's room.

"So I'm in the men's room, I'm trying to come down just enough to stay on this planet, and I've got my face pressed against this tile. I'm leaning against it because it's cool. And – blam! – someone kicks the door in and it's 'Trane. [*Makes shrieking jazz noises, as if playing a sax*] He's doing that and by this point he's burning! Burr-ning! [*Makes more squalling jazz-orientated noises*]. Skee-sa-wee-eek-swark! And I'm up against the wall. He doesn't even know this little fake kid's in there. He's playing in there because it's a good sound. And at

that point my mind ran out of my nose in a puddle on the floor!...

"I realized that there were levels that I could never get to but, suddenly, I could see what direction I wanted to go in. There were things that jazz musicians could do that I could never hope to do. I'd listen to the chords McCoy Tyner played and they weren't in my world. I had never heard those chords. I knew that somehow I wanted to reach for more. I wanted to move from [Broadway standard-turned-folk tune] 'They Call the Wind Maria' to 'Trane playing 'My Favourite Things'. Now, I feel I had a direction."

FOUR JC 2: MATTHEW CARTER, TYPE DESIGNER

From a profile in *The New Yorker* that I ripped out years ago. In 1960, Carter travelled to New York: "'I was made abruptly and forcefully to realise that I knew nothing.' He felt that he was faced with two choices: to slink home or to resolve to stay. 'The cowardly part of me could have gone back to England and pretended I hadn't seen all of this design'...

"In the spring of 1960, The John Coltrane Quartet played its first engagement. Carter was in the audience. Over several weeks, he heard them three or four times. 'Sometimes they played the same songs in the second set as they played in the first... Not because they were lazy, but because they wanted to surpass themselves, or find something in the music that they hadn't found earlier in the evening. They were that acute.'

Listening to them, he decided that he owed it to himself to try and stay in New York. 'Their seriousness of purpose was a lesson... I could have been dishonest enough to return to England and say I hadn't seen great design. But I couldn't somehow pretend that I hadn't heard The John Coltrane Quartet.'"

FIVE INDULGED ROCK STAR GIBBERISH OF THE WEEK

"The Oslo hotel where you can sleep with your favourite rock star [projected onto the bedsheet next to you]" blah'd *The Guardian*... "The idea came from A-ha's Magne Furuholmen, Coldplay's Guy Berryman, Mew singer Jonas Bjerre and producer Martin Terefe, who together make up the pan-European supergroup Apparatjik." They were given carte blanche to decorate the Thief hotel.

Then comes the gibberish: "'We started by going around tacky gift shops trying to find things to make the room as kitsch as we could and create a sort of "disco combat" feel,' explains Furuholmen. 'We found pixelated carpets, retro fabrics, lots of vinyl, and something every hotel room needs: a disco ball for the bathroom.' Furuholmen and his band mates took these treasures and created *Apparatjik World*, an eclectic mix of art, video, music and installations – including projections of band members dressed as semi-nude muscle men with bulging silver posing pouches ('we like a costume: it gives us freedom,' says Furuholmen). The result? 'Quirky... with a touch of insanity,' is how Stordalen describes his new suite."

Oh, those buzz words that rock musos so love... quirky, tacky, kitsch, retro... reaching a nadir with that deathly phrase "disco combat feel". I mean, how dated is that? Didn't U2 give us that about twenty years ago?

Wednesday, November 13

ONE A GREAT PHOTO
Jane B and Serge G, from a new book of her brother Andrew's photos, *Jane & Serge: A Family Album*.

TWO A GREAT LYRIC
Jimmy Webb interview by Dave Simpson, *The Guardian*
"The lyrics to 'MacArthur Park' infuriate some people. 'Someone left the cake out in the rain / I don't think that I can take it / 'Cause it took so long to bake it / And I'll never have that recipe again.' They think it's a psychedelic trip. But everything in the song is real. There is a MacArthur Park in Los Angeles, near where my girlfriend worked selling life insurance. We'd meet there for lunch, and there would be old men playing checkers by the trees, like in the lyrics.

I've been asked a million times: 'What is the cake left out in the rain?' It's something I saw – we would eat cake and leave it in the rain. But as a metaphor for a losing chapter of your life, it seemed too good to be true. When she broke up with me, I poured the hurt into the song. It was always around seven minutes long – not twenty-two as has been written.

"Bones Howe, a fellow producer, had asked me to create a pop song with classical elements, different movements and changing time signatures. 'MacArthur Park', more of a suite than a song, was everything he wanted, but when we presented it to his new act, The Association, they refused to record it.

It was the late 1960s and I was doing music for an anti-war pageant with some Hollywood stars, including Mia Farrow and Edgar G. Robinson. Richard Harris and I started hanging out after rehearsals and drinking Black Velvets: 50 percent Guinness, 50 percent champagne. One night after a few, I said: 'We ought to make a record'. He'd starred in the movie *Camelot* and sang every song in it beautifully. A few weeks later, I received a telegram: 'Dear Jimmy Webb. Come to London. Make this record. Love, Richard.' He always called me Jimmy Webb.

"I got a flight and stayed with Richard in Belgravia. Over the course of two days, we tore through 30 or 40 of my songs. I was playing the piano and singing. He was standing there in his kaftan, waving his arms and expressing excitement at some songs, not so crazy about others. The best went into his debut album, *A Tramp Shining*. 'MacArthur Park' was at the bottom of my pile. By the time I played it, we had moved on to straight brandy, but Richard slapped the piano. 'Oh Jimmy Webb. I love that! I'll make a hit out of that, I will.'"

"I recorded the basic track back in Hollywood, with myself on harpsichord accompanied by session musicians The Wrecking Crew. We rehearsed it a few times, then played it right through, using the first take and adding the orchestra painstakingly later. When Richard did the vocals at a London studio, he had a pitcher of Pimm's by the microphone. We knew the session was over when the Pimm's was gone. I never could get him to sing the title correctly. He'd say: 'Jimmy Webb, I've got it!' Then he'd sing: MacArthur's Park..."

THREE A GREAT EBAY LISTING: WILL POST, BUT ONLY TO UK...

Yes. It's a record shop on eBay...

FOUR A TERRIFIC GUITAR

At a press brunch for Southern Tourism, and again at the *Hatch Show Print* exhibition, we hear Trent Dabbs and Amy Stroup face an intimate bunch of strangers and entwine their voices beautifully while singing smart, literate songs from the latest alt-end of Nashville. As a bonus, Trent's got quite the nicest Gibson J-200 I've ever seen, tobacco-brown and sweet-toned. Late 80s model, and he told me that he had to prove he was worthy of it by playing a set of songs to the guy selling it.

FIVE FAKE BOB!
Steve tells me of a dream he had the other night where Bob Dylan was a dog walker. So I made him the album cover.

Wednesday, November 20

ONE IN BOB NEWS...
Watch *this* ▶. THE. MOST. JAW-DROPPING. MUSIC VIDEO. EVER. The world of US TV skewered with humour, with shades of Bob and Larry Charles' dystopian nightmare *Masked and Anonymous* hidden in the glossy surface (watch those news channels again and look at the ticker-tape lines – BANKS STILL DEALING IN IMAGINARY MONEY, for instance). A triumph of technology and imagination, it's also very funny. Channel hop "Like a Rolling Stone" and find that everyone is singing it, whichever channel you land on, from soap opera to *The Housewives of Wherever* to shopping channel to the news. Love the Kanye West quote. Hats off to VANIA HEYMANN, who had the idea.

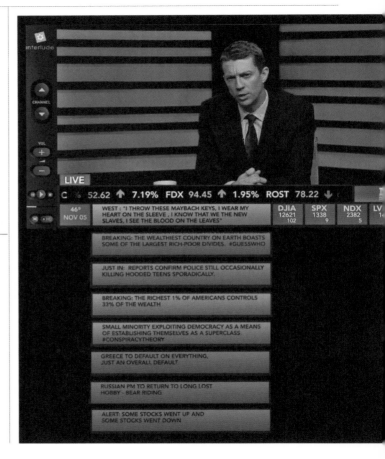

{FIND IT AT | VIDEO.BOBDYLAN.COM}

TWO **BOB NEWS 2**

Hugh and I wander over to Bond Street for the press view of Bob's *Iron Range* at the Halcyon Gallery. Hugh is disappointed that rough and rusted metal has been so highly varnished that it looks like cookware rather than sculpture.

Downstairs are Bob's huge re-Photoshopped magazine covers (very strange and not very good) and his Gangster Doors, vintage car doors riddled with gunshots. At this point, I confess I felt like Mr Jones.

THREE **OH, GEORGE! YOU CARD!**

Tom Junod, in *US Esquire*: "Being Clooney, he does not only write to Brad Pitt, however. He also writes as Brad Pitt. A few years ago, he even had some stationery made up with Brad Pitt's letterhead. Then he found a book about acting and accents and sent it to Meryl Streep, with an accompanying note. It said, 'Dear Meryl, this book really helped me with my accent for Troy. I hope it helps you too.' He signed it 'Brad Pitt'.

Then he sent another letter to Don Cheadle on 'Pitt's' stationery. As long as Cheadle has been acting, he has dreamt of playing Miles Davis. So the letter informed Cheadle that Pitt's production company had acquired the rights to Davis's life story. The letter said that Pitt wanted him to star in it. As Charlie Parker."

FIVE **TRIPTYCH FROM MARRAKECH**

Drummers in the Jemaa el-Fnaa Square. Always go to the barbers with the painting of Liberace on the door for a shave. I understand this list of chefs and restauranteurs, but was puzzled by the inclusion of Ray Charlz.

Wednesday, November 27

ONE **"THE BEST BLACK, GAY, ONE-EYED JUNKIE PIANO GENIUS NEW ORLEANS EVER PRODUCED"**

There are certain people so musical that everything they *are* is musical. Their movements, their voice, their atmosphere. James Booker was one of those people. Not that he wasn't a truly colossal pain in the ass to those around him, but the fact that many stayed with him and attempted to help his journey

"David, little David, help me now, c'mon little David..."

EXCERPTS FROM DAVID HOOD Q&A, SOHO HOTEL CINEMA

Audience member: *Do you have a theory about what the magic of Muscle Shoals was?*

DH: I think it's a group of young people who wanted to make good music, that was the driving force. We never thought we'd be famous, we never thought we'd be Beatles or anything like that... Always my role has been a supporting role. I was the guy by the drummer, playing and trying to do whatever I could to make the artist sound good. We all had the same goal, and that was to play great music and to hear it on the radio. And that was a thrill... It's still a thrill.

I was interested in the fallout from Aretha's appearance in the Shoals and her sudden departure after Rick Hall and her husband, Ted White, came to blows. I asked: *Was there a difference in feel, working in New York, where the sessions relocated, compared to the Shoals?*

DH: Well, it was a lot more formal. There were union guys saying "You can't unplug that amplifier, we gotta have someone come in." We did the Letterman show three weeks ago in New York and we're setting up and I wanted to move my amplifier, and... In Muscle Shoals, we were the guys, that's the thing. [But in New York] once we got in there, got in our positions, playing the music, it was the same...

Our little studio, 3614 Jackson Ave., when Paul Simon came and recorded there – he came to record "Take Me to the Mardi Gras" because he had heard "I'll Take You There" and wanted those black Jamaican musicians to play, so he came and booked the studio time. He booked four days for that song, and

{PAUL SIMON | "ST JUDY'S COMET" *for the Swampers lightness and Pete Carr's guitar*}

when he came in it was raining – and the studio leaked... I don't know if it's polite to say this, but the sound engineer [Jerry Masters] taped tampons across the back of the control room roof, because the water was dripping on the control board.

We got "Take Me" on the second take, so we had three more days. Paul Simon's not going to give up the studio time he's paying for, so we cut "Kodachrome" and those other things... [Those other things included "Loves Me Like a Rock", "One Man's Ceiling Is Another Man's Floor" and the luminous and delicate "St. Judy's Comet", showing the deft touch that made them perfect collaborators. Just listen to Pete Carr's guitar fills, Hood's super-melodic bass and Barry Beckett's cool vibes. The Rhythm Section also cut "Still Crazy After All These Years" and "My Little Town" with Simon.]

So, very primitive facilities that we had... but it's the sound of the musicians – it's not the room, it's the musicians. Many, many accidents happen in music. At the end of "Kodachrome" you hear Paul Simon go "OK" – that's when he's trying to get us to stop, to do it again, and we keep playin' and it sort of becomes the record, so you never know on things like that.

My friend Alex asked: *In the film Rick Hall comes across as an eccentric, sometimes brutal character – is that a fair depiction?*
DH: That's some true depiction – to this day. The session where you see [in the film] Candi Staton recording "I Ain't Easy to Love"...
ALEX: *He's all over it, isn't he...*

DH: He was *so typical* Rick Hall. He was still as awful as he ever was. "No man, that's no good! That's not what I want..."
Audience member: Is it a love/hate thing?
DH: Mostly love [audience laughs]. He gave me my start. I would be nowhere without him... I tell him that every time I see him. It's a small town where we are. You either love each other or kill each other!

Other than the fact that I missed there being any mention of Eddie Hinton [add the name of your own overlooked Shoals denizen here], the film captures something of the time and

place that those wonderful records came out of. Read Mick Brown's lovely piece, "Deep Soul" – that tells you what you need to know.

I caught up with David after twenty-five or so years – the last time we talked was in his office at 1000 Alabama Avenue. I wore the T-shirt the studio had given us, and Alex took a picture on his phone. The quote at the top is Mavis Staples' exhortation to David Hood in "I'll Take You There". The Shoals sign photograph was taken by me in '87.

through this world pays testament to their appreciation of his genius. In a film, *Bayou Maharajah*, comprised of great interviews, fascinating recordings, amazing clips (from local bars aplenty to German TV) and some wonderfully eerie black and white "ghostly" videos, this original native son of New Orleans vividly grabs your attention.

His voice – talking or singing – is hypnotic. His piano playing... well, that defies description. Neither "standard" Professor Longhair derivation nor straightforward funk 'n' boogie, but a weird hybrid of these things with a dash of Liberace's romanticism (don't laugh), and Chopin's and Rachmaninoff's melodies.

There's a distorted improvisation that slowly turns into "A Taste of Honey" and somehow deepens a piece of pop fluff right in front of your ears. And always – always – something bitter and sweet mixed in. Often you watch him play an outrageous passage with a hard glint in his eye, a steely focus and drive, and as he ends it, a sly, shy smile to himself, as if to say, "There, *that's* what I can do..."

My favorite interviewee (and there are some great ones) is Harry Connick Jr., who knew Booker as a slightly wayward uncle figure (well, more than slightly) since Harry's father, the district attorney of Orleans Parish, had befriended and helped Booker at various times.

His recall of the night that Booker phoned him at two in the morning to ask Harry to come rescue him from some drug escapade gone wrong ("James, dude – I'm twelve years old!")

was extraordinary. He tells of recording Booker's phone calls, and you can see that he's still unsure to this day why he did. He says something along the lines of "I just loved hearing him talk, and I thought if I taped him, I'd always have his voice to listen to." Watch as Harry shows, beautifully, how Booker added layer upon layer of complexity to a tune. Mesmerizing.

TWO I'VE FOUND MY HARMONICA, ALBERT...

Bathed in the warm glow of Bob's band, a Dylan concert to really enjoy. On stage at the Royal Albert Hall Charlie Sexton still has the moves of a heartthrob (let's not forget that he fronted the bar band in *Thelma & Louise*), Donny Herron's like a engineer at his desk, working tirelessly on all manner of instruments and sounds, and the New Orleans engine room of George and Tony just keeps rolling on, making even the most ordinary twelve-bar come to life.

Yes, it had its up and downs. Michèle, up until then an enthusiastic applauder, said "I'm not clapping that" after a particularly calamitous "Spirit on The Water". I was with her – it was like a drunken showband at the end of the pier, with Les Dawson on piano.

But the high points were high. A malevolent "Pay in Blood" that far surpassed the studio take. A great re-visit of "All Along the Watchtower" with a left turn, two-thirds through, into a spacey and atonal breakdown, before a thunderous climax.

A lovely "Waitin' for You", a song written for the soundtrack of *Divine Secrets of the Ya-Ya Sisterhood*, highlighted by a Sexton solo that sounded for all the world like the great Grady Martin. A gorgeous "Forgetful Heart". Oh, and a beautiful and soulful "Blowin' in the Wind" to end with.

THREE *GOOD VIBRATIONS*

It's the story of Terri Hooley, godfather of Belfast punk (he started a record shop called Good Vibrations), and it's nominally a feel-good music film but is actually pretty hard-nosed about the difficulties of Belfast in the seventies. The fast-cut collage that follows the opening scene takes our main character from childhood to 1976. It's brilliantly done, in a kind of kinetic pop-art way, packed with news images of the Troubles, and edited to Hank Williams singing "I Saw the Light". As it progresses it becomes more and more distorted, and finally the song disappears among swirls of echo, to be replaced by a hum of feedback and soundwash.

FIVE BRUCE SPRINGSTEEN, "NEW YORK CITY SERENADE", ROME

I remember a night in Sheffield, in 1974, when my friend Mike and I played this track (newly released) to Colin Graham, old family friend, editor of *Angling Times* and big-time "Jazz Buff". We were trying to prove that rock musicians could play their instruments and felt the combo of Bruce and David Sancious was a good bet... or something like that. In a game of what Charlie Gillett would turn into Radio Ping-Pong, we were searching through the records we'd brought with us (oh for an iPod) for

something that we thought could pass muster.

I wish I could recall what Colin, pipe in mouth, thought of it. Watching this recent performance of it, beautifully filmed and played, gives a Proustian rush back to the time I spent obsessively listening to *The Wild, the Innocent & the E Street Shuffle*. Apparently I bought it at Dobell's, and it was £2.99.

I approached Jim Sherraden, the man who saved Nashville's Hatch Show Print, with some trepidation. I felt guilty. In the late 80s, having discovered the wonderful world of Show Prints (posters, often printed on card, that would be nailed to telegraph poles, placed in barbershop windows, pinned to noticeboards), I'd decided to get some printed for a 12-inch single cover. I'd seen some of the famous Hatch prints (Elvis and Hank) but had thought they were no longer a going concern. The only contact I could find for a Poster Shop was in a magazine article about Tribune Showprint, of Earl Park, Indiana.

So I wrote them, and they sent me a set of forms to fill in. I sent them back with an International Money Order and waited. Three weeks later, a package of twenty-five posters arrived, on the "Rainbow" card that I'd requested, a favorite of mine from a Mighty Clouds of Joy poster that was on a wall at Mus-

cle Shoals Sound. Our single didn't sell, but about six months later, Tom Petty's *Full Moon Fever* came out with a faux version that just leaves you thinking, Why not go the whole hog and get the real thing?

Jim saved a great American institution, coining the phrase "Preservation Through Production". He writes excellent lyrics to songs by Jonas Fjeld, a Norwegian national treasure (and

{ERIC ANDERSEN | "BLUE RIVER"}

at various times musical partner to Eric Andersen and Rick Danko). He signed my much-loved copy (rather brilliantly, as he spoke to me, telling me not to feel guilty, Tribune were great and still going strong) of the book about Hatch that came out a bunch of years ago. He told my mother a funny story about Levon Helm and kissed her on both cheeks, making her, and my, evening. A hero.

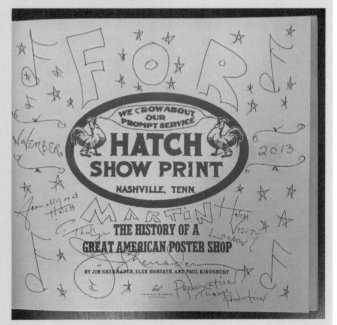

{DANKO/FJELD/ANDERSEN | "DRIFTIN' AWAY"}

Wednesday, December 4

ONE FAVOURITE KICKSTARTER PLEDGE REWARD OF THE WEEK

I can't get enough of documentaries on the musicians behind some of the finest pop music ever made. Motown's Funk Brothers in *Standing in The Shadows of Motown*, The Swampers in *Muscle Shoals,* Booker T. and the MGs in *Respect Yourself: The Stax Records Story*, and now *The Wrecking Crew*.

This is, to quote Danny Tedesco, son of the great guitarist Tommy Tedesco and director of the film, "a documentary about an elite group of studio session musicians in Los Angeles in the 1960s who played on hits for the Beach Boys, Frank Sinatra, Nancy Sinatra, Sonny and Cher, Jan & Dean, The Monkees, Mamas and Papas, 5th Dimension, Tijuana Brass, Ricky Nelson, Elvis Presley and Phil Spector's Wall of Sound, and that's just a few! The amount of work in which they were involved was tremendous." A thousand buck pledge will get you legendary Wrecking Crew pianist/arranger Don Randi's services for

a recording session – and he'll buy you lunch as well!

TWO THIS WEEK – 3 TOP-NAME ATTRACTIONS!

The Jet Set somehow don't sound like the right support group, do they?

THREE FANFARLO, WATER RATS

What are the chances of stumbling across a really good band in a London pub? One in a hundred? One in a thousand? Whatever, Fanfarlo are terrific (apart from their name, possibly). A cracking drummer, two keyboardists who double on violin and trumpet, a frontman with a beautifully pared-down guitar style and a bass player who looks like a bass player should. They've described their current sound as "Space Opera meets Spaghetti Western". I can't do any better than that. They also cover one of my most favourite songs, "Witchi Tai To", written by jazz saxophonist Jim Pepper and based on a Native American chant. The hit version was by Harpers Bizarre, purveyors of Baroque Pop, produced by Van Dyke Parks, and with The Wrecking Crew aboard by the sound of it.

FIVE *THE MAN WHO BROUGHT THE BLUES TO BRITAIN: BIG BILL BROONZY, BBC FOUR*

"I met some big shot and I was ready to make a record. I wrote a guitar solo called 'House Rent Stomp' about those rent parties. No words, just pickin' those old guitar strings, making the first two, E and B, cry, making the G and D talk, and the A and E moan." That's the best description of blues guitar I've heard.

Wednesday, December 11

ONE SPECIALIST SUBJECT: JANIS JOPLIN

On the BBC quiz show, *Mastermind*. My score, 5. Competitor's score, 12. He was extremely good, but he had actually revised for the show I'd guess...

TWO MARTIN SHARP 1942–2013

From the obituary in the *New York Times* by William Yardley: "He painted Marilyn Monroe blooming in a van Gogh vase, devoted decades to documenting the cultural significance of Tiny Tim and was sentenced to prison for breaking obscenity laws in his native Australia.

Martin Sharp, who died on Sunday at 71, pursued his distinctive Pop Art for half a century without much concern for whether it was popular. But for a brief period in the late 1960s, his muse helped shape the imagery of rock music.

It started with a beer at a bar in London in 1967. Mr. Sharp had arrived the year before to start *London Oz*, an extension of the irreverent Australian magazine *Oz*, for which he had been artistic director.

At the Speakeasy Club on Margaret Street, he befriended two musicians. When Mr. Sharp mentioned that he had written a poem that might make a good song, one of the musicians said he had just come up with new music but needed lyrics.

Mr. Sharp scratched out his poem and his address on a napkin. A couple of weeks later, the musician dropped by and gave him a 45 r.p.m. record. He was a guitar player for a band called Cream. His name was Eric Clapton. On the A side of the 45 was 'Strange Brew'. On the B side was Mr Sharp's poem put to music, 'Tales of Brave Ulysses'."

178

THREE BONNIE RAITT, BBC FOUR SESSIONS

Bonnie, wine bottleneck slide on finger, Shubb capo at the second fret, calling up the ghost of Lowell George. What I first thought was a ridiculous manicure was, in fact, a set of white plastic fingerpicks. Every solo was a thing of controlled emotion and dexterity in the service of soul and beauty. She also had Mike Finnigan on keys (who played on *Electric Ladyland* and toured in Maria Muldaur's astonishing band in 1975).

My friend Mark was there and said they all seemed a little tired, and the production team kept asking for retakes, but certain things really worked on TV. Hutch Hutchinson's use of a small travel bass on "I Can't Make You Love Me" was great, there was a tremendous "Million Miles", where she articulated the words way better than Bob, and Finnigan got all Mose Allison on its ass… (not that I much care about articulation, but the song seemed all the more desperate for it).

And "Love Has No Pride" nailed you to the wall. Against simpatico bass and pump organ, Raitt played her 1972 classic and brought forty more years of a life lived to it. All X Factor contestants should be forced to watch this performance.

FOUR MIDNIGHT AT THE OASIS (SOHO BRANCH)

Reminded of Maria Muldaur at Ronnie Scott's, a gig I failed to get into, I look up some reviews on Rock's Backpages. I remember that I spent a week hassling Barbara Charone in the Warner Bros. press office trying to get an interview with Amos Garrett. I don't know why. I was at art school and had no journalistic credentials. I think I just wanted to tell Amos how great I thought he was.

Karl Dallas in *Melody Maker*: "She is backed – if that is an adequate word for so brilliant an aggregation – with quite the tightest, most talented little six-piece band any singer was ever blessed with, which came out from behind her and featured pianist Mike Finnigan as singer once in each set.

Everything about this band is a joy – from the cool, right-on drumming of Earl Palmer, to the twin guitars of David Wilcox and Amos Garrett, so contrasting and yet so complementary." Earl Palmer! *Earl Palmer!* Rock 'n' Roll History right there. However, neither this review or Charles Shaar Murray's in *NME* mentioned the fact that the bassist was James Jamerson, which is bizarre. How could you not mention James Jamerson? (Murray also found the performance bland beyond belief, but then he sneered about Springsteen at the Hammersmith Odeon, and he was wrong there, too.)

FIVE BRAIDS, XOYO

At sea in a roomful of hipster beards and square-rimmed glasses. Of course, there's no obligation to like the music made by

relatives or friends, but there's nothing nicer than when you do, here in the shape of the ferociously talented Austin, Taylor and Raphaelle [Taylor is my cousin's son]. Down to a trio from a four-piece, what before was impressive loop-driven modern ambient music has now become thrillingly visceral and really emotional.

They were aided by the best sound I have ever heard in a club, or maybe in any venue. Their soundman, John, puts the drums, keyboards and guitars through the PA, using no amps (he previously worked for the legendary Clair Brothers, leaders in the field).

It was whisper-quiet – something I've literally never heard before – and it allowed the music to form, in pin-sharp detail, in front of your ears. Each mallet stroke or snare lick or signal-processed synth effect or treated vocal sat exactly where it should in the mix, allowing the performance to build to a fantastic climax. Incredible.

Wednesday, December 18

ONE **I'D NEVER HEARD OF DIANA DAVIES...**

I came across her by chance and found these really interesting collections at the Smithsonian. Great early Newport Folk Fest, and lovely NYC folk scene. Here's a few favourites: Butterfield, Mother Maybelle, Howlin' Wolf, Son House, Phil Ochs & Eric Andersen, Bob 'n' Don...

THREE **AT THE 100 CLUB**

With Hugh to the last lunchtime gig put on by Tony Leppard, one of the redoubtable mainstays of the Ken Colyer Trust. Live New Orleans Jazz sounds great, especially at lunchtime in a

{BRAIDS | "LITTLE HAND" †}

FOUR FOR MY BIRTHDAY...

Dotter gives me Shaun Usher's wonderful *Letters of Note*. Here's an excerpt from a proposal by Steve Albini [recording engineer and producer extraordinaire] to Nirvana. This is not in the book, but is one of my favorites on the website:

"#5: DOUGH. I explained this to Kurt but I thought I'd better reiterate it here. I do not want and will not take a royalty on any record I record. No points. Period. I think paying a royalty to a producer or engineer is ethically indefensible. The band write the songs. The band play the music. It's the band's fans who buy the records. The band is responsible for whether it's a great record or a horrible record. Royalties belong to the band.

"I would like to be paid like a plumber: I do the job and you pay me what it's worth. The record company will expect me to ask for a point or a point and a half. If we assume three million sales, that works out to 400,000 dollars or so. There's no fucking way I would ever take that much money. I wouldn't be able to sleep. I have to be comfortable with the amount of money you pay me, but it's your money, and I insist that you be comfortable with it as well. Kurt suggested paying me a chunk

dark basement. Hand-hewn, there's something so emotionally warm about the entwining horns and the grainy, sifty rhythms that within seconds you're caught up, and May-to-September couples start jiving behind you...

Mike Pointon drolly MC's, adds great trombone, and picks a fine set of songs – "The Glory of Love", "Lady Be Good", some Bunk Johnson blues – and everything swings beautifully. Favourite moments: When drummer Emile Martyn plays the fire extinguisher, on the wall behind him, to punctuate a chorus. And when Adrian Cox on clarinet goes up a gear near the end of his solo on "Lady Be Good" and raises the roof.

which I would consider full payment, and then if you really thought I deserved more, paying me another chunk after you'd had a chance to live with the album for a while. That would be fine, but probably more organizational trouble than it's worth.

"Whatever. I trust you guys to be fair to me and I know you must be familiar with what a regular industry goon would want. I will let you make the final decision about what I'm going to be paid. How much you choose to pay me will not affect my enthusiasm for the record.

"Some people in my position would expect an increase in business after being associated with your band. I, however, already have more work than I can handle, and frankly, the kind of people such superficialities will attract are not people I want to work with. Please don't consider that an issue."

FIVE AND ON ANOTHER SHAUN USHER SITE...
Some fine examples of musicians' letterheads...

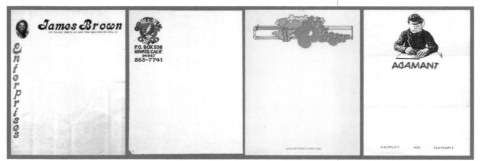

Wednesday, December 25

ONE COVER GIRL: JULIE LONDON
Michèle's request for a Julie London Christmas album hits a snag. She never did one. But with a little internetting and some InDesign, Julie's Miss December (from her album, *Calendar Girl*) becomes a fully-fledged seasonal treat.

TWO "OH THE SHARK, BABE, HAS SUCH TEETH, DEAR..."
Michael Gray on Bobby Darin "Bobby Darin's singles were part of my adolescence, and all these decades later I'm still impressed by his work, the multiplicity of his talent and his human decency.

He was a songwriter, singer, actor, pianist, guitarist and men-

{GOOGLE | "MICHAEL GRAY BOBBY DARIN"}

tor to Roger McGuinn; he conquered the pop charts and then dinner-jacket showbiz, yet came to see that turbulent times called for songs of social conscience. As a person he was gracious, articulate, sharp and funny. He was a talented actor... nominated for an Academy Award for Best Supporting Actor [in 1963].

"As for his records, well OK, not 'Splish Splash', but 'Dream Lover', produced by the Erteguns, was one of the most shimmering records of 1960 – and was followed, very surprisingly, by the best version of 'Mack the Knife', with Darin unarguably the master of this radically different genre.

"Then came 'Beyond the Sea', a more than worthy successor that didn't try to replace the Charles Trenet original ('La Mer', a timeless track blemished only by the ridiculously over-hearty male voice choir at the end). I still love it. I loved a number of his later records too, though often preferring the B-sides... Neil Young said this of him: 'I used to be pissed off at Bobby Darin because he changed styles so much. Now I look at him and think he was a genius.'

"He sang duets on TV with an extraordinary range of people from Stevie Wonder to Judy Garland, from Dinah Shore to Clyde McPhatter and from Linda Ronstadt to Jimmy Durante. He sang 'I'll Be Your Baby Tonight' with Judy Collins in 1969; he could sing 'Cry Me a River' and 'Lonesome Whistle Blues'; he could play bluesy harmonica and convincing drum solos; and do fine imitations of Hollywood stars."

Lovely, and true. Check the version of "Lonesome Whistle Blues". In a week where I watched Mumford & Sons' self-regarding documentary, *Big Easy Express* (loosely inspired by *Festival Express*), the ability to inhabit a Hank Williams song is not to be sneezed at. Darin's really there, the young pretenders not even in the same state.

THREE THINKING OF BOBBY DARIN...

I remembered that MAD MAGAZINE's opinion of him was less complimentary. Somewhere I have this issue, but I found what I was looking for on BobbyDarin.net: "In October 1961, the pop culture magazine MAD Magazine introduced a feature entitled 'Celebrities Wallets'. It was drawn by George Woodbridge and

written by Arnie Kogen. The Magazine stated, 'With this article, MAD introduces a new feature, based on the proposition that you can tell an awful lot about a person by the scraps of paper and cards and bills and photographs and money he carries around in his wallet. Since we are all basically nosey, we thought it would be exciting to see what famous people carried around in their wallets. So we sent out a special research team to pick some famous pockets... Bobby Darin was their first subject."

FOUR *EMIL AND THE DETECTIVES*, NT

I know it's a kids' show, but I was one once, and this – well, this was my favourite book. My copy, foxed with age and with its black and white line drawings badly coloured in, is a treasured possession. I was not let down, especially by the extraordinary Expressionist set design and the Weimar-esque pit band, led by Kevin Amos. Their verve, and the wonderful score by Paul Englishby, added immeasurably to the experience. The choreographing of the children, the commuters and the cycling is really clever, and the use of light to create a city and its sewers, breathtaking. If you're around, find an excuse to go...

FIVE **ON THE WAY TO AND FROM** *EMIL*...

In sheet rain, almost vertical, turning the Hungerford footbridge across the Thames into a swimming pool: tuba and melodica, playing "Winter Wonderland". Tuba. Melodica. Now that's a combination. Then a clarinettist, playing only the sax solo from Gerry Rafferty's "Baker Street", but looping it and using the echo to play around himself. Fabulous. I don't know if we were paying them for their inspired choices or their fortitude...

Well, that's a hundred posts reached. Whew! All best to every one of you reading, and have a sterling seasonal sojourn. Back, in some form, in 2014.

Monday, December 31

A few of my favourite things this year.

ONE **WORDS AND MUSIC, BOX, COX & ROBERTS**

Found when moving, the sheet music for "Across the Great Divide". Ghost Riders on the trail of the Lonesome Pine, before fetching up in Woodstock...

TWO **DOUGLAS/ LIBERACE**

In *Behind the Candelabra*, the single most vivid Hollywood performance of last year. "Why do I love you? I love you not only for what you are, but for what I am when I'm with you. I love you not only for what you have made of yourself, but for what you are making of me. I love you for ignoring the possibilities of the fool in me, and for accepting the possibilities of the good in me. Why do I love you? I love you for closing your eyes to the discords in me, and for adding to the music in me by worshipful listening."

THREE DONALD FAGEN, SUBTERRANEAN IN GESTATION, *EMINENT HIPSTERS*

"I must have been about 8 years old when my father, like so many second-generation American dads, decided to get his family the hell out of the city and make a run at upward mobility in the suburbs. After a couple of years and a few false starts, we finally settled into a ranch-style home nestled among hundreds of its near-identical brothers in Kendall Park, New Jersey, a typical housing development circa 1957. The development was not very developed. I was not happy.

Sawdust still hung in the air. To walk out of the sliding glass doors onto the slab of concrete that was the patio and stare across an ocean of mud at one's doppelganger neighbors was, well, awesome. My parents, gazing out the window of the kitchen of the future, delighted in the open space, the gently curving streets and the streamlined look of the cream Olds Dynamic 88 all cosy in its carport. But for me, a subterranean in gestation with a real nasty case of otherness, it was a prison. I'd been framed and sentenced to a long stretch at hard labor in Squaresville."

Fascinating stuff about The Boswell Sisters (check out "We Just Couldn't Say Goodbye") and Henry Mancini, and I'm only a third of the way in.

FOUR FAVOURITE SONG OF THE YEAR

Lorde, "Royals". Synth bass. Beats. No other instruments, just a punchy lead and great backing vox. A top melody. And pop-star skewering lyrics to die for:

"I've never seen a diamond in the flesh / I cut my teeth on wedding rings in the movies / And I'm not proud of my address / In the torn-up town, no postcode envy

But every song's like gold teeth, Grey Goose, trippin' in the bathroom / Bloodstains, ball gowns, trashin' the hotel room...

But everybody's like Cristal, Maybach, diamonds on your timepiece / Jet planes, islands, tigers on a gold leash..."

Followed by her curtly dismissive:

"We don't care, we aren't caught up in your love affair."
Thrilling.

FIVE DAN PENN, "ZERO WILLPOWER"

The *Muscle Shoals* documentary made me listen again to Dan Penn's album *Do Right Man* from 1994. Writer of "The Dark End of The Street" and "Do Right Woman, Do Right Man" among others, Penn recorded the album in the Shoals and it features many of the town's greats. This track was always a favourite, and listening again to the perfectly weighted rhythm section of Roger Hawkins and David Hood – like the suspension on a bridge – to the stately horns and organ, to the helicopter-like tremolo of Reggie Young's guitar, I'm struck by its perfection. Nobody plays more than the song needs, or less than it deserves.

SIX **ROBBIE FULKS, "THAT'S WHERE I'M FROM"**
Bob Dylan said in 1990, "There's enough songs in the world. The world don't need any more songs…" and I knew what he meant. Bob weakened his case, of course, by writing "Love Sick", "High Water (for Charley Patton)" and "Sugar Baby" a few years later. In some genres, you may as well give up – modern country music especially. As the country mainstream does the thing it does every decade or so and flirts with AOR, and the alt-end just gets more singer-songwritery (i.e. like smooth-sounding versions of Lucinda Williams), I didn't expect to find a new Fulks album so moving.

Do I need another acoustic bluegrass 'n' country album? Well, yes. Especially one recorded in three days by Steve Albini in Chicago. Ken Tucker, writing for *npr*, puts it perfectly: "With *Gone Away Backward*, Fulks has made an album that feints in the direction of nostalgia while grappling very much with the here and now. Even for a singer-songwriter known for his clever twists and turns, it's a considerable achievement… It partakes of folk, country, bluegrass and honky-tonk even as the shape of the songs and the content of the lyrics close off much chance of any one of these genres claiming the music as its own."

Fulks had recorded "That's Where I'm From" a few years

back in a more trad arrangement with a band and pedal steel, and it's interesting to compare and see how much deeper the song's become, supported this time round with a couple of guitars, bass and mandolin. A sound that's totally naked – you could be sitting in a room with them. Every note perfectly placed. And a lyric that summons the fantastic "Cosmopolitan Country" of the late 60s, of Tom T. Hall and Tammy and George, as it limns the thoughts of a man far from his past:

"Back in the driveway / The end of the workday / How fast that world disappears
A fresh lawn, a pine tree / A neighbor just like me / Who's worked all his life to get here…"

And he thinks back on…

"Dad doing battle / With dirt hard as gravel / And summers the crops never came
We'd shoot down a pheasant in flight / And sing songs about Jesus all night…"

And the chorus kicks in…

"That's where I'm from / Where time passes slower /
That's where I'm from / Where it's yes ma'am and no sir
You can't tell I'm country / Just you look closer / It's deep in my blood…
A white collar, a necktie / That's where I've come / Half-naked in the moonshine / That's where I'm from…"

Then, after a glorious interlude of guitar interplay, the killer couplet: "If you've ever heard Hank Williams sing / Then, brother, you know the whole blessed thing…"

2014

DON'T STOP ME NOW, I'M HAVING SUCH A GOOD TIME, I'M HAVING A BALL, DON'T STOP ME NOW...

Wednesday, January 7, 2014

ONE **STEVE MCQUEEN,** *LIVE FOR MYSELF,*
ANSWER TO NOBODY **EXHIBITION, TOP FLOOR OF**
THE BERWICK STREET CAR PARK, SOHO

Strange but brilliant exhibition space, although a little too big for this mixed cars 'n' chassis show. Photographer Barry Feinstein was such a great chronicler of a certain strain of '60s and '70s celebrity, and the McQueens are no exception.

From Dave Brolan's introduction to the book of these pics, *Unseen McQueen*: "During his long career, Barry photographed presidents, rock musicians and movie stars. He was always looking for some way to make an interesting picture; for him it was always about the picture, not the subject. When the Beatles played their last ever concert at San Francisco's Candlestick Park in 1966, Barry was there with a movie camera; he needed footage of screaming fans for his movie *You Are What You Eat**. He did not film the Beatles because he 'didn't need them'! Bob Neuwirth, Dylan's confidant and tour manager, told me that of all the people on the 1960s scene, Barry was really the cool one that everyone was drawn to and wanted to hang out with... Lord Buckley [dubbed him] 'His Triple Hip-ness'."
**A film notable for using the Band to back Tiny Tim on "Be My Baby" and "Memphis, Tennessee" for its soundtrack, around the time of the* Basement Tapes. *I think someone (Pauline Kael, maybe) called* You Are What You Eat *"the sort of film about youth that Spiro Agnew might make".*

THREE **GHOSTPOET (OBARO EJIMIWE),**
SIXTY-SECOND QUESTIONNAIRE, *MAKING MUSIC*

Have you got a favourite sound? "I really like the reverb in tunnels. It really inspires me. I live in Dalston, and in Shoreditch there's a tunnel leading from Shoreditch High Street to Liverpool Street. There's sometimes a saxophone player in there. It sounds great."

FOUR **US** *ESQUIRE,* **WHAT I'VE LEARNED**

Gregg Allman: "People always lean toward who's the best guitar player, who's the best singer? I don't see it that way. They're all the best, you know? They've all gotten your attention, you've admired them, you've tried to sing like them. That makes them the best, each and every one of 'em."
Dickey Betts: "I only play slide when I have to. I like to play acoustic slide. I like that. I just... I can do it, you know. But it ain't my cup of tea. I think it was probably standing next to Duane all these years. I mean, he was so damn good at it. Duane used to say, 'I'm not playin' guitar when I play slide. I'm playin' harmonica. I'm thinkin' like a harmonica player.'"

Wednesday, January 15

ONE **"AS THE RADIO SPIT OUT CHARLIE RICH /**
MAN, HE SURE CAN SING, THAT SON OF A BITCH..."
— *Tom Waits, "Putnam County"*
Bob sends me a link to an outstanding piece from the *Oxford*

{THE ALLMAN BROTHERS BAND | "STATESBORO BLUES"}

American's Tennessee Music issue. The writer, Joe Hagen, finds a way to add new things to a story where the subject is not only dead but was heavily profiled (and more) by the peerless Peter Guralnick while alive. He finds a way in through the people who were around Charlie and a suitcase full of fan mail.

Here's a taster: "Williams, his publicist, was charged with motivating him and keeping him off the booze. But the music business seemed to make Charlie miserable. For a magazine profile in 1974, he returned to his old farm in Arkansas to visit CJ, the black field hand who taught him to play piano, joined by Williams, Epic executive Dan Beck, a reporter named Carol Offen, and a female photographer, Raeanne Rubenstein. Offen recalls that Charlie was tortured by his heavy schedule, showing her on his calendar where he'd penciled in 'Make love to Margaret Ann.' The only way to cope with touring, he told her, 'is with pills and booze and that kind of crap—and I don't want to live the rest of my life like that, and why should I?'

"... Visiting CJ at his dilapidated shack in rural Arkansas, Charlie seemed as happy as anybody had seen him, with a 'beatific smile on his face.' CJ, in a blue porkpie hat and suspenders, started fingering the blues on his out-of-tune piano, singing a B.B. King song. 'That's it! That's where you put the hex on me, right there!' Charlie yelled out. 'Now, you talk about some soul!' He told Offen it was the first time he'd relaxed in four years.

"What began as a tightly controlled PR junket soon turned into a beer-soaked misadventure, going from a local house party in the afternoon to a pizza parlor at midnight, where Charlie, getting increasingly smashed, asked that they play the somber 'Feel Like Going Home,' the B side to 'Behind Closed Doors,' on the jukebox over and over again. By 'home,' he didn't mean back in suburban Memphis with Margaret Ann, but on his old property in Colt, Arkansas..."

TWO AND ALSO IN THE SAME ISSUE, RIDING WITH THE KING...

A fantastic reminiscence by Norbert Putnam, Nashville bass player and producer. Here's a taster from that: "I received an unusual phone call from Felton [Jarvis, Elvis's producer]. He was wondering if I could drop by his house and assist him as he brushed the teeth of his pet boa constrictor. This was a job that very few of his friends accepted, but I was appreciative of all the work he sent my way, so I agreed to go over." This leads on to the a weird story of faking a week's worth of overdub sessions on an Elvis album so that The King could impress his new bride, Priscilla. You have to read it to believe it.

THREE ALANNA NASH, IN *VANITY FAIR*, ON A LOVELY PHOTO OF (POSSIBLY) ELVIS AT 15, IN NORTH TUPELO, PUBLISHED FOR THE FIRST TIME

"It's the location of the photo that cinches the deal. The boy in the frame stands at the intersection of North Spring and Jefferson, the epicenter of black and white Tupelo. The establishments on the west side of North Spring—a pool hall, barber

shop, and military surplus store—catered to a mostly black clientele. The businesses to the east—a grocery-and-seafood market, a furniture store—served white customers. [Elvis's old friend Sam] Bell, who still lives nearby, remembers many Saturdays when the block was the busiest spot in town, where some shoppers arrived from the country in horse-drawn wagons."

Wednesday, January 22

ONE **C.C. PHIL SPECTOR!**
Dave sends me this great letter from Paul McCartney to Alan Klein.

14th April, 1970.

A. Klein, Esq.,
Apple Corps Limited,
3 Savile Row,
LONDON, W.1.

Dear Sir,

In future no one will be allowed to add to or subtract from a recording of one of my songs without my permission.

I had considered orchestrating "The Long and Winding Road" but I decided against it. I therefore want it altered to these specifications:

1. Strings, horns, voices and all added noises to be reduced in volume.

2. Vocal and Beatle instrumentation to be brought up in volume.

3. Harp to be removed completely at the end of the song and original piano notes to be substituted.

4. Don't ever do it again.

Signed

PAUL MCCARTNEY

c.c. Phil Spector
John Eastman

TWO **"EVERYBODY WANTS TO RULE THE WORLD"**
By Lorde, from the *Hunger Games: Catching Fire* soundtrack. Things I don't like about this version: the way Ella Maria Lani Yelich-O'Connor sings the word *rule*. Things I do like: everything else.

THREE **"HEY, SUPE, PICK UP ON THIS, MAN... ALL HIGHWAY PATROL SECTIONS. SUSPECT VEHICLE: 1970 DODGE CHALLENGER, WHITE IN COLOUR!"**
Vanishing Point. It's got night, neon and narcotics, and that wonderful ingredient of seventies movies: it looks like it's shot by a photojournalist. Beautiful stills of road vistas, strip towns, old lined faces, the angles of gas stations and wells. It sounds fantastic, the throb of a muscle car engine on heat-haze roads, or cutting arcs in the Nevada Desert to tremolo'd guitar. Banjos frail and sirens wail.

It's got Cleavon Little, two years before *Blazing Saddles*, playing a blind DJ in full flight (The Big Bopper was the model, and Little's performance undoubtedly an influence on Robin Williams in *Good Morning, Vietnam*). It's got Delaney & Bonnie as a Christian rock band at a desert festival. It's got implacable Barry Newman, here reminiscent of James Gandolfini. It's got a race with a customised E-Type Jag, soundtracked by squalling guitars and hi-hats... For two-thirds it's a great film (the

{PAUL MCCARTNEY | "THAT WAS ME"}

flashbacks and hallucinations, not so much). If you liked *Two Lane Blacktop* and *Serpico*, check it out.

FOUR *DALLAS BUYERS CLUB* TRAILER

In the smallest cinema known to man – around twenty seats – and at a bizarre angle to the way-too-close screen, we see two trailers using music to different effect. *The Monuments Men*, a film set in the Second World War, features crashing R&B/hip-hop to try to convince a younger audience that George Clooney and Matt Damon are worth taking a punt on even if, hey, it's all old-fashioned looking and about saving paintings.

Dallas Buyers Club, on the other hand, goes for the stamp of authenticity (if not accuracy – it's set in 1985), using the raw emotion of the Alabama Shakes' "You Ain't Alone" to spill between cuts of Matthew McConaughey giving what looks like his best performance yet. And, dammit, it works.

FIVE "BLUE MOON" IN *BLUE JASMINE*

Woody Allen's music editor must wince every time they start a new film. "Shall I go and get the King Oliver, Mr Allen?" This anachronistic schtick, classic jazz in the present day, got old about twenty years ago – now it's just bizarre, a stylistic tic that means nothing. Yes, I get that Jasmine is a character out of time, Blanche Dubois in a Bernie Madoff world, played by Cate B, acting with a capital A. But bleating on about "Blue Moon" – playing when she met her beau – to a succession of uninterested people is just weird. Added to which, I can't get the image of

Woody Allen sitting in his room writing a character who leaves his wife for a teenage au pair out of my head.

Wednesday, January 29

ONE FOLK MUSIC HAS ANOTHER MOMENT...

A fitting soundtrack to a fascinating documentary, *The Naked Rambler* (some Nick Drake, I think, and Tom Paxton's "Rambling Boy"). The Joan Baez documentary I've not quite finished watching. BBC Four showing Murray Lerner's *Festival* (about the 1963-65 Newport Folk Festivals). The opening of *Inside Llewyn Davis* and the attendant media blitz. And lastly, all the obits for Pete Seeger. Yes, folk's been all over *everything* in the last week or so.

My favourite act in Lerner's film were the amazing Blue Ridge Mountain Dancers, clean-cut college kids looking for all the world like cousins of Buddy Holly and Annette Funicello, high-stepping and twirling, accompanied by Seeger's banjo-playing, to a standing ovation from the crowd.

From BLUERIDGEMOUNTAINDANCERS.COM: "In 1962 from in and around the little mountain town of Hendersonville, NC, the so-called 'Dancingest Little Town in America', a group of teenagers and one adult, 24-year-old James Kesterson, started the Blue Ridge Mountain Dancers."

THREE HAPPY TRAUM ON FOLK MUSIC

Happy: "It seems to me that folk music is a very funny form musically, because it can be easily a kind of dead issue. I think that's the way many people do folk music; when it's put in those terms, it really can lose the vitality that it's supposed to have. So, naturally I'm attracted to people who can take folk songs and make them alive and make them exciting.

"I mean, you could play folk songs with a symphonic orchestra or you can play folk songs with a rock and roll band, but it will very often lose the essence just as much as if somebody's doing an old Burl Ives imitation, which also loses the essence to me.

"But when Ry Cooder plays a folk song, most of the time he keeps the essential things about that music that attracts me to it and yet at the same time adds something which is fresh and different. So that's one of the reasons why I think both he and Taj Mahal are very important. Because they take those old songs and add a life to them." From ROCKSBACKPAGES.COM.

FOUR EXCERPT FROM NEIL YOUNG'S GRAMMY SPEECH (PRODUCERS & ENGINEERS WING)
It's fascinating to hear Neil Young talk about process and technology in such an informed and open way.
"So this is a cool night because we're all here together… A lot of us, you know, producers and engineers – I'm kind of a producer, partially, an engineer, I'm not really good at either one, as anyone who's heard my records can attest. But we're performance-oriented: technical things don't matter that much. That's only one way of making records. A lot of you out here are craftsmen:

beautiful records, and take great care with every note. And I know I'm not one of them. I like to capture the moment. I like to record the moment.

I like to get the first time that I sung the song. **I like to get the first time the band plays the song.**

"So there's a lot of compromises we make to get that feeling, but in the long run, that's where the pictures are when I hear my words and when I see the pictures when I'm listening. So that's what we try to record…

"I love all you people, because I know what you're doing, and the more crazy you are about all the things I don't care about… Sometimes you make great records, and it's fantastic. They're not like my records… Sometimes I can't feel them, but I can really appreciate them.

"No, sometimes I can feel them and I go, 'Holy shit, how did they do that? How did they make that record? I know they layered it – it's not like a documentary where something happens and you took a picture, cinema verité.

"This is a movie: somebody created all the scenes, and they talked, and there was a dialogue, and then they did the dialogue again, and they Foleyed the sound, and they did all the stuff, and everything's perfect – but it's still good.'

"It's just a different way of doing it than I could ever do, because I have so little ability… That's why I'm flat, that's why it doesn't matter that there's bad notes. That doesn't mean it's not production – it just means it's the kind of production we do.

"Some people are here tonight that I've worked with over the ages that are just really incredible people. Al Schmitt's here tonight... [Schmitt had recently recorded Dylan's album of standards, *Shadows in The Night*] because he's the father of what's going on here, and he's still here.

"And he was recording a way that I want to record now, and I'm going to make a record with Al – we're talking about making a record together where there's only one mic, but we are doing it with a huge orchestra.

"We're not going to mix it, we're going to do it and mix it while we do it. Everybody can get in the right place, and if it's not right – well, we'll move the bass closer. It's not loud enough? Move the amp closer, then! It sounds good, but it's just too quiet, so move it up. Or if it's a string, move it in. And the drums? Leave it over there, go back farther. OK, good. Thanks. Do you know how much fun that is to do? That is so much fun. It's like playing music – it's not making music, it's playing it...

"The thing we do is, we create great stuff in the studio and then we just kiss its ass goodbye. Nobody's ever going to hear it. That's unfortunate, and it didn't used to be that way. That's something that happened to us – that's an injury we've sustained, and it deeply hurt us.

"So the time has come for us to recover and to bring music back to the people in a way that they can recognize it in their souls – through the window of their souls, their ears."

So they can feel and vibrate and so that they can get goosebumps. We cherish those fucking goosebumps. We really need those."

FIVE **SOME NON-FOLK: I WALKED BETWEEN THE RAINDROPS...**

...to work, eschewing my usual Boris Bike, and "Day Dream", the Ellington/Strayhorn song on Allen Toussaint's *The Bright Mississippi* album, sneaked into my earphones. It's really something, and I'd never properly listened to it before – Joshua Redman on burnished tenor duetting with Toussaint's exquisite piano. It makes time stand still as I walk past a hundred people standing in the rain in Rathbone Place, victims of a fire alarm drill. It comes to an end as I cross the coffee shop threshold, usurped by Thin Lizzy's "The Boys Are Back in Town" as I stand in line behind Ian Hislop and Andy Hamilton catching up with one another.

NB: from Michael Hill's liner notes on Nonesuch Records' website: Apparently, Redman nailed his solo on the first take. Toussaint praises Redman's "beautiful tone. I'd love to catch him on a street corner somewhere. And everyone was hip to him much more than I was. When I told my son about him, he said, 'Oh yes, he's the bomb.' And my son was right. Joshua is a marvelous musician. He's finely tuned to what he's looking for in his sound; he doesn't accept stock."

Wednesday, February 5

TWO THAT DYLAN-CHRYSLER-SUPERBOWL-HALFTIME AD

"So let Germany brew your beer, let Switzerland make your watch, let Asia assemble your phone… we will build your car." In the era of globalisation let's not forget that Chrysler is an Italian-owned car company. I was pleased to discover Jody Rosen's blog on *New York* magazine's website. He was terrific on the Grammies, and great on this:

"As Dylan, age 72, moves into the twilight, he can see the boldface obituaries, rearing up on the horizon: 'BOB DYLAN, AMERICA'S GREAT PROTEST SINGER, DEAD.' There is clearly nothing on earth that irks Bob Dylan more than the specter of those wrongheaded and inevitable headlines. Dylan hasn't recorded a protest song in decades, but make no mistake: The car ad and the yogurt ad, they're protests."

Of course, lots of people thought this a ridiculous, untenable position, and Conan O'Brien did a very funny uncut version. But, visually slapdash as the ad is, I like the way that, as Dylan says "cool", it runs into the motorcycle revving along the highway.

THREE "AS I WALKED OUT TONIGHT IN THE MYSTIC GARDEN / THE WOUNDED FLOWERS WERE DANGLING FROM THE VINE"

Hugh sends a link to a great blog: *Gardening with Bob Dylan*, "Written by a working gardener, with regular updates, easy ideas and thinking aloud. I have a garden of my own in Kent on clay soil and in a droughty area. I have recently acquired another, in Piemonte, Italy, higher and more continental in climate. I'm female and not very young. Other enthusiasms are garden literature and Bob Dylan. He has something to say about everything, even gardening."

From the *About* page: "I'm no kind of aesthetic theoretician. But I have always believed that a successful piece of art will finger the synapses of your brain and your emotions together, setting up sparks between them. With luck you get a multiplicity of resonances, bouncing around, throwing light on both the world and yourself in it.

"For me, that is what Dylan does; it's not just music and singing, it's an open act of creation which you, the listener, have a hand in and a responsibility for. You have to listen. You have to concentrate. You develop meaning together with the singer and your own understanding of the world.

"To be more prosaic, you need new thoughts as you work in a garden; otherwise you're going round and round the yearly practices, the endlessly repeated nuggets of advice. I like those thoughts to open and widen the vista in the mind, to go beyond the plant or the material, or the practice. To join things up, to express something beyond themselves, to be part of life. Let me out of the fenced enclave, however beautiful! Dylan's songs will always lead me somewhere. They'll connect me up, charm or amuse me, and lead me back to myself again, to what I'm doing, or what I care about. So I write my posts carefully, sticking to one song each time and enjoying the challenge of tying the song to a gardening preoccupation, or the lessons I have learnt in many years of making gardens."

FIVE "EVERYTHING DIES, BABY, THAT'S A FACT..."
Levon Helm, singing "Atlantic City", in *Ain't in It for My Health*, a documentary where mortality weighs heavy as we follow Levon going to a variety of specialists for invasive procedures as he puts together his final album, *Electric Dirt*. Some thoughts:

1) It's fascinating to see Larry Campbell struggle with Levon's anger. "I would go out on that Grammy night if they could tell me what good it's gonna do for Rick and Richard... They never wanted to do a thing for 'em when they'se around."

2) There's a fine version of Randy Newman's "Kingfish" with Levon on funky acoustic rhythm guitar.

3) And as eloquent a summation of what the Band meant as I've ever heard, from Barney Hoskyns.

4) Levon's great memories of the Woodstock Festival: "Fortunately I'd taken some of that brown acid!" he cackles.

5) Does anyone else remember Jesus, thinner-than-thin with long straight hair? Always shedding his clothes to dance at the Marquee or Reading or the free concerts in the park? More often than not, he was there. And appearing here, in some Wembley '74 footage of the Band playing "Chest Fever".

6) "In the Pines", played to his new grandchild. Starting as a lullaby, it gets more and more intense as it goes on. As Levon plays his Gibson mandolin, a montage plays of him drumming through the ages. "The best seat in the house" he'd say, as he tub-thumps behind Ronnie Hawkins in the Hawks, behind Dylan in '65 and '74, and in the Band. The baby's mother, Levon's daughter Amy, can't stop herself from joining in.

Wednesday, February 19

ONE A GIFT FROM BOB & SANDY
In which stunning clay figures mash the Day of the Dead with celebrity icons. Name all six, Win A Prize!

TWO PRINCE'S PLECTRUM FROM HIS FIRST VISIT TO LONDON, 1981

As Prince plays small gigs in the capital, from front rooms in Leyton to the offices of The Guardian, *a look back…*

I knew of Prince because my friend Mick had given me *Prince*, the album. I was working in my first job at the *Radio Times* and went to the Lyceum show with two friends from work, Sue and Ruby. I remember it being virtually empty, as there hadn't been much publicity. It was the *Dirty Mind* band of Andre Cymone on bass, Lisa Coleman and Matt Fink on keyboards, Bobby Z on drums and Dez Dickerson on guitar. The keyboardists were disguised (Matt Fink had some kind of radiation suit on) and the frontline wore underwear and trench coats. Quite mad.

It was a spectacular show, with Prince's guitar playing outstanding, and they went down a storm with the few hundred people there (mostly music-biz types, I think). I was right at the front (well, the whole audience were, actually) and close enough to catch Prince's plectrum.

I have a memory of Prince being bad-tempered, not with the audience but at the empty hall. He stomped off at the end, throwing his pick rather petulantly… and cancelled the rest of the tour. I recently read the brilliant Ian Penman on this gig. He hated it. Really, really hated it. See for yourself in this cut-down excerpt [I know I shouldn't, but it is pretty long]:

"For a wolverine habituee of the sharper clubs and bars of our capital such as myself, this tawdry 'gig' was something like a step into the horrors of Hieronymus Bosch from the accustomed gilt-edged decadent sumptuousness of Klimt! The dry ice and fright lights – whose calculated effect is undermined and rendered pretty pathetic by way of the Lyceum's half-emptiness – turn out to be a good index of the Prince live repertoire's ancient grasp of sub-cultural subtlety: the plot doesn't thicken, it keeps its consistency. Heavy, stodgy, overdone, tasteless, lacking in spice or space – you get the picture?

'Outfront', Prince prances in unison with his two guitar cohorts – they walk it like they talk it, as the saying goes, every song split down the middle or battered to bed with the tedious exaggeration of third-rate Heavy Metal. Someone remarked to me the next day that oh, you know what these young chaps are like with their Hendrix fixations.

Hendrix? It never began to shimmer with a hint of the historical avant-shapelessness or spirited slipstreams or sexual harangues of a Hendrix! My two fellow funkateers and I unanimously elected to wander away from the endlessly guitar wrenching spectacle after about half an hour – we didn't really even 'walk out'; it was more of an embarrassed shuffle."

I, on the other hand, was obviously taken in by the dry ice and the third-rate Heavy Metal. I still am.

THREE ANNIE CLARK REVIEW, FROM OUR FRENCH CORRESPONDENT, STEVE WAY

"St Vincent was awesome at La Cigale – small theatre venue, great fun – she has the arty moves, channeling a deranged Barbie rock android. Did the whole gig, including climbing steps, on high heel strappy black pixie boots. Fiona most impressed."

FIVE OH, AND I THOUGHT I MIGHT WRITE ABOUT THE SOUL-SAPPING BRITS...

... but *Every Record Tells a Story* does it better. Except he fails to mention the strange absence of any discernible talent in Ellie Goulding, Kate Moss's voice (don't speak, don't break the illusion), the pitiful MasterCard plinth, Pharell's Club Tropicana trousers (I said he'd look back in six months and rue the day, but Miche pointed out that six hours might be more accurate), and the absurd bigging-up of host James Corden by most of the bands (why? He was so poor). OK, that's it.

Wednesday, February 26

ONE *OF TIME AND THE CITY*

I caught twenty minutes of Terence Davies's great half documentary / half memoir, his love letter to Liverpool. From the Korean War footage, overlaid by the Hollies' "He Ain't Heavy, He's My Brother" – a mixture that shouldn't work, but does – through Terry's hilariously voiced-over *Yeah Yeah Yeah*s when the Beatles come on-screen, to the stunning slum clearance / building of the tower-blocks sequence set to Peggy Lee singing "The Folks Who Live on the Hill", it never fails to move.

JASON WOOD: "The film shows you a Liverpool beyond the Beatles and football, which is what people tend to think about when they think about the city. Your narration is very significant. It lends character because it is so impassioned."

TERENCE DAVIES: "What was odd was that I was writing this commentary as I was doing it and recording it as a rough guide. We got someone to do part of the narration, but it just didn't work and the producers said, 'No, you must do it.' I was worried that when you hear your own voice, it can sound a bit like the Queen Mother after she died. All my films have strong Liverpool accents. It always makes me feel a bit embarrassed...

"At one point they asked me to put in how I lost my accent and I said, 'You can't be serious? You really can't be serious? I'm not doing that.' I was worried, and I was staying with my sister Maisie and I said, 'When did I lose my accent?' and she said, 'You never had one!'

"I have no illusions about my work but I must add I have no illusions about anybody else's either. I am very strict with myself and I think, 'No, that could have been improved.' It was what I thought was right at the time – and you have to stand by that. And if it completely fails, you have got to say, 'But that is what I meant at the time.' There's a line by Vaughan Williams – I think it's on his *Sixth Symphony* – when he says, 'I don't know whether I like it, but it is what I meant.' And that's a wonderful thing to say upon your own work."

TWO **TIM SENDS A LINK**

...to Postmodern Jukebox's rather lovely twenties-styled version of "Sweet Child O' Mine", perhaps inspired by Bryan Ferry's take on his back catalogue. "My goal with Postmodern Jukebox is to get my audience to think of songs not as rigid, ephemeral objects, but like malleable globs of Silly Putty. Songs can be twisted, shaped, and altered without losing their identities – just as we grow, age, and expire without losing ours – and it is through this exploration that the gap between 'high' and 'low' art can be bridged most readily." – *Scott Bradlee, founder.*

Well, OK, Scott! File alongside the Ukulele Orchestra of Great Britain and Pink Martini. Oh, and the Sad-Faced-Clown version of "Royals" rocks, too.

THREE **A QUOTE I REALLY LIKED**

Laura Barton talking to Willy Vlautin, singer/guitarist with Richmond Fontaine: "We're sitting in an empty London pub, where the clipped twang of Vlautin's Nevada accent seems to lift the gloom. 'I've used escapism as a crutch my whole life,' he says. 'I hated being a kid, so I escaped. But I never thought of myself as a rich guy driving a Cadillac... I was pragmatic. My big dream was to have an uncle that owned a wrecking yard and then I could just work there, and he'd actually like me and he'd make me dinner. And I would live in that fantasy world. I'd wake up every morning and check in.'"

He'd actually like me and he'd make me dinner... That's a line that could make you cry.

FOUR **LIVE MUSIC EXTRA:**

1) BAND OF GOLD. Dotter scolds me for not mentioning her "awesome" wedding band. And it's true. I was so tired after the wedding I could barely think what to say. The band (*Jazz. Nice.*) was put together by Mike Pointon, who I collaborated with on Ken's book [*Goin' Home*], alongside Ray Smith. It was made up of musicians who had played with Ken Colyer (Mike, since he was nineteen), supported by sons of Ken's peers on drums and bass. They really swung.

One guest, bowled over, assumed they'd been together for years, and at the end asked Mike how long "The Lavender Hill Mob" (the venue was on said hill) had played as a unit, and Mike answered, "About three hours." The acoustics were great, the sound of the musicians tight and warm, and the repertoire wide-ranging. Even when they were playing softly during the meal, people were applauding the solos. I've never seen that happen at a wedding before.

2) JAZ DELOREAN AT THE ALLEYCAT. At the *Iko's Record Shop* night, it was Lee Dorsey time, the highlight of which was Dom Pipkin's wonderful re-imagining of "Working in the Coal Mine", in which he left the rhythm section behind and proceeded to conjure up all sorts in a trance-like meditation. I heard Scott Walker, Stravinsky, Booker, and Dr John before he got back on the straight and narrow...

The evenings are always fairly ramshackle, with misses and hits, but there's usually something like this to treasure. Jaz

for that matter. Allergic to songs." A pretty succinct description, if you ask me, and their first gig doesn't disappoint. I'm a sucker for funk drumming and trem-bar harmonics / histrionics, and they sound wonderful together in this blanket-covered demobbed bunkhouse, playing forty minutes without a safety net. Tom has a lovely line in, er, tom/cymbal interfacing, and it's always fun listening to Mark (below) trying to avoid anything as shocking as a melody.

Headliners Horseless Headmen were tight and fascinating. Stand up, G. Painting (guitar, effects king), Paul Taylor (trombone, fabulous tone), Nick Cash (drum kit and percussion, check out the upside-down water bottle) and Ivor Kallin (fretless bass guitar and chopsticks in beard). I love a gig that almost

Delorean (above) delivered my favourite band performance with a terrific take on Louis Prima's medley of "Just a Gigolo / I Ain't Got Nobody" on the crowded, tiny stage, featuring fabulously sleazy horns and a winning vocal from the guitarist (with the crowd on the chorus). Anyone trying to get to the women's bathroom had to run the gauntlet of the four horn players (and an accordionist) who couldn't actually fit on the stage.

3) AVANT-IMPROV AT THE HARRISON. Mark and Tom describe their band, Throttling Tommy, as "the unlistenable in pursuit of the unplayable. A blues-rock power trio without the Marshall stacks and the bass player, who hasn't turned up. And who have forgotten how to play blues. Or rock. Or anything else,

ends when an audience member shouts as an improvisation closes, "That was brilliant! You'll never top that!" and the band actually have a discussion about whether playing another number (which there's time for) is a hostage to fortune...

FIVE FROM OUR WOODSTOCK CORRESPONDENT

JOHN CUNEO REPORTS: "Saw Prince a few times myself. Once in Denver he came out while Vanity 6 was setting up, sat down at a piano to the side of the stage and played for half an hour. No mic, just for himself. The most mind-boggling stuff. We were up front and close enough to hear. If memory serves, I believe the Time came up after Vanity and before Prince. One of the funkiest nights of my life. I was levitating."

Wednesday, March 5

ONE WHAT'S NOT TO LOVE? OR KILL?

Looking for, I don't know, some picture of something, I noticed a few really interesting images come up in my Google search, and that they belonged to a blog, *Murder Ballad Monday*. I've only just begun to delve into it, but if the post devoted to Norah Jones's "Miriam" is anything to go by, it's riveting. Highly recommended. A few weeks ago I caught NJ doing the revenge songs from the album this song was on, produced by Brian "Danger Mouse" Burton, on Sky Arts' *Live from the Artists Den*. Standing at the keys, she had an intensity at odds with her rep and a terrific band to boot.

TWO THE GRIT STAYS IN THE PICTURE

Why do so few documentary makers retouch or clean up or adjust the exposure of the photographs they use? *Studio City*, a really likeable doc about the Van Nuys, Los Angeles, studio where Buckingham Nicks met Fleetwood Mac and Nirvana recorded *Nevermind* is particularly bad on the Lo-res/Over-exposed/Scratch scale. I understand if you can't source the originals easily, but the amount of "shit on the blanket" (as the printers used to say) was catastrophic. I could barely concentrate on the talking heads for exclaiming each time another '80s promo pic or candid studio Polaroid covered in gunk was lovingly panned over.

THREE ACCENT – UP THERE WITH MERYL STREEP!

André Benjamin catches Jimi's voice amazingly well in *All Is by My Side*. And I'm not ashamed to say I'm really looking forward to this.

FOUR TWO PARAGRAPHS...

from a lovely post on Robbie Fulks' website about flying / snow/ grandfathers / children/ rock clubs and Fats Waller...
"I must admit that I have had it with rock clubs. Airports have their hassles and troublesome personnel. But after navigating through them, something definite happens: you get from one place to another. After navigating the shoals of silliness at a rock club, you're right where you started: obscure, penniless, and a little sad.

It seems to me that the daily operational grind of these places – wiping down last night's spilled drinks and body fluids with strong bleach, stocking the bar, transporting in the sound man and one dozen other miserably paid mortals, hauling in the drums and other big pieces, setting up hospitality, sound-checking, and so on up to load-out – is not commensurate to the social value of the service, which is to let young people exhibit their talents (usually imaginary) to an audience (also known as a handful of acquaintances cajoled and shamed into coming) in a professional production environment (!), so that the act can ultimately gain enough of a toehold, through multiple appearances in these disreputable sick wards, to climb to a height in the music firmament from which it can create artistic works in financial security and perform for acres of ecstatic consumers, forevermore, amen (and for this pipe-dream, there is no number of parenthesized exclamation points equal to the author's derision)."

Wednesday, March 12

TWO JAZZ NAMES

In a pile of things, I find the launch issue of *The Rocking Vicar*, Mark Ellen's pre-*Word* "magazine", which grew out of an early email newsletter. My favourite nugget is David Quantick's Jazz Names: adding your dad's nickname to the place you live. Mine at this time? Bilco Fitzrovia. Send in more!

FOUR CARLA JEAN WHITLEY CALLS...

and she's writing a book on Muscle Shoals, and she's found a picture that I took of the sign, "Welcome To City of Muscle Shoals, Hit Recording Capital of the World" [SEE PAGE 172]. Looking for images for her, I find my favourite picture, of Heather and the great bass player Bob Wray, recording at 1000 Alabama Avenue, and this business card from Barry Beckett that I didn't know I had.

Rewatching the film on BBC Four, I found myself wishing for less of the Singing River stuff, waaaaay less of Bono (he ever record there? No. His music influenced much by what was recorded there? No.) and for much more music. What was there was fantastic, especially the Wilson Pickett sessions (love the look on Roger Hawkins' face when he recalls Pickett complimenting him on his drumming) and, of course, Spooner at the Wurlitzer playing those immortal chords...

Wednesday, March 19

ONE SAMMY RIMINGTON, MARTIN WHEATLEY, CUFF BILLETT, VIC PITT, CHRIS BARBER, KENNY MILNE, CAMBERLEY CRICKET CLUB

An unprepossessing room, but a great evening, with music ranging from New Orleans to St Louis and New York, via Hawaii (for Martin Wheatley's cracking solo performance of "Laughing Rag"). Hadn't seen Chris play for years, but nice to get a chance to thank him for his contributions to British & Ameri-

can music. And lovely to make the acquaintance of Martin, too modest to tell me that he was part of the Bryan Ferry Orchestra, but keen to share a love of Hawaiian guitarists in general and Roy Smeck, the "Wizard of the Strings", in particular.

TWO WHISTLE TEST '70s CALIFORNIA SPECIAL

Two highlights (apart from the obvious ones – Little Feat's "Rock 'n' Roll Doctor" and James Taylor's pellucid, almost weightless, guitar playing): JD Souther doing "Doolin-Dalton" with the accompaniment of a bass player who switched to piano for the bridge and coda, playing beautifully... just a shame that JD wasn't handsome enough to join the Eagles, eh? And Ry Cooder's fantastic take on Sleepy John Estes' "Goin' to Brownsville" with quite the most violent mandolin playing ever committed to video.

FOUR MY NEW FAVOURITE BLOG: *MY HUSBAND'S STUPID RECORD COLLECTION*

"Alex and I have lived together for 9 years. In those 9 years we have packed up, moved and unpacked his record collection 5 times. It's about 15 boxes, about 1500 records – "that includes the singles and stuff, which you're also going to have to review" is what Alex just said to me from the other room.

"This project was my idea, inspired by maybe one too many glasses of wine last weekend, when I was in charge of changing the music... Here are the rules I've set for myself. Start with the A's... Listen to the entire thing even if I really hate it. And make sure to comment on the cover art. Are you with me? Let's see how far I can go."

Two excerpts: "There is an article by Ralph J. Gleason on the back cover of this album called *Perspectives: The Death of Albert Ayler* which is very good and making me wish I liked this music more. Maybe it's an acquired taste. While I already knew that this type of jazz existed, this is probably my first time listening to an entire album of it all the way through and intentionally."

"I really love these liner notes. For the song 'We All Love Peanut Butter' by the One Way Streets it says: 'One hot summer day in 1966, two mom-driven station wagons pulled up outside Sunrise Studios in Hamilton, Ohio and out piled 4 insane teens. While their moms set up a table on the lawn outside and played bridge and drank lemonade, the One Way Streets were inside the studio shredding their way through 2 songs they felt would create a major disturbance. As a finishing touch to their wild afternoon, they ripped off an eighty-dollar mike on their way out the door and haven't been heard of since.' Every single detail about that anecdote makes me very, very happy."

FIVE "HATE" IS A STRONG WORD, TIM CHIPPING, *HOLY MOLY*, THURSDAY, MARCH 13

Just when you thought New Zealand singing teenager Lorde could do no wrong, she goes and upsets reggae fans. Lorde somewhat confusingly wrote on her blog: "I hate Reggae, Reggae makes me feel like I am late for something." She's not welcome at the offices of newspaper the *Jamaica Star*.

Writing in the paper's *Roun' Up* section, columnist Keisha says: "International artiste Lorde say she hate reggae music. Everybody nuh haffi like everything but HATE is a very strong word. Lorde, you always look like Smeagol from *Lord of the Rings*. You always look like you a have seizure when you deh pon stage a try move you crawny body. If you need fi HATE anything, you need fi HATE you age paper. A nuh our fault say you a 17 and look like 3 million. A nuh our fault say you caan sing live. Gwaan from ya, Miss One Hit Wonder."

Would anyone mind if we spent the rest of the day saying "gwaan from ya"?

Wednesday, March 26

ONE **IT'S NEW ALBUM DISPLAY WEEK AT 5 THINGS!** These may be my favourite two album covers, ever. Jimmy Reed's a study in perfect fifties still-life, and Blind Blake (or rather, Blake Alphonso Higgs, not Blind Blake the bluesman) looks like some proto-Neville Brody illustration (if you

remember his illustrated 12-inch singles from the '80s, that is). The guitar neck and peghead is fantastic, and the fingers are a little like Robert Johnson...

TWO CHECK OUT THE WONDERFULLY NAMED *DUST & GROOVES*

You could spend a lot of time on the DUST & GROOVES website. This week I found the interview with record (and music ephemera) collector Jeff Gold, and there's much to enjoy here. Dig Jimi's personal album collection, the Rolling Stones' eponymous debut album – "the first pop album with no type on the cover, thanks to their innovative manager, Andrew Loog Oldham" – and the great see-through Faust album, which I remember owning (and liking for the cover more than the music) but can no longer find! Be sure to catch the bizarre German cover for David Bowie's *The Man Who Sold the World*, which folds out to a two-foot circle...

FOUR FROM THE BLOG WITH *JUST A HINT OF MAYHEM*

"Don't you just love Elton John's 'Bennie and the Jets' from his 1973 double album *Goodbye Yellow Brick Road*? I certainly do. I knew that it wasn't a live recording but the applause included on the track makes it sound as though it is. Did you know that the applause wasn't even recorded at an Elton gig? In fact it is drawn from recordings of the audience clapping and shouting at Jimi Hendrix's Isle of Wight festival set in 1970. I know of another occasion where that kind of thing has happened too. The sound of the crowd used on the title track of David Bowie's *Diamond Dogs* album is actually the applause taken from a live album by the Faces... Can any of you offer any similar gems?"

FIVE A LITTLE MORE *LLEWYN DAVIS*

Llewyn Davis has become our background music of choice over the last few months. I'm not sure why, as the album is not consistently good (in fact, I think the best things on it are Dave Van Ronk's "Green Green Rocky Road" and Dylan's "Farewell", the only original tracks) but it creates a great mood. So a few more *ILD* bits:

1) ANNIE CHARTERS: I wanted to know what Annie thought of the film and was pleased that both she and Sam loved it, while realising that it, of necessity, played loose with the truth of actual life in the village in 1962. Sam produced *Inside Dave Van Ronk* for Prestige (apparently the cat was only there for a couple of frames as the cover was shot, but it was enough for the Coens), with Blue Note legend Rudy Van Gelder as engineer, which I hadn't known.

Annie took the lovely pic of Terri Thal and Dave on a Village rooftop. She said that she and Sam were both mouth-agape at the re-creation of Moe Asch's office (where he offers Llewyn Davis a coat instead of royalties). Apparently the walls really were covered with terrible paintings that Moe was convinced were priceless, and he left some to Sam and Ann in his will.

2) OSCAR ISAAC: "Here's a crazy story. I was doing this really small movie and there was this guy in the scene – he was an extra, he's in his sixties and he's playing a drunk in a bar. There was this guitar just sitting there on the set, and in between takes he picked it up and started playing. So I asked him what his story was, and he said that he was a guitar player

from New York. So I told him that I had this audition coming up and that the part was based a little bit on Dave Van Ronk. So he says that he played with Dave Van Ronk.

And then he told me to come by his place, and I asked him where that was and he told me that he lived above the Gaslight on MacDougal Street and that he'd lived there since the seventies. It was like this time capsule. He had these stacks

{DAVE VAN RONK | "DID YOU HEAR JOHN HURT?"}

of records and guitars all over the place. And he doesn't start playing Dave Van Ronk, he starts playing the stuff that Dave Van Ronk was listening to, like the Reverend Gary Davis and Lightnin' Hopkins.

And then he introduced me to Dave Van Ronk's widow. And this was all before the audition. So I felt this... was meant to be. So then I started playing with him. I'd go along to coffee houses and open up for him and we would share the basket. And that really immersed me in the whole scene and allowed an organic folk sound to come out."

3) RICHARD WILLIAMS: "I've seen it a couple of times and was impressed by the faithful portrayal of the Greenwich Village folk scene as it prepared for the transition from Pete Seeger to Bob Dylan (although, as a friend pointed out, nobody tied a scarf with a loop in the way Oscar Isaac, who plays Davis, does until about ten years ago)."

EXTRA! **GOODBYE CARD FROM ILLUSTRATOR DAN MITCHELL...**

...as I leave my job. Thanks, Dan!

Wednesday, April 2

ONE OXFAM REMEMBERS THE GREAT SKIP JAMES, MARYLEBONE HIGH STREET

TWO JESSE WINCHESTER: NOT DARK YET

...although news travelled around that it was. Looked out his great first album, on Ampex (a tape manufacturer's short-lived attempt to run a record label), and listened again to a fine set of songs, helped along by Robbie Robertson's light-handed production. And what now seems an envelope-pushing fold-out sleeve...

THREE LOVED THIS PATTI SMITH QUESTIONNAIRE

Favourite song that no one else has heard of: "The song that I think of is 'If I Can't Have You' by Etta and Harvey. Etta James used to sing with Harvey Fuqua and it's an awesome song. No one knows about it – I've asked a million people, do you know this song by Etta and Harvey? And there's just something so... it's a very sensual... it's a badass song!"

Etta was really nonpareil... Check the elongated "I" just before a minute in, and the "Well-a-hooo" that Harvey follows with. Sensational. And in the week that my sister-in-law gives birth to a baby girl called Etta, most appropriate.

FOUR LUNCH WITH SAMMY & LOUISE RIMINGTON

1970 Jazz Fest poster, bass drum in the basement (with a calf-skin head that Sammy had fitted), Sammy playing his 1982 Fender Telecaster Elite (a commercially unsuccessful attempt

to do a Fender version of a Gibson Les Paul Recording model) and the mandolin that Sammy will take to this year's Jazz Fest for his string band with Sava Venet.

Wednesday, April 9

ONE I GOT THOSE OL' SUBCOMITTEE BLUES AGAIN

"As thousands take their seats Thursday night at New York's Barclays Center to watch Kiss, Cat Stevens and other artists be inducted into the Rock and Roll Hall of Fame," writes Marc Myers in *The Wall Street Journal*, "Cecil 'Big Jay' McNeely will be preparing dinner in his one-bedroom apartment in the Baldwin Hills section of central Los Angeles. In the late 1940s and early '50s, Mr. McNeely helped pioneer rock 'n' roll. His wailing blues saxophone and feverish R&B concerts set new showmanship standards for many rockers who followed—including Little Richard, Elvis Presley, Jerry Lee Lewis and James Brown. He also helped integrate R&B, paving the way for rock's mass-market ascendancy in the second half of the 1950s...

"'Having more early R&B artists inducted would be great, but ultimately it's the decision of the subcommittee,' said Rock and Roll Hall of Fame Foundation president and CEO Joel Peresman. 'Then their recommendation needs to garner enough votes among nominating-committee members to get on the ballot.'" That last sentence on Big Jay McNeely's omission from the Rock and Roll Hall of Fame makes you question the very notion of a Rock and Roll Hall of Fame, doesn't it?

TWO "AND THE AUDIENCE LAUGHED AT LESTER MADDOX, TOO"

Bob G. sends me a link to a site where eloquent strippers talk about music and politics, and one of the choices leads me to this discovery about Lester Maddox. As Wikipedia says: "Maddox's name... appears in the opening lines of Randy Newman's song 'Rednecks' in allusion to his appearance on *The Dick Cavett Show*:

'Last night I saw Lester Maddox on a TV show / With some smart-ass New York Jew / And the Jew laughed at Lester Maddox / And the audience laughed at Lester Maddox too. / Well, he may be a fool but he's our fool...'"

He was a populist Democrat and a staunch segregationist, refusing to serve black customers in his Atlanta restaurant in defiance of the Civil Rights Act. Amazingly, Maddox was the seventy-fifth governor of Georgia (from '67 to '71). After his 1974 gubernatorial bid, and with his political career seemingly over and with massive debts, Maddox began a short-lived nightclub comedy career in 1977 with an African-American musician, Bobby Lee Fears, who had worked as a busboy in his restaurant.

Sears had served time in prison for a drug offence before Maddox, as lieutenant governor, was able to assist him in obtaining a pardon. Calling themselves "The Governor and His Dishwasher", the duo performed comedy bits built around musical numbers, with Maddox on harmonica and Fears on guitar. Truth, truly stranger than fiction.

THREE DUKE FAKIR, FOUR TOPS SINGER, HOW WE MADE "REACH OUT, I'LL BE THERE"

From *The Guardian*: "We were all in the studio one day when Holland-Dozier-Holland said they wanted to try something experimental. They had this thumping backing track played by the Funk Brothers – it had an amazing drum beat created by timpani mallets hitting a tambourine. The sound was fabulous, but then Eddie said they wanted Levi Stubbs [the Four Tops' lead singer] to do Bob Dylan-type singing over it. Levi was uncomfortable at first. He said: 'I'm a singer. I don't talk or shout.' But we worked on it for a couple of hours, recording it in pieces, talking part after talking part.

"Eddie realised that when Levi hit the top of his vocal range, it sounded like someone hurting, so he made him sing right up there. Levi complained, but we knew he loved it. Every time they thought he was at the top, he would reach a little further until you could hear the tears in his voice. The line 'Just look over your shoulder' was something he threw in spontaneously. Levi was very creative like that, always adding something extra from the heart. The finished song didn't sound like the Four Tops. We just assumed it was some experimental thing that would go on an album.

"A few weeks later, Motown boss Berry Gordy sent us a memo: 'Make sure your taxes are taken care of – because we're going to release the biggest record you've ever had.' He called us into his office, and I remember one of us asking: 'So when are we going to record this great song?' He said: 'You already have.' We're all

thinking: 'Huh?' Then he played 'Reach Out' and we said: 'Hold on, Berry, we were just experimenting. Please don't release that as a single. It's not us. It has a nice rhythm to it, but if you release that we'll be on the charts with an anchor.' He laughed, but we left the meeting feeling very upset, almost angry.

"I was out driving when I heard the song on the radio for the first time. It hit me like a lead pipe. I turned my car round and drove right back to Berry's office. He was in a meeting but I opened the door and just said: 'Berry, don't ever talk to us about what you're releasing. Just do what you do. Bye.'"

FOUR MISTAKEN WALL PAINTING. DON'T HOLD THE FRONT PAGE

I was waiting in the car, when the sunlight drew me to something on the wall at the end of our street. And in one of those "doesn't that look like the face of Jesus in my burnt tortilla?" moments, I thought it was a version of the cover of The Band. I know – mad. What it actually is: the number £29,000. Which in itself is quite strange…

FIVE RONNIE SCOTT'S JOOK JOINT

Reading *A London Year* (a compilation of diary entries for each day drawn from myriad sources), I come upon this, written on March 27, 1776, by Edward Oxnard: "In the evening went to Drury Lane to hear the Oratorio of the Messiah. It is impossible for me to express the pleasure I received. My mind was elevated to that degree, that I could almost imagine that I was being wafted to the mansions of the blest. There were more than a hundred performers, the best in England."

I knew how he felt as I sat in the best seat in the house [*thanks H+E!*] and listened to Ronnie's super-talented MD James Pearson lead his house band through a soul-heavy set that was flatly astonishing. If you'd asked me beforehand if I wanted to hear "Proud Mary", I'd have politely declined. What could anyone bring to that karaoke warhorse, written by John Fogarty and pummeled into the ground by Tina Turner?

I reckoned without Michelle Jones and a band who played everything with taste and feeling. It's hard to know where to start. The first half had been the Alex Garnett quartet with Dave Jones on bass, fleet fingered but mountainously funky, Pearson on keys and Elliott Henshaw on drums, moving from the twenties to the seventies, jazz-wise, with ease. The same musicians became the nucleus of the band for the second set, joined by a five-piece horn section featuring, joy of joys, a baritone sax.

They also added three terrific singers and the sensational Adam Goldsmith, fresh from essaying every guitar style known to man in the *Voice* house band. A medley of Cop Theme Tunes was followed by a perfect "Night Train", hot horns to the fore. There was so much to enjoy here, especially Goldsmith's Curtis Mayfield–style licks wrapping around Polly Gibbons's sultry vocal on Ray Charles's "What Would I Do Without You?" and his angry soloing on "I'd Rather Go Blind", counterpointing Michelle Jones.

I could have watched Elliott Henshaw all night. I had to go up to him afterwards and tell him that he was one of the best drummers I've ever seen. In the jazz quartet it was "Big Noise from Winnetka" (expansive and dynamic Krupa-esque tom thumping) one moment, *Mister Magic*–era Harvey Mason (a model of funk precision) the next. His cymbal playing behind the soloists was hair-raisingly good, every intonation weighted and propulsive.

In the R&B/Soul second half, where they were reading charts for unfamiliar arrangements, he was just as jaw-dropping. Not a missed turnaround, not a bridge or chorus that didn't lift higher than the one before. Hugely recommended, the Jook Joint's on Sundays, once a month, with a shifting cast of great musicians.

Wednesday, April 16/23 (10 Things)

ONE KEITH HAYNES EXHIBITION, CHARLOTTE ST.

Knew Donovan's "Sunny Goodge Street", which features in another of Keith Haynes' vinyl artworks, but didn't know "Sunny South Kensington". Listening to it on YouTube, I

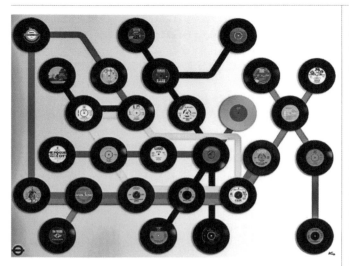

decided on balance I'd not missed a lot:

> *"Come loon soon down Cromwell Road, man / You got to spread your wings / A-flip out, skip out, trip-out, and a-make your stand, folks, to dig me as I sing / Jean-Paul Belmondo and-a Mary Quant got stoned to say the least / Ginsberg, he ended up-a dry and so he a-took a trip out East."*

TWO I LEFT MY HEART IN SAN FRANCISCO

Reminded when Bob sends this: "Here I am again in the cafe for my morning coffee and read. I like this place because it is a good mix of working class, tech and the poor. Like myself, I guess. Anyway, they again have turned the music selection to Pandora... Motown and related music is in the air, the customers are about to burst into dance. It feels like a Bollywood movie. What a great way to start the day. I exit to BB and the thrill is gone. *Bob/Sent from my iPhone*".

THREE ALLEN TOUSSAINT...

... may be the man to call if you need a Silent Film Pianist. During a concert at Ronnie Scott's, his evocation of childhood piano lessons and being taught "Chopsticks", segues into a cracking romp through his favourite classical pieces and culminates with "Rhapsody in Blue", via a car chase, a hurricane and some pratfalls. His intense version of "St James Infirmary" with a soupçon of moody "Summertime" is also a highlight.

But he saves the best 'til last. Richard leans over as he finishes his set and asks what he'll play for an encore, but I'm still hypnotised by the 20-minute-long nostalgiafest of "Southern Nights" with its evocation of Allen's childhood visits to his Creole grandparents in the bayou ("My father would take us there to show us where we came from, so we would know where we were going... We didn't care much about the philosophy... but we liked the ride").

I can't think, but Richard says, quizzically, "On Your Way Down"? "Freedom for The Stallion"? And I say it's unlikely that he'll do the former... and then he does. It's the moment of the night. From Richard's blog, THEBLUEMOMENT: "Something magical happened at the very end of Allen Toussaint's solo show at Ronnie Scott's last night. A very enthusiastic fan in the front row, who had been permitted to sing most of the lead vocal on "Brickyard Blues" earlier in the set, invited Toussaint to play "On Your Way Down" — a song that appeared on his album *Life Love & Faith* in 1972 and was unforgettably covered by Little Feat on *Dixie Chicken* a year later — as his encore.

The great man complied, and immediately led us into territory we had not visited in the preceding hour and a half. For a couple of minutes we were transfixed by a 76-year-old master's journey to the essence of the music with which he has lived his life: to the heart of the blues, of which "On Your Way Down", with the sober elegance of its contours and its wry reflection on the human condition, is one of the very greatest examples."

FIVE KING, SPRINGS

Seen on *WowHaus*: The Palm Springs estate Elvis and Priscilla Presley honeymooned at in 1966 is on the market for US$9.5 million. The house at 1350 Ladera Circle is "designed in four perfect circles, on three levels, incorporating glass and peanut brittle stonework for indoor-outdoor living." Boasting art deco design and furnishings throughout, the four-bedroom, five-bath estate was recently "restored to its 1960s splendor" and includes a pool, private garden, tennis court, fruit orchard and – because this was the King's castle – a stage.

It's nestled at the base of the San Jacinto Mountains, with "the honeymoon suite" offering a panoramic view of the Coachella Valley. But peanut brittle stonework?

SIX BRILLIANT SHELVING EXHIBITION ALERT!

I know, a shelving exhibition! But Martino Gamper's Serpentine Sackler Gallery show is fantastic, not only for the iconic shelving systems, but for the witty way that they're dressed.

Pictured is the most music related, but weakest of the exhibits. Go see the century brought to life through tiny things on shelves.

SEVEN THE BALLAD OF GEESHIE AND ELVIE

I don't feel qualified to even comment on the extraordinary piece that John Jeremiah Sullivan wrote this week for *The New York Times*. If this is a subject you're interested in, just read it. "In the spring of 1930, in a damp and dimly lit studio, in a small Wisconsin village on the western shore of Lake Michigan, the duo recorded a batch of songs that for more than half a century have been numbered among the masterpieces of prewar American music, in particular two, Elvie's "Motherless Child Blues" and Geeshie's "Last Kind Words Blues", twin Alps of their tiny oeuvre, inspiring essays and novels and films and cover versions, a classical arrangement."

And watch the beautifully made films accompanying it (photographs and video by Leslye Davis, production by Tom Giratikanon). And at the bottom, listen to the songs. And finally hear the Kronos Quartet's version of "Last Kind Words Blues", scored by Jacob Garchik, to hear another setting of a melody so singular, so strange and so unique.

TEN FARFISA ORGAN, STEPTOES & SONS SCRAP YARD, PECKHAM

"Yours for £150, or £80 if you take it now, as I'm closing and then I won't have to take it in."

THANKS FOR READING VOLUME ONE OF FIVE THINGS I SAW & HEARD THIS WEEK.
COMMENTS, CRITICISMS & ERRORS TO MARTINWORKBENCH@GMAIL.COM.
PLEASE FEEL FREE TO REVIEW THE BOOK AT AMAZON.CO.UK, AND FOLLOW THE
BLOG AT FIVETHINGSSEENANDHEARD.COM.

Printed in Great Britain
by Amazon

79000687R00121